A
PEOPLE'S RESPONSE
TO
OUR GLOBAL NEIGHBORHOOD

A PEOPLE'S RESPONSE TO OUR GLOBAL NEIGHBORHOOD

• • •

Dialogues on the Report of
the Commission on Global Governance

PUBLISHED BY BOSTON RESEARCH CENTER FOR THE 21ST CENTURY

OCTOBER 1995

Published by
Boston Research Center for the 21st Century
396 Harvard Street
Cambridge, MA 02138-3924

Edited by Michael Hays and Amy Morgante
Layout/design by Susan Brennan and Ralph Buglass
Cover design by Susan Brennan
Conference photographs by Jonathan Wilson and Susan Brumfield

Library of Congress catalogue card number: 95-43649
A people's response to Our Global Neighborhood:
Dialogues on the Report of the Commission on Global Governance.
p. cm.
"Sponsored by Boston Research Center for the 21st Century in
collaboration with the Coalition for a Strong United Nations and
the Commission on Global Governance."
ISBN 1-887917-01-2
1. International relations. 2. International organization. 3. United Nations.
I. Boston Research Center for the 21st Century. II. Coalition for a Strong
United Nations. III. Commission on Global Governance.
JX1391.P45 1995
327.1'01 — dc20

TABLE OF CONTENTS

· · ·

People's Response Speakers   *i*
Preface   *iii*
Foreword   Betty Reardon   *vii*

PART I:
May 13, 1995 United Nations Renaissance Conference:
A Response to the Report of the Commission on Global Governance

    Summary   5

    Overview of the Report   -   Olara A. Otunnu   9
                                                      Open Discussion   17

    Response Panel #1   Jacques Baudot   29
                                                  Dessima Williams   33
                                                  Robert F. Meagher   37
                                                      Open Discussion   45

    Response Panel #2   Betty Reardon   55
                                                  Eric Hauber   59
                                                  Winston Langley   63
                                                      Open Discussion   71

    Closing Remarks   Arvind Sharma   77

PART II:
May 25, 1995 Forum
Reforming the United Nations: What is Ahead for
Our Global Neighborhood?

    Summary   87

    Overview of the Report   Barber Conable   91

    "The United Nations in Trouble"   Anthony Lewis   97

    Response Panel   Richard Parker   103
                                                  Daniel Cheever   109
                                                  Virginia Straus   113
                                                      Open Discussion   117

    Closing Remarks   Barber Conable   129

PART III:
July 10, 1995 Luncheon Seminar
A Women's Response to **Our Global Neighborhood**

    Summary   135

    The Discussion   139

PART IV:
July 22, 1995 United Nations Renaissance Conference:
Creating a Civil Society in Our Global Neighborhood

Summary		167
Overview of the Report	Shridath Ramphal	171
	Open Discussion	183
Response	Helen Caldicott	187
Response Panel #1	Stephen P. Marks	199
	Nancy B. Roof	205
	Open Discussion	215
Response Panel #2	Guraraj Mutalik	225
	Virginia Straus	231
	Open Discussion	241
Closing Remarks	Shridath Ramphal	247

Afterword	249
Appendix	
Summary and Analysis of Questionnaires	257
A Call to Action	273

People's Response Speakers

JOSEPH BARATTA (Moderator)
Coalition for a Strong United Nations

MAGNE BARTH (Moderator)
International Peace Research Institute, Oslo (PRIO)

JACQUES BAUDOT
Social Development Division of the United Nations

SEYOM BROWN (Moderator)
Department of International Cooperation, Brandeis University

HELEN CALDICOTT, MD
Physicians for Social Responsibility

DANIEL CHEEVER
United Nations Association (UNA) of Greater Boston

BARBER CONABLE
Commission on Global Governance

ERIC HAUBER
Soka Gakkai International

WINSTON LANGLEY
*Department of International Relations and Political Science,
University of Massachusetts at Boston; UNA of Greater Boston*

ANTHONY LEWIS
New York Times

STEPHEN P. MARKS
School of International and Public Affairs, Columbia University

ROBERT F. MEAGHER
Fletcher School of Law and Diplomacy, Tufts University

GURURAJ (RAJ) MUTALIK, MD
  International Physicians for the Prevention of Nuclear War (IPPNW)

JAMES M. OLSON (Moderator)
  United Nations Association (UNA)

OLARA A. OTUNNU
  Commission on Global Governance, International Peace Academy

RICHARD PARKER
  Shorenstein Center for Press, Politics, and Public Policy,
  Kennedy School of Government

DANIEL PARTAN (Moderator)
  Boston University Law School; UNA of Greater Boston

SHRIDATH RAMPHAL
  Commission on Global Governance

BETTY A. REARDON
  Peace Education Program, Teachers College, Columbia University

NANCY B. ROOF
  Center for Psychology and Social Change

ARVIND SHARMA
  Department of Comparative Religion, McGill University

SAYRE SHELDON
  Boston University

VIRGINIA STRAUS
  Boston Research Center for the 21st Century

BARBARA SUNDBERG BAUDOT
  Saint Anselm College

DESSIMA WILLIAMS
  Department of Sociology, Brandeis University

PREFACE

• • •

In 1989, as the dust from the crumbling Berlin Wall and the failed ideology it represented began to settle, former West German Chancellor and Peace Nobelist Willy Brandt initiated a process that led to the formation of the Commission on Global Governance, the issuers of the report that is the focus of this book. That report, *Our Global Neighborhood*, articulates "a common vision of the way forward for the world in making the transition from the Cold War and in managing humanity's journey into the twenty-first century." In a happy coincidence, the work of the Commission — which had the reform of the United Nations as its centerpiece — culminated in the publication of this report in 1995, the year in which the United Nations marked the fiftieth year of its existence.

At the heart of the Commission's report is the belief that a global civil ethic ought to guide action within the global neighborhood, and that leadership infused with that ethic is vital to the quality of global governance. The idea that sustained their inquiry is wonderfully profound in its simplicity: "all people, no less than all states, have a right to a secure existence."

But even after reading *Our Global Neighborhood*, one might well ask why this report, insightful as it is, should have a more powerful and positive impact on the behavior of the world community than did the numerous other reports and ideas that have been promulgated over the years. Why should it have any greater efficacy than, say, the League to Enforce Peace that was established in 1915 under the auspices of the New York Peace Society? The League, too, offered impressive solutions to the seemingly intractable problems of global security, but to little avail. Likewise, the Kellogg-Briand Pact of 1928, which also aimed to outlaw war as an instrument of national policy, failed to achieve any long term results. And then, in more recent years, who could argue with the wisdom and insight of those independent commissions of the 1980's and early 90's that were inspired by the desire to strengthen our global community, for example, the Commission on Disarmament and Security Issues chaired by Olof Palme, Gro Harlem Brundtland's World Commission on Environment and Development, or Julius Nyerere's South Commission to mention just a few? It was, after all, through the efforts of these independent commissions that the groundwork for the Commission on Global Governance was laid.

Perhaps the difference between those commissions, pacts, and reports and the work of the Commission on Global Governance can be found in its vision, a vision that informs the title and is at the very heart of this *People's Response to Our Global Neighborhood*. Central to this vision is a deep understanding of the fact that we the people, not just governments, have a stake in the issues that define the challenges we all face at this important juncture in history. Daisaku Ikeda, the founder of the Boston Research Center for the 21st Century, showed a similar understanding of the importance of fostering civil society when he said, "My basic concept is that the United Nations will be properly reformed only when it succeeds in hearing and empowering the voice of the common people." It was with this understanding that Mr. Ikeda suggested in a peace proposal he wrote in January 1994 that the Center work with others to shape a UN reform proposal from an NGO point of view — a suggestion that inspired *A People's Response*.

The purpose of this volume is to open a space in which the "voice of the common people" can enunciate its many concerns. It is the beginning of what we hope will develop into a polyphony — a civil society comprised of the individual voices of women and of men, the fresh new accents of youth, the inflections of the south as well as the north, a blend of the voices of the first, second and third worlds joined in an ethos that has its source in what Mr. Ikeda describes as the "psychological tendency to favor harmony over opposition, unity over division, "we" over "I." That ethos and some of those voices resonate in this book.

While planning and developing this project, the Boston Research Center was extremely fortunate to have the able assistance of the co-hosts and co-sponsors of the various "People's Response" events chronicled in the following pages, including the Commission on

Global Governance, the Coalition for a Strong United Nations, United Nations Association – USA, United Nations Association of Greater Boston, International Physicians for the Prevention of Nuclear War (IPPNW) and Physicians for Social Responsibility.

In addition to the speakers, participants, and co-sponsors of the four "People's Response" events, we would also like to express our deep appreciation to the many people who contributed their time and talents to the preparation of this book — Dan Bilello, Susan Brumfield, Kathy Dewey, Anne Hudson, Kali Saposnick, and John Smith for their great support and assistance and Jonathan Wilson for his photography; to Rosemary Loomis, Alvin Winder, and Curt Young for the extraordinary writing assistance they provided, and to Michael Hays for the quality, thoughtfulness and intelligence of his editing.

FOREWORD

• • •

Our Global Neighborhood, the report of the Commission on Global Governance published on the occasion of the 50th anniversary of the United Nations is not only a "Call to Action," as indicated in the final section of the report; more importantly perhaps, it also constitutes an invitation to reflection and debate on the part of that global civil society to which the report assigns significant responsibility for the future of the "neighborhood." The present volume offers a constructive initiation into that process among members of the American public committed to supporting and strengthening the United Nations by bringing together a series of four programs conceived by the Boston Research Center for the 21st Century, as *A People's Response to Our Global Neighborhood.*

I am sure that all the other respondents will agree that it was both a privilege and a challenge to be invited by the Center to participate in these sessions. It was a privilege to be among a group committed to developing ways to humanize world society; and it was a challenge to offer comments and suggestions on such a ground-breaking report. Like most of the respondents in these discussions, I sought to support and extend the insights and possibilities offered by the report by bringing a constructively critical approach to bear on its analysis of the needs and realities of the world it seeks to change. Ultimately, though, the challenge constituted by the report cannot be met by a series of discussions, however constructive they may be, nor by any particular reflections on them, such as those that will be found in this foreword.

We can only stand up to this challenge through ongoing and ever widening public inquiry into the nature of the problems we face as a world community, and through systematic strengthening and extension of our capacities to respond to and resolve the problems outlined in the report. In short, we need much more intense — and inclusive — discussion among all of the world's "neighbors," discussion, that is, that includes those as yet unaware of the challenges and responsibilities we face, the "people out there" in the neighborhoods such as those invoked by Helen Caldicott in her response to Commission Co-Chair, Shridath Ramphal during the conference at Columbia University in July.

This fact in no way diminishes the importance of these four sessions as a beginning, though. The individual presentations and responses of the Commission members — Otunnu, Conable, and Ramphal — were straightforward and enlightening. They provided their audiences with insights and an understanding of the purposes and perspectives in the report that reading alone could never offer. In this respect, their overviews of the report reinforced the sense of privilege in participating in these events and served as a reminder of our responsibility to continue the inquiry their work has opened. The discussions included here also show that in all four sessions the responses to the Commission's statements were articulate, constructively critical, and thought provoking. In the remainder of this foreword I will simply outline a few of the more salient aspects of these responses.

Almost without exception the respondents commended three elements of the report along with the recommendations that arose from them. These three were: its identification of the fundamental values essential to transforming the global neighborhood into a human community; its recognition of the significance of and the need to assign to civil society a major role in the development and maintenance of the community; and its acknowledgment of the individual person as the locus of both responsibility and security. In sum, the report is understood as an effort to reinforce the principle of the universality of human dignity and as a call for a global transformation that would bring this principle into practice.

Wherever the report is criticized, these criticisms to some degree represent efforts on the part of the respondents to identify what they thought to be omissions and obstacles in the Commission's work. These are usually coupled with constructive suggestions for extension and continuation of the report's recommendations. Such points are also raised by the audience during the open and wide-ranging exchanges that followed the formal presentations. Among these, the points that seem to me most in need of further inquiry are: 1) the privileged perspective from which the Commission and the respondents spoke concerning those not represented in the exchanges — the marginalized, deprived and the vulnerable; 2) the emphasis on economics that obscures the perspectives and needs of the deprived; 3) the possibility arising from these first two that some groups and individuals will continue to be excluded because of the perpetuation of "global otherhood"; 4) the lack of specific references to women and children; 5) inadequate attention to the excessive power of transnational corporations and to issues directly related to 6) the environment and 7) human rights.

All the speakers and respondents addressed one or another of these points in a manner that opened possibilities for expanding the "Call to Action." Dessima Williams, for example, calls for enlisting the participation of women at all decision making levels to help close the leadership gap and Jacques Baudot adds "service" to the list of fundamental responsibilities. In a related set of comments, Richard Parker emphasizes the power of the committed individual. Turning to the realities of the present, Anthony Lewis reproaches the UN for its "failure" to halt the carnage in Bosnia, and Stephen Marks insists on the centrality of human rights, reminding us of the sobering fact that states often tend to be hostile to civil society. Helen Caldicott urges us to take moral responsibility for the life of our dying planet.

All these comments and the other criticisms offered in the four discussions clearly attest to the useful and provocative nature of the report. They demonstrate that it can (and will, I hope) be a vehicle for the development of that larger discourse all the speakers see as an urgent necessity in order to move the United Nations and world society toward support for a socially and ecologically sustainable planetary community — the community we must have if human history is to continue beyond the next century. As Shridath Ramphal suggests, human fallibility, if not culpability, is responsible for our global crises, but he, like his fellow Commission members and the respondents, believes that human responsibility can rise to the challenge. As Helen Caldicott states at the end of her devastating analysis of the condition of the planet and the shallowness of our response to this condition: "We can save the planet." The upshot of these comments is nothing short of a demand for a series of cultural transformations that will make this possible.

I see the discussion around *Our Global Neighborhood* as a significant component of that transformational process, especially since a growing number of internationalists have begun to attend seriously to the report. It is a focus of discussion where the UN is seen as a major tool for reorganizing the planetary order. And although the report has received some criticism leveled in far harsher tones than the critiques articulated in the four sessions reproduced here, even these other assessments, some of which reject the report in its entirety because of specific shortcomings, contribute to this potentially transformative discourse initiated by the report. There have, for example, been accusations that the report panders to transnationals and states; that it undermines the most constructive work the UN has achieved through specialized agencies; that it retains a narrow and elitist view of "civil society;" and that it lacks clarity in its distinction between government and governance.

Perhaps the gravest omission is the report's failure to focus on half of humanity. Writing this foreword while fresh from China and the Fourth World Conference on Women, nothing speaks louder to me of the limitations in these discussions than the absence of the voices of women and the substantial exclusion of a gender perspective. These two missing elements demonstrate the need for an ongoing discussion about the specific injustice that most thoroughly violates the principle of universal human dignity — the universal inequality between women and men sustained by a patriarchal structure that neither the report nor its critics have sufficiently addressed.

Unless and until gender becomes a major perspective on the issues we address as a world community, the values upon which *Our Global Neighborhood* is based are not likely to be realized. Despite Vienna (Human Rights Conference 1993), Cairo (Population Conference 1993) and Beijing, where the consideration of gender made possible significant advances for women and, thus, for human rights and population control, women's perspectives and gender issues, essential and necessary to a just and democratic neighborhood, cannot enter the main policy discourse without the equal participation of women in future commissions or indeed in any ongoing initiatives of the Commission on Global Governance. Dessima Williams observed that only 6 out of 28 commissioners were women; they were outstanding women, but nonetheless too few to assure that the report would take full note of the fact that the majority of the marginalized, deprived, and vulnerable are women, or of how an inordinate portion of the global burdens they seek to remedy fall upon women, or insist that women's voices be heard and that gender be factored into the review and recommendations of such commissions.

Women have traditionally been the maintainers of community, the advocates of the common good, the stewards of the environment, and the guardians of the future in their local neighborhoods. Through civil society they are doing the same for the global neighborhood. Recognizing these factors and bringing them into the discussion of issues of global governance should be a primary item on any agenda set to discuss this publication or other efforts to promote reflection or debate on the future of our global neighborhood.

A People's Response to Our Global Neighborhood is a significant contribution to the discussion of that future. Readers will find a wide range of reflections and suggestions about both civil society and the inter-state system. To continue, extend, and share in the exploration of these issues is of vital importance to the whole human family. Human dignity is manifest in human responsibility. *A People's Response* is an invitation to accept responsibility for the human future.

> – **Betty A. Reardon**
> *Columbia University*
> September, 1995

Boston Research Center for the 21st Century, site of the May 13th and May 25th conferences and the July 10th luncheon seminar.

Panelists brought diverse backgrounds and perspectives to this conference series.

Jonathan Wilson

The Presentations proved both informative and lively.

Jonathan Wilson

Classical music warmed up the atmosphere at the May 13th conference.

Jonathan Wilson

Professor Winston Langley of the University of Massachusetts at Boston (left) and Eric Hauber, Soka Gakkai Permanent Representative to the UN (May 13th).

Jonathan Wilson

Professor Arvind Sharma of McGill University and Virginia Straus, Director of the Boston Research Center for the 21st Century, review the day's successful proceedings (May 13th).

Jonathan Wilson

Olara Ottunu and Dessima Williams share thoughts following their presentations
on May 13th.

CONFERENCE PROCEEDINGS

United Nations Renaissance Conference: A Response to the Report of the Commission on Global Governance

. . .

MAY 13, 1995

Boston Research Center for the 21st Century
Cambridge, Massachusetts

PROGRAM OF THE DAY

• • •

Welcoming Remarks
> *Virginia Straus, Boston Research Center for the 21st Century*
> *Joseph Baratta, Coalition for a Strong United Nations*

Overview of the Report, *Our Global Neighborhood*
> *Olara A. Otunnu, Commission on Global Governance;*
> *International Peace Academy in New York*

Open Discussion

Response Panel
> *Magne Barth (moderator), International Peace*
> *Research Institute, Oslo (PRIO)*
> *Jacques Baudot, Social Development Division*
> *of the United Nations*
> *Dessima Williams, Department of Sociology,*
> *Brandeis University*
> *Robert F. Meagher, Fletcher School of Law*
> *and Diplomacy, Tufts University*

Open Discussion

Response Panel
> *Seyom Brown (moderator), Department of*
> *International Cooperation, Brandeis University*
> *Betty Reardon, Peace Education Program,*
> *Teachers College, Columbia University*
> *Eric Hauber, Soka Gakkai International*
> *Winston Langley, Department of International*
> *Relations and Political Science,*
> *University of Massachusetts at Boston*

Open Discussion

Closing Remarks
> *Arvind Sharma, Department of Comparative Religion,*
> *McGill University*

3

SUMMARY

• • •

Olara Otunnu, member of the Commission on Global Governance, set the stage for the discussion of the report, *Our Global Neighborhood,* by providing the context out of which the report was derived. In the 1970s and 1980s, a number of sectorial reports were produced. "We wanted," he said, "to see if a more global vision might emerge out of these sectorial preoccupations, but we also wanted to see if there were ideas in the earlier reports whose time might have come."

In addition, he said, the Commission recognized that with the end of the Cold War, there were several trends: (1) the development of a more cooperative international atmosphere; (2) a growth and deepening of international interdependence; (3) the advent of civil society within various countries and its slow emergence at the international level as well; (4) the burgeoning movement worldwide for democratization; and (5) the erosion and, in some cases, the collapse of ideological certainties.

Ambassador Otunnu went on to clarify major concepts discussed in the report. The term *global governance,* he elaborated, is an approach, a way of looking at problems. It means having a global approach to the problems that affect everybody worldwide but it is not, he was clear, about global government or world government.

Following a discussion of the recommendations of the Commission on Global Governance, Mr. Otunnu observed that global governance cannot be achieved within an ethical vacuum. There must be a sense of shared values. At a minimum, because we are each other's neighbors, there must be a sense of neighborhood values. Further, Mr. Otunnu said, "It is not possible to construct any form of global governance without people and without leadership. In the end, this must be translated into men and women who are committed to taking up ideas, mobilizing them, producing a clear vision, and translating it into action at the local, national, and international levels. The global neighborhood, Mr. Otunnu summarized, remains an aspiration, a clarion call, a goal toward which we must strive.

In the panel presentations and open discussions that followed, the Commission was praised for recommending that there should be an indefinite extension of the Nuclear Non-proliferation Treaty and that there should be the eventual and complete elimination of existing nuclear weapons.

There were expressions of concern about the cynicism and lack of confidence in government that exists at all levels. Applying the comments specifically to the United Nations, Mr. Otunnu responded:

> *I think what the UN must now try to do is shape a more balanced and manageable agenda. My own fear is that the UN might move from having taken on too much — a much too ambitious and intrusive agenda without the proper means for success — to undertaking too little. I think both dangers must be avoided. What one wants is a balanced agenda for the UN which allows it to play an important but manageable role.*

Conferees raised a number of issues during the open discussions and response panels, many of them centering on the acknowledgment that the United Nations as founded in 1945 was a very different United Nations from that which can — and ought to — exist in the '90s and on into the millennium. There was a particular emphasis on the specific need to find ways to address intrastate as well as interstate strife and to establish that people have the right to shape their own national destiny.

Response panelists Dessima Williams and Betty Reardon placed special emphasis on the need to address the gender issues and ecological perspectives more fully than they have been addressed by the Commission.

An animated and earnest discussion focused on the values that underlie the report and that must somehow unite all peoples and institutions if we are ever to achieve global governance. As Mr. Otunnu said, we must teach people beginning in childhood to understand that we have a materialist, scientific dimension to our lives which is very important but also a deeply spiritual, ethical aspect that must be developed fully.

Conferees praised the Commission on Global Governance for insisting on the importance of changing ideas, ways of thinking, and processes, and for the underlying optimism in the generation of this report which recognized that one may transform society in part by seeking to transform individual lives. Eric Hauber added that "Dialogue is an essential vehicle for democratization and for bringing the voices of the people to the workings of the UN, which is currently dominated by the voices of states and state interests."

"What this report does," Winston Langley observed, "is affirm rights while coupling them with responsibilities. That is a major contribution."

As Mr. Otunnu responded to the comments and criticism proffered during the day, he summarized:

> *Hope posits faith in human capacity. It recognizes that within us there are many forces at play, some of them very dark and ugly, but despite that, there are also other elements that can be very powerfully beautiful and transforming. Ultimately, this is where faith and hope come together — in the belief that the capacity exists, in spite of present evidence, in spite of present realities, to transcend the ugly, the negative, and to achieve a measure of healing, reconciliation, acceptance, and embrace.*

Arvind Sharma concluded the day's sessions with a conceptual framework of four paired concepts: morality and law; order and justice; government and governance; and justice and equality. Elaborating on the first pair, he asserted that "law represents a failure of morality" and stressed our great need for common values. Regarding the second, he felt that while we can have order without justice, we cannot have the opposite: justice without order. "Any attempt," he suggested, "to achieve justice means that the prevailing order will have to be disturbed." As for the third pair of concepts, Mr. Sharma maintained that "you can't have governance without government." He also observed that "We have to address the basic problem of government. And what is it? In my opinion, the basic problem of government is that the business of coming into political power and staying in political power consumes so much time, energy, and money that there is no time or energy left to do anything creative with that power."

Finally, hearkening back to the theme of reconciliation that had just been sounded by Mr. Otunnu, Professor Sharma reflected that one theological concept that will be extremely helpful in this context is forgiveness.

Overview of the Report
OLARA A. OTUNNU

• • •

Olara Ottunu, a member of the Commission on Global Governance, is President of the International Peace Academy. He practiced and taught law and served as a member of Uganda's interim parliament before becoming Uganda's Permanent Representative to the United Nations. He has served as his country's Minister of Foreign Affairs and was a professor of international relations and law in Paris.

I propose to divide my remarks as follows: I will briefly discuss the main considerations that animated the work of the Commission on Global Governance. Then I will move on to what we understand and mean by "global governance." Third, I will discuss some of the key recommendations contained in our report. Then, I will offer some concluding remarks, looking to the future in particular.

First, there are two developments in particular regarding the main considerations that animated our work. One set of developments could be called quantitative and historical, by which I mean the various sectorial reports which were produced by several independent commissions in the late 1970s and '80s, in particular the Brandt Commission on International Development Issues, Brundtland on the Environment,

> **"It is not possible to construct any form of global governance without people and without leadership. In the end, this must be translated into men and women who are committed to taking up ideas, mobilizing them, producing a clear vision, and translating it into action at the local, national, and international levels."**

Palme on International Security, the Sadruddin Aga Khan — Prince Hassan Gin Talal Commission on Humanitarian Issues, and finally, the South Commission chaired by Julius Nyerere.

All these were sectorial commissions that dealt with a single question and produced a comprehensive report. We wanted to see if a more global vision might emerge out of these sectorial preoccupations. We also wanted to see if there were ideas in the earlier reports whose time might have come; for example, the Palme Commission stressed the need to apply the concept of "common security," but at the time the report came out — in the middle of the Cold War— many commentators laughed this out of court. We wanted to revisit these reports to see if some ideas that had not gained favor in the '70s and '80s might be revived in the '90s. If so, they might serve to produce a sense of common purpose, a common vision, and highlight some main themes that needed to be operationalized in the '90s.

The second set of developments which animated our work was more qualitative in nature. I refer here to the end of the Cold War, to the emergence of a more cooperative international atmosphere, and to the growth and the deepening of international interdependence. I refer as well to the advent of civil society within various countries and its slow emergence at the international level as well. And I refer to the burgeoning movement worldwide for democratization, the most dramatic being, perhaps, the conversion of various forms of military dictatorship in Latin America into democracies and the spread of democracy into the former communist bloc of Europe. The final qualitative development has to do with the erosion, and in some cases the collapse, of ideological certainties.

Taken together, these developments made us feel the time was right to embark on the project which came to be known as the Commission on Global Governance. Now, what did we mean by global governance? What were the main assumptions behind our work? First of all, global governance is an approach. It is a way of looking at problems, a manner of responding to challenges at both the local and international levels. It means having a global approach to the problems that affect everybody worldwide, while at the same time stressing the need to respond to problems where they most affect people, which means at the local level. It would also treat and respond to problems systematically rather than sectorially or on an ad hoc basis, thus providing a response informed by an overall vision of the situation in which we live today.

Global governance is most certainly not about global government, or world government. Perhaps the concept closest to global governance is what the British often refer to as "good government." The term has nothing to do with any particular government or whether one approves or disapproves of this or that government. Instead it relates to a method of governance that is transparent, that is accountable, that stresses fairness and mechanisms for appealing administrative decisions within the system. That is what "good government" means, and it is very close to what we mean by "global governance." Even though the United Nations is the only universal organization that exists today, and although it is very much at the center of efforts toward global governance, we were not exclusively concerned with the role of the United Nations. We addressed ourselves to all the spheres and actors in today's world. We had the United Nations in mind, but also national governments, regional organizations, civil society, transnational corporations — the entire cluster of actors who now animate the international scene.

The third part of my remarks will focus on the recommendations that we put forth in our report. I want to stress in particular six of these recommendations. The first of these has to do with the concept of the security of people. This, as many of you will recognize, is not a new concept. Indeed, many of you in this room have used it, popularized it, and discussed it in your papers. What we have done is take a concept that had rapidly entered public discourse, clarify its parameters, and popularize it further. And out of that, some practical implications, like those in terms of sovereignty, have emerged as well.

If sovereignty is about providing for the security of people, it provides a shield to those who are the keepers of that state. But the term also implies a responsibility to ensure not just the security of the state, but the security of the people who live within a country. If those who govern fail to live up to their responsibility, that should cause the international community as a whole to get involved to ensure that the people of that particular country can live in security. Here we move from the level of concept to practical implications. We recommend that the United Nations find ways by which, in situations of gross and systematic abuse of the rights of people, it can get involved; this means scaling the wall of sovereignty.

Out of this comes the right of petition, which is recommended in our report. It arises from the consideration that in various sectors within the United Nations system today there are provisions for non-official actors to have input, except in the area of peace and security. Areas such as human rights, the environment, and women's rights have all developed major NGO input. But in the province of the Security Council there is no arrangement in place for those who are not states to insert an item on the agenda, testify, suggest a possible course of action, or raise an alarm. And so, in providing for the right of petition and the council of petition, we are trying to provide an entrée for those who are not official actors to have input with regard to peace and security matters. This, then, is the first recommendation, which elaborates on the concept and the practical implications of the security of people.

The second recommendation has to do with the reform of the Security Council. Again, what the Commission is recommending is not entirely new; various permutations of these ideas have appeared elsewhere. There are three specific ideas that the Commission has put forth with regard to the reform of the Security Council. First, that there should be a two-stage approach, with some aspects of reform implemented now, and a more comprehensive review conducted within ten years. In the short term, the Commission is recommending that, in addition to the five permanent members who will retain their places, five standing members should be given terms longer than two years — perhaps ten-year terms. Then, in addition to the present ten non-permanent members, three others should be added. This should be tied in with the notion of a full review ten years hence, thus creating a two-stage approach to something more comprehensive. This recommendation has been animated by our concern that the Security Council as presently composed is outdated. It reflects neither the real power structure in the world nor the growing spirit of democratization worldwide. For both reasons there is need to reform and reconstitute the Security Council.

The third recommendation is that there should be constituted an Economic Security Council which plays a similar role to the political Security Council, but with its membership constituted differently. Let me stress here the role of the Economic Security Council as a strategic policy forum. Those of you who are familiar with the background to the establishment of the Economic and Social Council will immediately recognize that, in the beginning, this was the role that had been conceived for that institution. Unfortunately, in practice it has not evolved in such a way as to perform that role, and various efforts to reform it along these lines have not had great success. So we are recommending the formation of a new organ within the UN that would perform this particular function at the highest political level. The practical implication would be that the Economic and Social Council (ECOSOC) would be abolished and other subsidiary bodies within the UN system that are not performing as well as they are supposed to would be reviewed, reorganized, and, in some cases, abolished. Thus, we recommend a review of the United Nations Conference on Trade and Development (UNCTAD) and the United Nations Industrial Development Organization (UNIDO) and of the roles and usefulness of all of the regional economic agencies within the UN system.

The fourth recommendation concerns the Trusteeship Council. We noted what is obvious: the Trusteeship Council has been so very successful that it has fully accomplished its mission. There are no longer any trust territories to be administered by it, but the Trusteeship Council continues to exist within the UN system. We recommended that the Trusteeship Council might be converted into a council with a mandate not over colonial and trusteeship territories, but over the global commons.

The fifth recommendation is for what we have called the Forum of Civil Society. Let me explain this a bit. Again, this is not a totally new idea. There is already in place the NGO forum that meets every year prior to the General Assembly session and highlights issues they would like delegations to take up when the General Assembly session convenes. What the Commission is first seeking to do is give a higher political profile to this body — more visibility and formal recognition within the UN system — so it would no longer be an informal, ad hoc operation. It would meet in the General Assembly hall, and the items that it took up would be a direct part of the later considerations of the official delegations. We deliberately decided not to elaborate on the precise terms or structure by which this might be conducted. We said this should be for the members of international civil society — the various NGOs who have become very active and articulate and reasonably well-organized — to elaborate. We merely propose the idea of such a forum.

The sixth and last area to which I'd like to refer pertains more to the domain of the rule of law. Having said that we believe that the rule of international law, generally, should be given a higher place within international governance, we proceeded to make several very specific recommendations. I should like to highlight three of them in particular. First, as a way to give even greater prestige to the International Court of Justice, we are proposing a one-term mandate for judges who are elected to it. As you know, today, a judge can be reelected indefinitely. And with that obviously comes the vagaries of the political process. We felt that a one-term mandate of ten years would strengthen the role of international law and of the International Court of Justice and give it a greater sense of integrity and prestige.

We've also recommended that the Secretary General be given the prerogative to refer a matter directly to the International Court of Justice. As many of you know, the other main organs of the UN have this prerogative; the General Assembly and the Security Council can seek an advisory opinion from the International Court of Justice. It is a very important tool that they have at their disposal. The Secretary General, on the other hand, who with the Secretariat constitutes an organ within the UN system, does not have that prerogative. There have been various abortive attempts in the past to create this possibility, so we are recommending that this initiative should be taken up again.

Finally, we are also recommending the establishment of an international criminal court. Although it did not originate with us, we are seeking to highlight this proposal and to give it more political prominence. Many people, including some of you here today, have advocated this for a number of years.

In conclusion, let me stress the following points: the first is that I do not believe global governance, however constituted, can in fact be achieved within an ethical vacuum. There must be a minimum of a sense of common, shared values. There must be a minimum sense of neighborhood values. Are we indeed each other's neighbors? That to me is a basic requirement. Otherwise, whatever we speak about in terms of global governance will fail to coalesce and become operative. It must be grounded on a very basic ethical foundation. Unfortunately, as we speak, the relative ethical vacuum is wide and growing wider.

Ironically, the erosion of ideological certitudes to which I referred earlier has only broadened that gap.

The second consideration to bear in mind is that it is not possible to construct any form of global governance without people and without leadership. In the end, this must be translated into men and women who are committed to taking up ideas, mobilizing for them, producing a clear vision, and translating it into action at the local, national, and international levels. One of the poverties of our era, generally speaking (there are many illustrious exceptions), is a poverty of leadership. Without leadership everything we are speaking about here will come to naught. Ideas do not become action by themselves. They pass through people.

Third, it is true that our report speaks of a global neighborhood. We believe in that notion with all our heart. There are two senses to this idea of a global neighborhood that I want to share with you. One is very concrete, almost physical, as exemplified by the way in which the Ebola tragedy in Zaire reminded us how diseases break out and travel; by the ways in which commercial and financial transactions are carried out around the world; by the ways in which information and people circulate; and by the ways in which environmental degradation affects everybody. In that physical sense the global neighborhood is very much a reality. We cannot escape this fact.

But there is a second sense of neighborhood which is very different and in some ways more fundamental. This involves emotion and spirit; something that springs up from inside. It is a sense of solidarity that is quite distinct from the ways in which we may be physically connected. After all, you can be neighbors physically but not have a sense of neighborliness. I fear that the world in which we live today is rather like that — that we are in fact physically neighbors but the neighborhood is not mediated by a sense of solidarity. So what the Commission is recommending stands as a clarion call, an aspiration; it is where we want to go, where I hope you will help take us. But we are not yet there. In many ways, we are very far from that goal.

These, then, are the considerations I want to leave with you. The report is out, there are many reasonably useful ideas in it, but unless you and others are prepared to fill the ethical vacuum, to provide the leadership of which I spoke, to go from a sense of physical neighborhood to actual solidarity, this report will come to nothing. I have hope

— based on the efforts I have seen being made in Boston and on your presence here this morning — that you, like the members of the Commission, are interested in providing what it takes to put this report into action. Thank you very much.

OPEN DISCUSSION

(In some cases, participants in the discussion did not identify themselves and are not identified herein.)

Unidentified: I was struck by the suggestion in *Our Global Neighborhood* that nuclear weapons could be eliminated in ten or fifteen years. I'm very much for that, and I wonder if you could recall for us any more of the details about that proposal?

Olara A. Otunnu: With regard to nuclear weapons, we had two recommendations. Actually, one of them has just become a reality. The Commission was perhaps the first to give prominent voice to the idea that there should be an indefinite extension of the Nuclear nonproliferation Treaty, and a day and a half ago that is exactly what has transpired at the United Nations. But, there is still a bone of contention. Such a decision cannot mean very much, and it will remain a very lopsided achievement, if it doesn't go hand in hand with measures that are aimed at the eventual and complete elimination of existing nuclear weapons. The spread of such weapons is one thing; their elimination is another. The achievement in New York a few days ago, significant as it is, remains incomplete unless we move toward this second goal. We did not propose specific measures as to how that may be done. We hope others may take the idea and run with it now that we have highlighted the need for nuclear powers to proceed in a serious way towards a process that will eventually eliminate existing nuclear weapons.

Mubiru Musoke: I have two questions. The first one has to do with your comments on sovereignty and the concept of sovereignty as a shield that governments — especially in Africa — used when they abused human rights. This concept has also come up within domestic law. Africans are making constitutions, and the idea that the people are sovereign now is the current understanding of this concept. Can you reconcile this idea of the state being sovereign with that of the people being sovereign? I think one overrides the other — they can't coexist. I need your comment on that.

The second question has to do with the idea that an international criminal court should be established. There isn't very much content to international criminal law. If and when this court is established, how are you going to avoid retroactivity? This court may come into existence two years from today, for example. Are you going to prosecute those who committed crimes like Idi Amin? I know that Nazis are still being hunted and brought to justice. There are so many other criminals in Africa. How are you going to apply the concept of international criminal law and avoid retroactivity?

Otunnu: Well, let me begin with the second question. There already exist within the national jurisdictions of various countries, and also within the notion of crimes against humanity, as well as the convention against genocide, standards which are internationally established that apply to certain kinds of actions, though they may still be incomplete. The difficulty has not been so much the absence of rules in this respect; it has been the lack of a forum, a court where people could be taken and tried. Measures on an ad hoc basis have been taken with regard to former Yugoslavia and Rwanda, for example. The Security Council has established special tribunals for these two cases.

Our idea in the report is to try to fill that gap, but obviously filling it won't be enough. In addition, one will also have to proceed to build a body of laws that are accepted internationally as well as within national boundaries, that can be applied by the proposed court. But, even as we speak, there are laws that could be applied if that forum existed. The question of retroactivity should not arise with regard to standards which exist. Where standards do not yet exist, they will have to be created, but not applied retroactively. That would be against all notion of justice.

Now, with regard to your first question, my response would be this: it has a lot to do with what kind of a state one has. If you are a democratic state in which those who hold power are elected and accountable and can be thrown out by the people, there is no contradiction between the shield and responsibility because they interact directly — the one affects the other. The contradiction arises when those who retain power, who are the guardians of the state apparatus, are not elected, have no accountability, and cannot be removed from power. Then the people have no sovereignty except in name. Their sovereignty has been appropriated by those who are the guardians of power within the state. So, we cannot speak about the issue of sovereignty, the role of people, or the security of people without at the same time speaking about the reform of the state into something more democratic, more accountable, more transparent. And that must be linked with the worldwide movement towards democratization of which I spoke earlier. Those two considerations are critical.

Secondly, I would say that the people actually enter the picture in both instances. They come into the picture locally because, within a given polity, people must be given the right to shape their own destiny — be given the opportunity for cultural expression, for social and economic initiatives to develop their communities. People shaping their own destiny in these ways is an expression, a measure of their sovereignty within the national polity. But if you have a nondemocratic state, where the guardians of the state become the oppressors and use the notion of sovereignty as a shield to keep away the outside world, our recommendation is that you then scale the wall of sovereignty and allow the international community to get involved as an expression of solidarity.

Valerie Epps: I'm part of the Coalition for a Strong United Nations. I have a general remark to make, and then I will address my question specifically to the area of international courts. I think that shortly after the breakup of the former Soviet Union there was a great deal of euphoria and support for notions of international governance. We saw this in the initiatives taken by the United Nations in expanding the role of peacekeepers and in the creation of a couple of new international courts. There was a moment when there was tremendous hope and belief in a general internationalized system. Unfortunately, that rapidly eroded, and after some unfortunate peacekeeping missions such as that in Somalia, there is now increasing cynicism with regard to the notion of international institutions in general. There is also an increase in rampant nationalism and in isolationism. The United States is a prime example of the latter at the moment.

My question to you is this: given that we go through waves of belief in international institutions and then experience a retrenchment that brings rampant nationalism with it again, what do you think are the conditions that must exist for international governance to become a reality? More particularly, if you look at the area of international courts, one of the recommendations in the report is that all nations accept the compulsory jurisdiction of the International Court of Justice. The difficulty, of course, is this: the percentage of United Nations members that accepted the compulsory jurisdiction of the court was quite high when it was initially created because there were only fifty-odd members, but now there is an ever smaller number of nations that accept the compulsory jurisdiction of the court. Currently only one of the permanent members of the Security Council, the United Kingdom, accepts it — and with considerable reservation. So, what are the conditions which must exist before we can move towards the acceptance of international governance in general, and particularly, the compulsory jurisdiction of the court?

Otunnu: I agree with you that there is a deep sense of disillusion with international governance, but I would go one step further. There is also a generalized sense of disillusion with governance at the national level, and not just in countries such as those to which Dr. Mubiru Musoke referred, which are clearly nondemocratic or dictatorial. That is an easy category. But in democratic societies, like Italy, Japan, or this country, there is hardly a brimming sense of confidence in governance at the national level. Quite the opposite. What distinguishes what is happening today in the US, Italy, Japan, or France to some extent from what is happening in some countries in Africa, is that the one has a very democratic arena, while the other involves a struggle to achieve democracy. I think that the need to rejuvenate a sense of confidence in governance exists at all the levels, and that is one reason our report stresses not a particular structure of government but a method, a way of responding to problems that can be applied at all levels — the international, the national level, and the local.

Concerning the failure of the United Nations, especially in peace-keeping, you are right. With the end of the Cold War, a more ambitious, more intrusive, more confident sense of what the UN could do in the area of peace and security emerged, and the UN took on a tremendous amount. Some of these efforts have been quite successful, such as the efforts in Cambodia, El Salvador, Mozambique, Nicaragua.

Others have been tragic failures. The continuing quagmire in the former Yugoslavia, the earlier failure in Angola, the retreat from Somalia clearly represent major setbacks for the United Nations. I think what the UN must now try to do is shape a more balanced and manageable agenda. My own fear is that the UN might move from having taken on too much — a much too ambitious and intrusive agenda without the proper means for success — to undertaking too little. I think both dangers must be avoided. What one wants to see is a balanced agenda for the UN which allows it to play an important but manageable role.

Finally, you spoke of compulsory jurisdiction for the International Court of Justice. In our report, among the things that we stressed is a call for all nation states to accept the compulsory jurisdiction of the International Court of Justice. You are right that in percentage terms the actual number of countries that have UN membership has gone up, and the percentage of countries that accepts the compulsory jurisdiction of the ICJ today is much lower than in 1945. What is needed is greater vigilance at the national level by citizens who feel strongly about the jurisdiction of ICJ, or the idea of global governance generally, urging their own governments, as well as at the international level, because the process of greater democratization, transparency, and better governance is needed at all levels at whatever pace is possible.

Brian Aull: I am from the Baha'i community of Cambridge which is involved in the Coalition for a Strong UN. The Coalition just had a conference on social and economic development, and one of the basic feelings expressed at this conference was that we have to overcome the idea that there are only two approaches to economics — one based on socialism and the other on so-called free markets. There have to be new methods of economic governance that use vibrant market forces but that are also accountable to the social and environmental imperatives of a larger global neighborhood. I know that your commission deliberated a lot about this before recommending the economic security council, but I'd like to know if you had any insights that were not reflected in the report — insights about changes of values, culture, or structure that might lead to this new system.

Otunnu: I will make just three brief comments. One is that our report is infused with, and ends with, the notion of values. That is fundamental at all levels. What we do must be informed by a greater sense of ethical responsibility. But we have also called for the mobilization of all the actors who affect governance and life on earth, including, as I mentioned earlier, members of civil society, religious organizations, and transnational corporations. All the key actors who affect life on earth should be mobilized to work together with this sense of responsibility. Finally, we also injected a sense of intergenerational responsibility. Our obligation is not only to ourselves and to others in different parts of the world; our neighborhood values must also extend to those who will succeed us on the planet. We have tried to give a more comprehensive vision of what is required and who must be mobilized to make it possible.

Gail Thomas: I'm a professor of sociology at the University of Texas. I was very much struck by the report's attention to the local as well as the global, but they both still seem to be very macro. I'm very much concerned about the micro level that specifically involves youth and our young people. Really, the ethical vacuum that you spoke of has to be addressed by involving young people, so my question to you is this: what do you see as the mechanisms for linking up with the schools and providing greater leadership opportunities for young people to participate in this global forum?

Otunnu: I would say first of all that I'm deeply concerned about a set of conditions that has its origins in the era of scientific enlightenment in the West, when the spiritual realm was very sharply divorced from the material realm. A tremendous body of knowledge and understanding has been developed on the material/scientific front, but, on the other hand, a staggering ignorance has developed with regard to spiritual and ethical matters. A certain distance and even disdain has developed. I think we realize this all the more in the aftermath of the collapse of certainties of the ideological kind. So it is very important to educate people from the earliest level to understand that we have a materialist, scientific dimension to our lives which is very important but also a deeply spiritual, ethical aspect that must be developed, and developed unabashedly. There is no logical reason why this particular terrain should be the exclusive domain of fringe fundamentalist groups. This is a concern for everybody.

I think in that respect that the part of the world which is generally called "the North" has much to learn from what is generally referred to as "the South." There, these matters are taken more seriously, perhaps, than in the North. Having said that, it's also obvious that some specific projects must be developed at very specific levels to address each particular malaise as it manifests itself in one locality or another. In a given country it may be the question of generalized violence, or the problem of drugs or attitudes towards sex. In each society it will vary, and around those cluster of issues very specific projects must be developed. Beyond that, I can only say that I endorse the concern that you have just expressed.

Nancy Roof: I'm from the Values Caucus at the United Nations, and I want to congratulate you on the wonderful report. It's been very well received by the members of the Values Caucus. In reading it, though, there was one area where I had trouble. You seemed to make the social dimension of the global neighborhood — solidarity, ethics, values — secondary, and a department under the Economic Security Council. I wondered if we were going to be talking about money and economics and again excluding the quality of life, solidarity, and values that bring people together? Could you help me with that?

Otunnu: We, too, had trouble putting it together. As presently proposed, it is called the Economic Security Council, but our notion of security for the person — economic and social security — is a very broad one that would include exactly the concerns that you have expressed. Maybe the name is not the best, but I don't know what name would be more appropriate. But having said that, I must add that there were others within the Commission who felt that there should be a separate council. Indeed, in a different report, the one being prepared by Yale University and the Ford Foundation on restructuring the UN, which is coming out soon, I think they plan to recommend two separate councils. There would be both an Economic Security Council and a Social Security Council. Maybe that is a better way of cutting it, I don't know. We had both ideas on the table and in the end we settled with the idea of a single organ — an economic security council. I suppose part of our concern was the problem of having too many major, high-level organs. Just creating something which is analogous to the Security Council will be a tall order. If, in addition, you talk about another council, you make it that much more difficult. Everything you say makes sense, conceptually, but on the practical level, it would be a good deal more difficult to achieve.

Rod Morris: I'm from the Center for Global Citizens in Oneonta, New York. Can you tell us a little bit about the reception of this report around the world? What is the prognosis for the future and, more specifically, do you have any evidence that there's been a response by the Secretary of State or by the President?

Otunnu: My sense is that, first, the report has been circulating on a worldwide basis. There are a number of groups such as this one now taking up and discussing either the entire report or various aspects of it. So, at what you might call the popular level — ordinary citizens, groups, civic associations — it has been very well received and it is generating lively debate. At the leadership level, we've made efforts to introduce the report to the highest political circles. We shall not know for sure until later this year what kind of response it is receiving in high government circles, but all the heads of state and relevant ministers now have copies of the report. When the General Assembly meets an effort will be made to initiate some formal process around the report. We shall then know exactly what governments feel deep down. In the media, it has been given reasonably wide coverage — not always favorable coverage, but wide coverage in different parts of the world.

Unidentified: First of all, the situation in today's world is quite different than it was at the time the UN was founded, and its membership and direction has also changed. Furthermore, entities other than the UN and national governments have become significant. In the last five years, during the post-Cold War era, there has been a rise in ethnic strife around the world. We have roughly two hundred UN member states and 15,000 nationalities (if we define them by existing languages) in the world, and I think that will continue to be a source of strife into the twenty-first century. To what extent has the Commission addressed the following three problems, and to what extent has it incorporated them within the proposals you've outlined in terms of reorganization and an economic security council: how can one get the transnational corporations to play a part by exercising not only their rights but also their responsibilities; to what extent is the trusteeship council going to be responsible for the rights and responsibilities of minorities such as the Kurds that have been divided between five states; and to what extent are you going to allow civil society, the NGOs, to participate in the work of the UN?

Otunnu: I'm very grateful to you for laying out the situation so very clearly. We are conscious of the fact that the UN as founded in 1945 was a very different UN and arose in a very different world situation from that of the 1990s. In 1945 the key actors on the international scene were clearly governments. The dominant strife that preoccupied those who sat at the table was interstate conflict as exemplified by World War I and II. All that has changed. And as you correctly say, there are a number of new actors who have come on the scene who have become very important; in some cases governments hardly have any control over what they do. What we stress is that the task of global governance is now larger and more complex than can be undertaken by governments alone. Others must join in. Second, we say that, even without reinventing or reconstituting the UN, there must be greater input by those others into what the United Nations is doing. The United Nations would then indeed involve, in the words of the Charter, "We the peoples of the world." We also call for autonomous activities by these other actors in their spheres of particular interest. Both are important.

Quite a few of our recommendations address these concerns specifically. The right of petition would allow aggrieved peoples to appeal directly to the Security Council. The Forum of Civil Society would give greater voice to international civil society, and so on. We may not have elaborated in great detail how this will happen, but the approach is there. It offers a more comprehensive response to the problems of the world that governments, even if they had the will, couldn't possibly undertake by themselves.

Mohammed Nawawi: There is an irony, a dilemma that we must face, and I hope it will inform the discussion later on. The problem is this. On the one hand, unlike twenty years ago, we do see different faces, different colors, different looks here today. There is also an increasing, international sense of community. But although brotherhood is increasing, it is really a very limited, rather elite brotherhood. At one point in the past, ten percent of the West dominated the world. That ten percent has, today, become varicolored, but it still dominates the world. So, on the one hand we have increasing unity at the highest level, but increasing disparity between that level and the rest of the world.

On the level of international business, for example, it seems clear we are really a small village; I can reach Japan via my modem whenever necessary. But there is also an ever-increasing disjunction between rich and poor locally as well as globally that is part and parcel of the increasing unity among the elite elsewhere. How do we resolve this dilemma? Americans feel very disgruntled about the growing distance between them and their government, but the American elite is ever more closely tied with the Indonesian elite, with Indian elite. Unless we resolve this dilemma there will be conflicts, not only between ethnic groups but conflicts like in those in Algeria and Egypt — real conflicts between the people and the elite.

Otunnu: I certainly accept your entire premise. There is a sense in which there are rich people and poor people and those in between, regardless of the country. It is true here in this country as well as in the many parts of the world you've mentioned. But I would add that we have not yet superseded the historical reality in which there are richer parts of the world and poorer parts of the world as well. That is also still true by and large. So we have both developments going on at the same time. Within every country there may be a stronger, richer, more privileged elite forming in relation to the bulk of the population. At the same time, the elites, worldwide, are developing a certain measure of inter-elite solidarity thanks to communication, travel, and education. But that does not negate the fact that there are still poorer parts of the world and richer parts of the world. We need to tackle both questions and build a solidarity which is informed by both these realities.

I have no easy solution to the problem, but I know that in a setup which is more democratic — politically, socially, and economically — such problems will be easier to mediate. I'm not just talking about the electing of officials; I'm talking about the distribution of resources between one part of the country and another, and between one social class and another. I'm talking about opportunities, about authentic democracy as opposed to situations of make-believe or fraudulent democracy.

Jack Backman: I was in the Massachusetts Senate for a number of years, where I worked on a lot of human rights legislation and campaigned with others for real welfare reform. I want to thank you and the Commission on Global Governance for the beautiful vision contained in your remarks and the Commission's report. I also want to raise a question about the Universal Declaration of Human Rights. I noticed with great interest that you mention it in only two places in your report. On page 244 you state that "the General Assembly has played a role of vital importance starting with the Universal Declaration of Human Rights," and on page 55 that "human rights has been furthered by the Universal Declaration of Human Rights." Nowhere else in the report do you make reference to it or its provisions. It is almost the same as the perfunctory comments made about someone who has come and gone in life. I would like your comment.

Otunnu: We felt two things. One was that an area in which the UN has real and important success is in formulating standards of human rights and, to some extent, in putting into a place a regime of human rights. We can argue about how effective or ineffective it has been, but the Commission on Human Rights, the system of Rapporteurs, the working groups, the infrastructure that began with the Universal Declaration of Human Rights have developed both standards and a framework for enforcement, or at least for bringing pressure to bear. The second impression we had was that whatever the weaknesses of the General Assembly and the various bodies below it, it has been relatively successful in shaping international public opinion, in putting certain things on the agenda. South Africa provides an example of the role that the General Assembly played in keeping the issue of apartheid on the international agenda until the end of that regime. Those were the points we tried to make. We were not attempting to develop a major discussion of the UN regime of human rights. We recognize their importance as an example of the kind of thing that can be done by the United Nations.

Response Panel #1

JACQUES BAUDOT

• • •

Jacques Baudot was Coordinator of the World Summit for Social Development held in March of 1995 in Copenhagen. A French national, he has spent his life in public service both in France and at the United Nations. He served at the French Planning Commission and Demographic Institute, and has worked at the United Nations Office in New York for the last twenty years.

The message of the Report of the Commission on Global Governance and the message of the World Summit for Social Development are very similar. To the notion of a "global neighborhood" — a beautiful expression which should capture the imagination of the young generations — corresponds the notion of "solidarity," which is one of the mottoes of the Summit. To the emphasis on values and on the need for a "global civil ethic," corresponds the acknowledgment by Heads of State and Government that "our society must respond more effectively to the material and spiritual needs of individuals." In both texts, the need for respect for the right of individuals is balanced by a call for a greater sense of responsibility on the part of all

"It is extremely important, I would even say comforting, to see in such a report mention of integrity and caring at the same level as liberty and respect for life."

actors on the world scene.

It is more important to stress such similarities than to look for differences. The reason is that there is a need, at the end of the twentieth century, for the concerted efforts of all people and all institutions of goodwill to identify the common good and the various paths to our common future. I shall, therefore, make a few comments on the conditions, as I see them, for a United Nations Renaissance.

The United Nations ought to make a contribution to the spirit of the time, to the ideas and emotions that shape the behavior of people and institutions, through its participation in global discourse — in its peacekeeping activity, but also in human rights, humanitarian affairs, or development. This means that the United Nations, as an organization, must be more than a pure reflection of the dominant culture and more than the least common denominator of the policies of its member-states. It means that the United Nations cannot be "neutral" and must offer an "added value" to the spirit of the time and to the dominant discourse. Please note that this conception of the United Nations implies that we do not accept a "providential history," or a determinism in human affairs created, for instance, by the evolution of our scientific ideas and the technologies they generate.

To contribute to the discourse on human problems and their solutions, the United Nations must have at its disposal criteria for sorting out the "good" and the "bad" aspects of the spirit of the time. Such criteria can only be derived from a set of universal values on which the institution is built, and which are interpreted, at this point in our history, through debates, resolutions of the General Assembly, and conferences such as the Social Summit. Hence the value, and the necessity, of the United Nations as a forum where the various political philosophies and political projects, as well as ideologies, are openly debated.

One of the most negative aspects of the spirit of the time is precisely to ridicule the United Nations as a forum (the "Talk Shop") and to ridicule the "philosophical debates." We badly need philosophy, not so much in the sense of a comprehensive theory on humankind, but more in the sense of a capacity to question our basic assumptions; and we badly need a passage between the theoretical, or the abstract, and the practical. To elaborate policies and measures for governments or for other actors in a conscious manner is precisely to bridge the gap between a philosophy and its practical consequences.

Is it possible to list the "universal values" which should assist the United Nations in sorting out the negative and positive features of our dominant culture? The values listed in the report of the Commission on Global Governance are both "traditional" and, I think, "revolutionary." We see "respect for life", "liberty," "justice and equity," and we see also "mutual respect," "caring," and "integrity." It is extremely important, I would even say comforting, to see in such a report mention of integrity and caring at the same level as liberty and respect for life. Without mentioning the various values which appear here and there in the Copenhagen Declaration, I should like to offer my own interpretation of this text by mentioning four moral orientations of the Social Summit.

The first is a subordination of the drive for the individual or national interest to the search for the common good. Whether for corporations, for public authorities, or for all individuals, the notion of responsibility vis-à-vis other human beings and the society at large is very much at the heart of the Copenhagen text. The second is related to the notion of service — not only public service, which, incidentally, ought to be strongly rehabilitated after decades of criticism, but also the notion of service to others, which is the most fundamental part of the exercise of power. To my mind, we, in the Copenhagen text, made a concession to the spirit of the time — should I say to political correctness? — by using the word "empowerment." However, we limited the potential damage that is attached to this concept by indicating that those who have the privilege to be in a situation of power — political, economic, or moral — ought to see such privilege as a source of obligation to the human community.

A third moral orientation of the Summit is the emphasis, not only on social justice and equity, but also on equality, a notion that is not very much favored in contemporary discourse. In many respects, there is a need in our societies for plain and simple equality between human beings. Lastly, permeating the text, is a sense of moderation in the judgment of contemporary problems as well as in the solutions which are proposed. Actually, the word solution is not used very frequently. We have tried to avoid the intellectual or political arrogance which too often divides the world between those who know and those who do not know.

For the United Nations to gain a moral authority and to be in a position to have a better discourse on world affairs, there are at least two conditions which ought to be met. A first condition relates to the participation of what is more and more frequently called the "civil society" in the deliberations and actions of the world organization. If we understand by civil society all institutions which are not part of government and the public sphere, and if we include in this concept the business community as well as the media, the churches, and the various associations pursuing global or sectorial objectives, then we can say that there is a glaring need for a more fruitful partnership between this civil society and the intergovernmental bodies which govern the United Nations system.

To the perfectly respectable notions of "advocacy" and "lobbying" for a particular cause — please note, however, that in order to be acceptable in the United Nations such a cause has to be compatible with the universal values we mentioned above — we must emphasize the notions of responsibility and accountability. Non-governmental organizations must see the United Nations not only as a forum for a dissemination of their views, but a place where they will have to report to the world community on their contribution to the common good.

A second condition for a "good" discourse of the United Nations is a moral continuity between the culture of the institution and the message it delivers to the world. We ought to be very demanding about the "virtues" that the organization should embody. Beyond the rather narrow concept of "efficiency," we should insist on intellectual probity, on respect for the other which, as we know, is more than tolerance, and on respect for the richness of life in society. The United Nations' discourse has, traditionally, been too technocratic. If we have, within the United Nations, a culture which refuses elitism and arrogance, then we shall be able to promote a type of international cooperation which would lead us to a better future. To the notion of mutual interest, we must add the notion of mutual respect and compassion for the weakest.

In many ways, the message of the Commission on Global Governance and the message of the Social Summit are "against the current." This is good and needed for the building of a global neighborhood in the twenty-first century.

Response Panel #1

DESSIMA WILLIAMS

• • •

Dessima Williams is a professor, social researcher and diplomat. She is former Ambassador from Grenada to the Organization of American States, and an NGO participant at the World Summit for Social Development in Copenhagen. Now a Visiting Associate Professor of Sociology at Brandeis University, she has also taught international relations and women in development at Williams College.

I begin with recounting a personal experience. On International Women's Day this year, as hundreds of women gathered for another day of international conferencing at the World's Summit on Social Development in Copenhagen, Denmark, one of my friends said to me, "Dessima, we have to do something special today. It's our day. It's women's day. You're the bold one in the group; what should we do?" Before I could celebrate, or protest, my reputation, or even try to uphold it, someone else said, "Let's sing. Let's give them some 'Mother, the Great Stone' singing here." "Mother, the Great Stone" is the anthem of the Caribbean Women's movement. It's sung when Caribbean women cross all divisions of class and profession and language and get together. We appeal to the mother of us all, the great Earth. It goes something like this: Mother, the great stone got to move,

> "The moral of the story is that people have power and can and must use it for governance and to push government."

Mother, the great stone, the stone of Babylon, Mother the Great stone got to move."

The expression, "great stone of Babylon," as you may know, is borrowed from our brother, Bob Marley. It's the stone of slavery and colonialism and of various forms of women's oppression. Everyone agreed that we would sing it, and we did. As soon as we got done with that, someone else said, "Well, we have to do something else." And before we could figure out what to do, someone said, "On the blue carpet, we'll all meet on the blue carpet." Over the next four days, about a dozen of us — joined intermittently by over a hundred conference delegates — fasted on a liquid diet only, sitting on a blue carpet in the middle of a passage for government delegates at the conference.

Women from Africa, the Caribbean, Canada, Japan, and the US joined this fast. It was our way of doing what *Our Global Neighborhood* asks, which is that people take action, and further, that as women we can — and must — exercise leadership. What then was our purpose? To establish a bridge, a visible, energized human bridge between the 1.4 billion people, predominantly women and children, who fast daily by force of the poverty born of their powerlessness, and the over one hundred heads of government — ninety-six percent men — deciding on social development.

What did the women's fast accomplish? We were able to open up a dialogue between power and human need. We were able to make a direct appeal to government leaders, some of whom acted on information we gave them. The moral of the story is that people have power and can and must use it for governance and to push government.

Now, my response to the Report, *Our Global Neighborhood*. It is an exciting development. Those of us who labored in the '70s and '80s for reforms within the United Nations system and within global political economy welcomed the recommendations therein. Indeed, it's the condensation, as Ambassador Otunnu said this morning, of a number of longstanding initiatives. For example, the idea of the sovereignty of the people can already be found in a particular reading of conventional international law; that is, a sovereignty that has been mobilized not only by governments but by peoples as well. To popularize this interpretation now is exciting, particularly in terms of the creation of the "people's shield," the right of petition against institutional abuses — the global war machine — to structural adjustment policies. Hopefully, the report will invigorate many with visions of a more equitable and sustainable twenty-first century.

I quote from the section of the *Call to Action* that deals with globalization. "Globalization is in danger of widening the gap between rich and poor." There is no danger of this happening in the future. The gap between rich and poor *has* occurred, and it *is* growing. Let me enlarge on that from the point of view of gender. It is very significant that the group that is the poorest, the most unemployed, and that constitutes the largest number of refugees, illiterates, etc., is made up of women and children. The United Nations Development Program (UNDP) captured that fact in its demonstration of worldwide resource distribution as a champagne glass structure. It is as follows: if we divide the world into quintiles, the top layer has access to and ownership of eighty-three percent of the resources of the world and the bottom twenty percent has control of less than two percent. Many of us like to think that we're in the great middle class, struggling for the remaining sixteen percent. The distribution — or maldistribution — of global resources, which is, in large measure, a consequence of globalization, is also defined by gender. At the very top, where power is most concentrated, we find a paucity of women. And at the very bottom, where power and resources are most absent, we find a concentration of women. If we take the UNDP's indicator, the human development index, which brings together life expectancy, standard of living, and literacy, nowhere in the world do women experience development equal to that of men.

Ambassador Otunnu talked this morning—as does the report—about the need for leadership. We need to bring together women (as the backbone, or as the Haitians say, the "poto mitans" of civil society) and the need for new leadership in our world today. Two years ago, a number of world figures were asked their opinion about the single most important idea necessary for the needed twenty-first century renaissance. Gabriel Garcia Marquez, South American author and Nobel literary laureate, said that the single most important thing that we could do to give ourselves a new chance would be to turn global management and leadership over to women. I'd like to ask that we think about that. And I'd like to suggest to Ambassador Otunnu that there are many wonderful women in civil society who in fact can make this kind of contribution. As he crisscrosses the world exploring the next stages of the work of the Commission, he might look into this possibility. And so might the rest of us. Finally, congratulations and thanks for the report.

Response Panel #1

ROBERT MEAGHER

• • •

Robert F. Meagher is Professor Emeritus of International Law at the Fletcher School of Law and Diplomacy, Tufts University, and a consultant on international economic law. He has lectured and taught in South Africa, India, Bangladesh, Thailand, the Philippines, and Australia, among many other places. Professor Meagher has authored a number of books and articles on international economic law, international financial aid, law and social change, international organizations, and environmental law.

L et me begin with a quotation from Wordsworth: "The world is too much with us late and soon, getting and spending." That is very true in this country. When Valerie Epps said there is a lot of cynicism here, she was absolutely right. But as Aldous Huxley said, "Cynical realism is an intelligent man's best excuse for doing nothing in an intolerable situation." Cynicism isn't going to get us anywhere, so I would like to be more positive as I move on. One last reference, a sentiment from one of e. e. cummings' poems: there's a hell of a good world next door; let's go. But we all know there isn't any such world. This is the only one we have, and we have to face a few things which are disturbing. The world today is radically different than the world of fifty years ago.

"Complex organizations, including the NGOs, all have problems of bureaucratization and power. And when you go into a country and begin to tell people what's best for them, which many NGOs do, they are trying to organize and implement policies that would be better left to the people of those countries."

The fifty countries who negotiated the UN Charter have now expanded to 184. That means that we live in a very complicated society. And, unlike the previous speakers, I'm not sure that the expression "global neighborhood" is a good one. I'm not sure because it makes the situation cozier and closer than it really is. I've lived in many countries where there are people who have never been to a city. They don't know about their own country, let alone the world. Though simplification is nice and pleasing, it also tends to distort reality. There are still a lot of problems that have to be discussed very seriously.

What is the underlying theme of this publication? The need for an international redistribution of wealth and power. We're not going to get there by being observers; we have to become participants. But if we become participants, a lot of the nice things we usually say will have to become a little cruder and a little rougher. There is no doubt at all that in the world today those who already have are getting more. Yes, we believe in democracy, but when things like the Charter of Economic Rights and Duties of States came up, the United States was one of the six countries that voted against it. We believe in democracy for us, but we don't believe that the eighty percent of the world's population that lives in the developing world should have as strong a voice as we do. We have wealth — that is our power — and we are not willing to give it up. We want to preserve power.

I listened last week to someone from the United Kingdom get up and say, "Look at how the UN has messed up in Bosnia." But who really messed up in Bosnia? Who refused to face the situation when it was faceable? Who refused to put up the money? When the Europeans said, "Well, we really don't want to get involved," the United States responded by saying, "This is really a European question." Then we kept playing the game, back and forth, and there was no money, no way to take care of the problem.

These things will not disappear, no matter how many laws we pass, no matter how many institutions we create. Having spent more than half my life living in Asia and Africa, I learned long ago that passing laws is easy, creating institutions is easy, but unless they're built upon a base of the people you're trying to affect, unless they come from these people they are irrelevant. Take a simple example from this country. We passed a Constitutional amendment against the making, sale, and consumption of alcoholic beverages: Prohibition.

It took two-thirds vote of the House and two-thirds vote of the Senate and ratification of three-fourths of the states of the United States, and there was probably more drinking between 1920 and 1932 than at any other time in the history of the United States. Unless law comes from the people, no matter what law you enact, you cannot automatically carry the day.

Does it really make any difference to most of the world who sits on the Security Council? No. Does it make a difference to the Japanese and the Germans? Yes. To the Indians, the Nigerians, and the Brazilians? Yes. They're interested in power. Their representatives are interested in being in a position to do things for their country. In other words, the internationalism of international organizations is in some ways exaggerated. There is still a great deal of provincialism.

However, having said those few negative things, I want to add that we are much better off today than we were before World War I, much better off than we were with the League of Nations, and we'll be better off in the future. The problem is that most people still believe that you can have revolutionary change. I am a proponent of incremental change. Not because I prefer things to go slowly, but because that is the way the world operates. You can't go into a complicated country, India, for example, and say, "change all your ways. There are only 900 million of you, it should be easy, we passed a law last week." What happened in the Soviet Union? We sent over American economists like Jeff Sachs. Does he want to work with existing Russian institutions and modernize them? No. He wants to give them the American banking laws, the American SEC; he wants to make the Russians Americans. There is an inability to understand that each culture is unique and that each institution that comes from within a society comes because the people there understand and want it.

We can speak about global neighborhoods and about core values, but let's sit down and think for a second. The world is basically divided into two types of societies. Individual societies, of which there are very few, and communal societies of which most of the world is composed. In economic terms, those translate in different ways. We talk about the command economies in the former communist countries. We discuss American market economy, but the one economy we never talk about, the one that predominates in the world, is the mixed economy. There are no market economies that are pure. We act as if there are. The Germans have dozens of public enterprises. The French do, the Italians do, and even the Americans have farm and other subsidies. Is that part of a market economy? There are hundreds of similar instances.

In the United Nations, which has 184 member states, developing countries, under the group of seventy-seven, control approximately 125 votes. They can pass any resolution they want. But fourteen countries contribute most of the UN budget. When push came to shove a few years ago, when the New International Economic Order fell, the US exercised its power and, as a result, there's been a muting of protest within the international system.

I think insufficient attention was devoted to transnational corporations in *Our Global Neighborhood*. I'm very familiar with their activities. I've advised many companies in many countries. There are problems there, since they are the principal source of capital for developing countries. These problems will get bigger year by year, since there is no international regulation of transnational corporations.

And, finally, an observation about non-governmental organizations, which represent the biggest change I've seen in international work in the past forty years. I want to add a word of caution, because I know many people here like NGOs very much. Complex organizations, including the NGOs, all have problems of bureaucratization and power. And when you go into a country and begin to tell people what's best for them, which many NGOs do, they are trying to organize and implement policies that would be better left to the people of those countries.

RESPONSE

By Mr. Otunnu

I'm very grateful for the very rich commentary from the panelists and I shall try my best to convey faithfully these sentiments to fellow members of the Commission. I would like to take up several of their comments briefly.

Mr. Baudot spoke of the "added value" that the United Nations ought to offer and of the way in which the UN is composed of, and yet should be more than, the sum of the component members. I want to stress my agreement with that. The UN cannot be divorced from the real power structure in the world. If it were, it would simply become a utopian project. So it must in some way relate to the power structure in the world. But at the same time, if it were no more than that, if it were simply a mirror image of the power structure in the world, it would become merely a mechanism of Realpolitik. What the UN must seek to do is reflect that power structure while going beyond it to promote and underline certain values and principles that can mediate international life. This is the kind of nuanced role the UN must strive to play.

Professor Williams spoke quite rightly about the problems arising from the allocation of power and resources and from the social differentiation which exists in the world. And it is true that the Commission didn't go into this at great length. The sectorial reports by the various independent commissions are both more focused and also deeper in their analyses and recommendations; the Commission's report is broader but obviously could not be as deep. That is why there are many areas where the Commission signals a problem and underlines a possible proposition but doesn't really develop it fully.

I also agree with Professor Williams that women are the most vulnerable and, in many societies, the most marginalized in the distribution of power and resources. Perhaps the only group that is sometimes more vulnerable is children. I also agree that more needs to be done to bring women into leadership positions, and that women may have more to offer than simply the leadership qualities that anyone who is a good leader may have. Having said that, I would add that it is also true that there are such things as poorer societies, poorer communities, more marginalized regions, more marginalized religious groups, and, although this does not contradict the fact that within each society women and children may be the most vulnerable and the most marginalized, we must keep this larger perspective in mind.

Professor Meagher spoke about the place of law, a subject that could lead us to a discussion about the place of democracy as well. It isn't sufficient to have laws and standards. It's not sufficient to have institutions. Yes, one must actually cultivate a whole culture, a whole way of responding to such problems. That is why I keep saying that what the Commission is underlining is an approach, a way of responding — something deeper than structures and laws. Take democracy, for example: one can have institutions and periodic elections, but in the end, enduring democracy can only grow from the local soil. It takes time to affect the actual outlook of the people within a particular society.

Concerning the reform of the Security Council, I would say that this project is not about democracy as ordinarily understood — democracy among people. Rather, it aims at the creation of a Security Council that more accurately reflects the power structure in the world than does the present Security Council. It's about updating the power structure. But it's also about democracy in the more limited sense of relative democracy between nations and different regions of the world as distinct from democracy among the people. There is value in such limited reform that we shouldn't lose sight of.

Finally on the NGO community: since I see a number of representatives here, let me say this. There are two challenges facing the NGO community. One is that the NGO world is not entirely independent of the international imbalance between North and South. It is disproportionately congregated in the North, and the NGOs from the North have disproportionately extended their tentacles into the South. This is something to take into account because, instead of correcting, this tends to reinforce the imbalances that exist in other sectors of international life. One should not overstate that case, but it needs to be underscored. Secondly, the NGOs have rightly stressed the importance of accountability and transparency in the affairs of governance at the national and international levels. But I think it is important for NGOs to be reflective and self-critical in this regard as well, both when operating within national boundaries and when working internationally. They too could do with a good deal more accountability and transparency.

OPEN DISCUSSION
Following Panel #1

Joseph Baratta: I've been trying to recall historical parallels to the work of the Commission on Global Governance. What private initiatives have historically resulted in some official reform of the order that we're talking about? One is the formation of the league to enforce peace under Hamilton Holt in 1915, which was influential on Woodrow Wilson in 1919. Another case is Solomon Levinson's article in *Christian Century* in 1918 which led to the movement to outlaw war and the Kellogg-Briand Pact ten years later in 1928. A third, closer to the Second World War, was the founding of the Commission for the Strengthening of Peace organized under James T. Shotwell in 1939, just as Hitler was invading Poland. That private initiative had some influence on the United States when the UN Charter was being drafted in 1944 and 1945. Still another instance was Winston Churchill's leadership between 1946 and 1948, which led to the great Congress in Amsterdam in 1948 and to the founding of the Council of Europe. Further examples would be Jean Monnet's work on Robert Schuman's proposal for a European Coal and Steel Community, and his Action Committee for a United States of Europe, which influenced the Treaty of Rome and led to the establishment of the European Community.

In the case of the United Nations, the only example I could think of was the Clark-Sohn plan in *World Peace through Law* (1958), which was part of a movement to exercise Article 109, which called for a review conference after ten years. That effort failed; a review conference has never been held. Now we have the Commission on Global Governance. In the light of these historical precedents, could someone on the panel reflect on the consequences your work might have?

Baudot: I would like to be the first to answer because I had nothing to do with the work of the Commission. First, all the historical examples that Mr. Baratta gave are obviously correct, but there is something that should have been further emphasized. Many commissions and reformers have insisted on changing structures, creating new institutions, or modifying the existing ones. The Commission on Global Governance did that, too. However, it did something else which is much more important. It insisted on the importance of changing ideas, ways of thinking, processes. That is much more important than any reshuffling of the current UN as an institution. And success in this respect is much more critical. It is something that none of us will be able to measure because there are so many things that will influence the way the UN and the international community work. To me, though, this is the main value of this kind of an effort.

Otunnu: Two contemporary examples stand out in particular. First, you mentioned Jean Monnet and the construction of the European Community. It is striking that what has become the European Union today began as modest, ad hoc, but determined efforts by private individuals. But it is *inconceivable* that it could have become what it is today without becoming a major pan-European project of governments as well as of peoples. That, to me, is evidence that if there is democracy and participation, many things can be done. The second example, more recent, is Arvid Pardo. Was he from Russia or the US? No, he came from Malta! And whose idea was it, his government's? No, it was an idea that came from him, from one particular individual, an idea about global management of the resources of the seas and open waters. That idea led to one of the most important projects of the United Nations ever, the Law of the Sea project. One individual fed this into the intergovernmental process.

Both these things occurred at a time when the ruling view was that these were areas for governments, not for individuals. People weren't as receptive to individual initiatives. Today, governments and others are more receptive to ideas regardless of where they come from. We must receive initiatives from wherever they come and simply judge them on their merits. Finally, it is obvious that, in order to succeed, initiatives — however they emerge — must be fed into the intergovernmental process sooner or later. That is why we have hope that what the Commission has recommended will eventually end up in some kind of intergovernmental process leading to major initiatives.

Meagher: I think another initiative that became extremely important was the informal talks between John Maynard Keynes and Harry Dexter White which led to the Bretton Woods institutions — the International Monetary Fund, the World Bank, and also an international trade organization that preceded the General Agreement on Tariffs and Trade. I think that is another example of two people doing most of the work almost by themselves.

Scott Mohr: Alfred North Whitehead said, "Ideas won't keep. Something must be done about them." I believe that's the attitude of this conference, so my question focuses on what is to be done about them? I also want to pick up on some remarks that were made earlier today about the fact that elites tend to talk to other elites while the vast mass of human society, as Newton said, referring to the ocean, "roar[s] along beside [them]." What is to be done to reach out and construct a base of power? This is an issue, as Professor Meagher pointed out, of power and influence. The world is run by very powerful people who make the decisions that determine the conditions of our lives, and this conference is proposing to change those decisions in significant ways on a global basis. That's absolutely breathtaking and astonishing, but in order to do that there must be some base of power, some lever to use which will make a difference. Otherwise, these recommendations will drift off as another irrelevant historical footnote.

It seems to me the Commission recognizes some of that, although I don't think it addressed it very directly. For example, one can find the following in the book: "People throughout the world tend to be guided by the media — and they are predominantly Western media — in determining when a problem warrants international action. Television coverage of a situation has become, for many, a precondition for action. Yet for most commercial networks, the precondition is crisis. There has to be large-scale violence..." It seems to me that if a power base is to be created for the kind of change that's being advocated here, that power base must somehow be achieved through diligent, sophisticated media attention on a global basis. I wonder if any thought has been given to how that might be accomplished.

Meagher: One of the points you made is very important: the media have had a tremendous impact all over the world. In Asia today, thanks to the Star Network, people who previously didn't know what was happening in the next village now look at programs and receive ideas from all over the world. And during the problems in Tiananmen Square, the fax machine and Internet became means for people in China to communicate with one another in ways the government could do nothing to prevent. As a result, a large number of people were empowered. The movement failed, but that happens to lots of movements. The point is that the new age of telecommunications is going to have a profound effect on political bases throughout the world.

Williams: I want to respond by returning to the question that was posed first. In the civil rights movement in the US there has been a tendency to see Martin Luther King first and Rosa Parks somewhere in distant second, with everybody else on the periphery. But as we think about what is to be done in terms of young people and activism in the US in the 1990s, we must review the past and take a look at the larger structure of what was a sustained and, to a large extent, successful movement made up of many, many individuals and not just an elite and its leader. We need that perspective now as we grapple with the moment.

The Commission was made up of twenty-eight members, six of whom were women. We believe that the leadership of organizations — whether the United Nations, academic institutions, or the media — has to be made up more and more of those whom we want to reach, and to whom we want the balance of power transferred. When we leave conferences like this, it is important to take this message with us when we return to the places where we work.

Secondly, I'd like to say that the research that we undertake is important in signaling this transfer of power and wealth — through the subjects we explore, who we involve, and how we manage the results of our work. We have a terrific initiative here on the part of the UN, but equally powerful undertakings are going on in places we don't know about, or to which we don't have access. That's important to bear in mind. I often tell my students that the world does not look like our middle class, northeastern United States classroom. Invert that model, and then we will see our mission if we are really interested in social change and democracy.

Lastly, I want to offer a focus for organizing our perceptions. In the publicity for a movie that is about to be released, an American says, "We are here to preserve democracy, not to practice it." I think we should think about that.

David Allen: Mr. Otunnu just cited the case of Europe and the building of Europe. If we use that example — groups joining together in Europe to create some sort of larger entity — to reflect on larger, global developments, presumably there are some parallels, and some interesting implications. In particular, Europe started out as an idea about simple interdependencies, largely in the economic realm. It has become much more than that. Indeed, there is now discussion of some sort of European government. Of course, there is resistance. Those on the more "liberal" side of the Western tradition, particularly in the United Kingdom, resist this, and yet over a period of several decades we've seen a movement from loose affiliations to much stronger, more coherent, more government-like affiliations.

I mention this in order to ask a question about a proposition in the Commission's report that the topic is governance and not world government. If we look at history, can we conclude that we can expect governance and not government over a period of time? Looking ahead, the answer may lie in the issues of bureaucracy and power that Mr. Otunnu referred to when he talked about reform of the Security Council.

Ottunu: The European example contrasts two possible approaches. One is construction by design. You begin with a grand design and construct to fit it. But the other is exactly the route that Europe followed: construction by planting facts, modest facts that, step by step, leave a trail that becomes a trend around which various standards and structures are built. That is the way Europe has been constructed. Personally, I'm very partial to that approach. It's an approach that might be explored in other parts of the world as opposed to a grand design model.

My second response to you would be this. Is it possible to build global government except around governments? History up till now leans in that direction. However, the international scene has also changed incredibly over the last many years, so there is not too much history to go on. If we examine the situation in 1945 and contrast it with just one area today — the role of transnational corporations — nothing in 1945 foretold what was to come. While history may not be a good guide, the realities of today — which I think will only grow in the future — tend to suggest that governance must certainly be about government at various levels, but also be about other actors. It is simply not possible anymore for government alone to respond to existing challenges. In any event, there are other actors we have to contend with who have become as powerful or more powerful than government.

I would suggest as an alternative perspective on history, to look at how things developed in Europe. If you look at individual nations, you will discover that before there were nations there were small duchies, sometimes fighting, sometimes working together. As time passed, larger, more powerful interests took hold, particularly at the commercial level. That is to say, there is an historical analog to the current global situation. The interesting question is, what path will humans take as they move to larger and larger forms of organization? It seems to me there is a danger in thinking that we must imagine government only in the ways we're used to conceiving of it. Instead, we should ask if we can define a democratic form which takes into account the human tendency to bureaucracy as well as prospects for abuse of power, and this includes all the powerful economic actors.

The historical trend is not linear by any means. As we speak we are witnessing at least two very contradictory trends. On the one hand it is true that, from duchies to nation states to a pan-European union, Europe is getting larger and bigger. But as we witness that process of integration, we also see the opposite, a kind of disintegration. In Africa, for example, it seems easier for Africans to speak of their pan-African identity: "We are all Africans;" and it's easy for them to say, "We are Baganda." But it's not always very easy for them to say with conviction, "We are Ugandans." These are contradictory realities and one simply has to find a way of managing both trends.

Unidentified: The previous question helps me to put mine better. I think it was Professor Meagher who used to insist that you should make your assumptions and premises explicit. I was excited at the beginning of this conference, but the more I hear, the more depressed I get. The cause is some of the concepts being used here, such as "poverty." Poverty implies inequality and tends to bring about conflict. As you try to devise remedies for inequality, you sometimes create conflict. Affirmative action in the United States is one of the best examples. The remedy becomes a problem. Since the concept of poverty is embodied in the very concept of the global neighborhood, I wonder if the panel can throw more light on it and how we can deal with it. Marxism began by proclaiming the elimination of poverty and the creation of equality and ended up destroying itself.

"Education" is another such term. Education can be used to eliminate poverty, but it can bring about inequality, too. Still another, "ideology." Ambassador Otunnu started by saying that the Cold War has ended, as if that means the end of ideological conflict. Ideologies by nature tend to be dogmatic and now, with the end of the Cold War, are we in search of another ideology? Is there an ideology embodied in this concept of spirituality? What kind of philosophy are you looking at? Are you saying that capitalism must triumph now, or some alternative? This has not been made explicit, and I don't understand where we are going. Another is "sovereignty." Sovereignty is important here because when you put it in the international context, it points to the problem of enforcing international decisions and norms. Who is sovereign? And who is going to enforce the decisions? The international community? The NGOs? Whatever we devise, whatever we propose, somebody has to enforce it.

Lastly, I was intrigued by Professor Meagher's contribution, especially the idea that you don't create institutions where they don't have the good soil in which to take root. The problem is that in Africa we've debated the concept of democracy and we've been told that democracy is not a universal concept. Africans need their forms, Asians need theirs. But I think this ignores the very concept of human nature — human nature seen as a universal element in world process.

Baudot: First of all, I don't think the increase in poverty in the industrialized world, whether it is in France or in the US, can be attributed to an excess of Marxism. Secondly, to have better taxes, to have a better system of distribution and, therefore, through that to reduce poverty is certainly not to build a system which is totalitarian. Thirdly, to talk about spirituality, ethics, and values is certainly not to deny the enormous amount of material poverty which has to be addressed. But to say that at the same time there is such a thing as a poverty of the spirit, that is very telling in our current contemporary societies.

Williams: I'll speak on the question of the material poverty that two-thirds of humanity finds itself in. As I indicated earlier, that two-thirds is overwhelmingly female and living in the Southern hemisphere. One of the ways in which those of us who work in this field conceptualize this situation is to say that it is the result of an imbalance of power. Part of that power involves an over-consumption of material and other kinds of non-material wealth in the North. The work of the Commission begins to grapple with that — not directly, but indirectly through issues of governance. I was very pleased, for example, to see references to an Economic Security Council that would take up the question of how to regulate transnational corporations. To the extent that there is some progress in that domain, we believe that the enlarged power the multinational corporations hold over the economies in many small countries will be reduced. But tackling the power imbalance is what I find most important, because poverty is less a question of resources than of political imbalance.

Meagher: It seems to me that the questions raised here have been answered. In terms of development, you can talk about efficient growth, which is what most economists talk about, and you can talk about growth with equity, which is what Third World countries talk about. You can also talk about growth and no development. These are large topics. Another way of looking at all this is to consider growth and the redistribution of wealth a zero sum game: if you gain because you're poor, I lose because I'm rich. Another theory supposes that if you create a big enough pie, everybody will have more. You choose the one you prefer.

In terms of the end of history, which Karl Marx and, more recently, Fukiyama, wrote about, we've always had people who believed that history had come to an end because their view of history was so narrow. When one particular thing happened, that ended it. I don't think the end of history has taken place, and I don't think capitalism as we knew it fifty years ago will be capitalism as we know it fifty years from today.

Jim Moore: I don't want anything I say to be interpreted as not being one hundred percent supportive of your report, but I would like to deal specifically with the Security Council issues. As I understand the report, you've suggested a change in size and composition of the Security

Council and the elimination of the veto. I would like to suggest that there may be some other things that ought to be considered if you want to have the report received favorably by some of the major nations. For example, the primary purpose of the UN, according to the Charter, is to maintain international peace. And to maintain international peace, I believe we have learned over the last fifty years that you need to have three basic items. You need to have sufficient force. We certainly learned that in Korea. You need to have financial resources backing that force. And we certainly learned that in Iraq where the United States felt that it needed to pass the hat to get support. And you need the will of the world behind the action. We learned that lesson all too painfully in Vietnam, where the United States was unwilling to put the issue to a UN vote. That is one of the lessons we learned the hard way.

I would like to suggest as well that you have not dealt adequately with the question of representation. I don't believe that the United States, the United Kingdom, Russia, or China would be willing to (forgive me Professor Williams) consider their votes equal to Grenada's vote. This has to do not only with power resources, but with financial resources. To induce the United States or the five major powers to give up a veto, perhaps you could consider substituting a different kind of vote. Perhaps, before an action is taken, you could have three votes: maybe a power vote, a financial vote, and then a will of the world vote.

One way of having a power vote would be for nations to pledge certain resources to the UN before any action is taken. Nations pledging financial resources before such actions would be given a vote. Or, perhaps, if we pledged a battleship or a unit of force we would be given so many votes. That would signal a balancing of representation on these very crucial issues. The same could be done in connection with the financing of a vote. Simply asking countries to give up the veto will not work unless you substitute some other mechanism. I would like to hear your reactions to this kind of an approach and the idea of getting it adopted by the major nations.

Jacques Baudot: I noted with great pleasure that the gentleman only mentioned four members of the Security Council, this seems to mean that France is ready to accept...

Dessima Williams: First of all, we are all equal, but if power is to be determined on the basis of who can send battleships to the front, I would encourage Caribbean integration — so Grenada can enlarge its size by aligning with Jamaica and Puerto Rico, Cuba and so on. But I would then also endorse proposals for the subdivision of the United States of America into at least ten independent states.

Otunnu: Your last point, about a more sophisticated method of voting is a very good one. It is one that needs to be explored further. After all, there are institutions in which similar things are now used. The Bretton Woods institutions have a very different system of voting: weighted voting. In ten years, when a comprehensive review is undertaken, there is no reason why that shouldn't be considered. I don't want to go into details, but it can be developed and discussed further. Secondly, you need have no fear that proposing equality within the Security Council — not between the members of the Security Council and much less between the members of the UN. What we are proposing is something which reflects your three indices of contribution, whether troops or military power, financial sources or political and diplomatic will. That should be reflected better than it is at the moment in the Security Council, and, certainly, other kinds of contributions which are now not fully recognized should be highlighted. Your thinking is not far from what the Commission is putting forward.

Response Panel #2

BETTY REARDON

. . .

Betty A. Reardon is the founder and director of the Peace Education Program at Teachers College, Columbia University, and of the International Institutes on Peace Education. She is a peace educator who has taught at all levels, from elementary to graduate, and has published widely in various fields related to peace education.

I want to express my gratitude at being invited to participate in what I believe is the beginning of the next phase of the Commission's work — the process of learning what is necessary to achieve the visions that were put forth in the Commission's report. As I thought about what I wanted to say and why I wanted to say it, I also thought of a joke that was told by the headmaster at a small school where I taught because it says so much about perspective and response as conditioned by experience. A first grade teacher who had just spent an afternoon in reading lessons with her seven-year-olds had an accident on the highway, a problem with her tire. She got out of the car, looked at the tire and said, "Oh! Oh! Oh! Look! Look! Look! Damn!

"The report makes reference to ethnicity and religion, but no reference is made to cosmology or to how people see the whole world...If we are going to be part of a community, we have to recognize those identities, bring together the richness of the multiple cultures of the Earth and try to fashion from it another dimension of identity and being for all of us."

Damn! Damn!" As I was preparing my remarks, I was reading student papers, so my comments will take the form of a paragraph containing an affirmation of learning achieved along with comments and suggestions on a learning agenda.

There is clearly a great deal of learning reflected in the Commission's report. It is a testament to the ability of persons inside systems to learn, and suggests that the systems themselves can learn. It seems to me that high marks have to be given on a number of points. One is the authentic global perspective. By this I mean that the report not only takes into account the entire system and all its actors, but gives serious attention to actors other than those belonging to state systems. But I want to repeat the cautionary statement about "global otherness" that was offered by the last speaker from the floor this morning. His remarks made clear to me something an Indian friend of mine has long been saying about Western universalism: in international arenas when we talk about universalism, many people interpret that universalism as the universalism of the West. While thinking about certain achievements — international human rights standards and so forth — I never fully comprehended that until this morning. It really sank in. I had an intuition about it though as I looked through *Our Global Neighborhood*.

Another very high mark has to be given for the fact that it is functionally futuristic. It has a vision of the future and of possibilities. When we involve ourselves in the process of peace education, we always find that there has to be some positive motivation for learning — some sense of where the movement could go. I find that very much present in *Our Global Neighborhood*. Another thing that is very important is the clear statement of core values. These values are conceptually fertile ground although more attention needs to be given them. The central value of respect for life could — and should — have been extended. Clearly, the respect for life that was mentioned was respect for human life. I am fully in accord with that value. However, I think we need a broader set of perspectives. This is my learning agenda. We need to take into account ecological, cultural, and gender perspectives as well as learning itself.

An ecological perspective would include all living systems, including the Earth, the planet as a living system. Last night, Randall Forsberg spoke about the practice of cannibalism. She said that it had been brought to an end, but if we look at it from an ecological perspective, cannibalism has not ended. We are consuming the source of our life as we once consumed the flesh of others. So, the concept of respect for life has to be broadened and deepened in terms of the spiritual element that Ambassador Otunnu mentioned. What is needed is not just respect, but reverence for life. One problem with the report is evident from this perspective. It arises with the concept of "sustainable development." It seems to me that we need to look into this. Is there a possibility of a replenishing development — a returning to, not just a taking from the Earth to the limits that it can sustain? We need to reflect a bit on the notion of a global commons in our learning agenda, because the exhausting of the global commons was a result of consumption for human purposes. The notion of sustainable development is embedded, as well, in the primacy of human purpose over other values. Sadly, it is not evident that this means better lives for all humans.

Another thing we need to look at again in the light of this universalism is culture. The report makes reference to ethnicity and religion, but no reference is made to cosmology or to how people see the whole world. It is through culture that people become people. We are who we are because of our cultures. If we are going to be part of a community, we have to recognize those identities, bring together the richness of the multiple cultures of the Earth and try to fashion from it another dimension of identity and being for all of us. Perhaps this is what is meant by UNESCO's "culture of peace."

The third perspective that deserves to be taken into account is a gender perspective. Very, very high marks to the report for its recommendation of an advisor on women's issues. However, gender is not a question of women's issues. Gender is not just a question of discrimination and oppression of women. Gender is related to the whole issue of relationships. When we talk about gender issues, we're talking about issues of changing relationships — not only gender relationships, but power relationships, economic relationships, the relationships of humanity to Earth as well. Relationships have to change and the way to see that most clearly is to see it through gender. Gender perspectives can enrich the discourse. It is not simply because of a need for equity that it is necessary to involve women in the discourse. It is necessary because through socialization, through gender roles, there is something else to be found. We need to have those perspectives as well as the ecological and the cultural, and we need to valorize the perspectives and experiences of women. We need to give social value to that which is done in the private and intimate spheres.

The changes and steps many of us have talked about today will require great courage and strength. Courage, for the most part, we derive from very intimate sources. We need to understand that. And if we talk of wholeness, of the ecological interlinking of all living social systems, the reality that the intimate parts of those social systems are interrelated with the rest has to be recognized and given its value.

Next, the learning perspective. I looked at the index first. I always do. No entry on education and no entry on learning. A way of seeing perspectives is to look through the index. And education — in the sense of intentionally learning — offers a perspective: if we're going to move from here to there, what do we need to know about? But it also means reflecting on experience and deriving new levels of awareness from reflection. I would like to talk more about education and learning, but since there is no time, I will just say that, in spite of some absences, the report leaves me with hope. It is a document that reflects great learning. A-plus for that.

Response Panel #2

ERIC HAUBER

• • •

Eric Hauber is Vice President at Soka University, Aliso Viejo, CA. He is the former Soka Gakkai International (SGI) Permanent Representative to the United Nations and is Vice General Director of SGI-USA. In this capacity he has been active in SGI's movement for peace, culture, and education for 23 years.

Before offering a concrete response to the Commission's report, I'd like to take this opportunity to say just a few words about the SGI and our relationship to the Boston Research Center. The SGI is a global network of lay believers in the Buddhist teachings of Nichiren, a 13th-century Buddhist reformer. Based on the principles of humanism and respect for the sanctity of life as they find expression in these teachings, we are pursuing a program of activities in the fields of peace, education, and culture. Our president, Daisaku Ikeda, is also founder of this Center. In this sense, the two organizations are cousins, or perhaps siblings. As a non-governmental organization, the SGI is principally involved in public information,

"This vision will only emerge through a process of dialogue; dialogue that is broad and open — that actively embraces all perspectives. One of the weaknesses of the NGO community is that we continue to spend too much time and energy preaching to the already converted. Our contacts and interactions with 'ordinary people' need to be expanded and deepened."

education in the most inclusive sense of the word.

This tradition reaches back to the inception of the organization in the 1930s, when our membership was drawn primarily from among educators, and to our first President, Tsunesaburo Makiguchi, who succeeded in bringing the sometimes abstruse ontology of Buddhism to bear on the problems of creating value and happiness amid the stringent realities of daily life in Japan at that time. Unlike many NGOs, we do not engage in lobbying or in direct efforts to influence policy-making. Rather, we seek — through a program of grass roots public education — to enrich and elevate the level of public discourse surrounding the many issues affecting the future of humanity.

Needless to say, the future evolution of the multilateral institutions that encompass the entire range of actors who will play a part in the processes of global governance are of central importance to the citizens of this country and of the world. Without placing any blame, I think it can be said that, up to now, neither the quality nor the extent of public interest and participation is at all proportionate to the importance of these issues. However, the situation seems to be changing. In order to support this change, we have recently undertaken a wide range of activities — organizing supporting symposia, exhibitions, open houses — that have sought to reach out to the public and increase involvement and awareness of the unique opportunities that UN50 presents. For example, we are preparing educational materials that can be presented at our 1,700 neighborhood-based monthly meetings. We are also planning training seminars as well as large-scale cultural events to help teachers bring UN50 into the classroom.

Now, to the report. It is timely, comprehensive; it has depth and specificity. In particular, though, we welcome the centrality that has been accorded the question of human values. Gandhi once said something to the effect that it is pointless to dream of a system so perfect that we would be freed of our obligation to be good. No matter how brilliantly the organizational diagrams of the UN system are rewritten on paper, without positively engaging people in the values that motivate them, no real progress away from the present chaos will be possible. A fundamental transformation of individual life is the central objective of Buddhism. At the same time, Buddhism holds that this transformation is the *sine qua non* of any meaningful or lasting systemic reform. Fostering this dynamic synergism is central to the SGI's activities.

We also welcome the underlying sense of hope that informs the report. Optimism implies neither a panglossian affirmation of present realities, nor a simplistic belief that things will work out for the best. It is all too clear that they won't. Optimism, fueled by a deeply held belief in humanity's ability to shape its own destiny, can set free incalculable inner energies and resources in people. In his most recent peace proposal, Mr. Ikeda writes that, "Now, more than ever, we require vision backed by a solid philosophy, and we have to work to realize that vision through actions rooted in a strong and dynamic optimism. We must never abandon confidence that no matter what difficulties arise, humankind has the capacity to overcome and to forge ahead."

It is this hopeful vision that we have all joined together to seek. The chairmen of the Commission make it very clear that this is the process that they have sought to initiate. But this vision will only emerge through a process of dialogue; dialogue that is broad and open — that actively embraces all perspectives. One of the weaknesses of the NGO community (and we academics — if I can speak on behalf of academics — might want to reflect on this point, too) is that we continue to spend too much time and energy preaching to the already converted. Our contacts and interactions with "ordinary people" need to be expanded and deepened.

At a Boston Research Center-sponsored conference on the UN and the World's Religions last year, Harvey Cox issued a heartfelt appeal for the practitioners of the many religions represented at the conference to make a further effort at engaging what he termed the "non-dialogic" elements of our respective traditions. As representatives of NGOs and as academics, some of us have our own hard core close to home with whom we've despaired of dialogue and whom, therefore, we neglect to engage. In other words, our immediate surroundings hold ample opportunities to extend the process of dialogue now. Dialogue is an essential vehicle for democratization and for bringing the voices of the people to the workings of the UN, which is currently dominated by the voices of states and state interests.

The report contains many important suggestions in this direction. Among them, the proposal for a Forum of Civil Society. This, linked with mechanisms to strengthen the regional solidarity of organizations in civil society and to redress the hemispheric imbalance of representation, could evolve into a vital channel through which the concerns of the world's citizens would be regularly reflected in the processes of global governance. This should also enable the very considerable spiritual and intellectual resources of civil society beyond the NGOs to be brought to bear in a more focused and coordinated manner on the many humanitarian, environmental, and developmental issues which face us. And while I would hope that these non-governmental contacts could become more regularized, it would be nice if some of the excessive formalities of state relations could be dispensed with as well.

As the report states, "the UN needs to cultivate intellectual interaction among leaders. At the present, they limit themselves to talking at each other through formal speeches or with each other mainly on a one-to-one basis. The opportunity for collective thinking does not exist." The report calls for global governance rather than global government. This represents a fundamental qualitative transformation. It finds parallels in what Joseph Nye here at Harvard has called the shift from "hard power to soft power," hard power being the unilateral imposition of will through overwhelming military, political, or economic force. Soft power, on the other hand is the discovery and clarification of mutual benefit and shared goals through dialogue.

We have to stop thinking in the old paradigms and unquestioningly moving along the old continuums, such as that between diplomacy and war, in which language serves as a substitute or a prelude to violence. In other words, there must be a qualitative transformation in all things, including the process of dialogue. It will not do to bring the people's voice to the UN if this does nothing more than amplify a cacophony of sectarian hate. Therefore, in closing, I would like to offer the following suggestion: that we begin thinking of the global civil society that is at the heart of the Commission's vision as a humane global neighborhood characterized by the civility of its discourse.

Response Panel #2
WINSTON LANGLEY

• • •

Winston Langley is Professor of Political Science and International Relations at the University of Massachusetts-Boston, and Vice President of the United Nations Association of Greater Boston. He has taught courses in international law and international relations, and has written widely on the subjects of human rights and the need for a transformed international system.

I would like to make six points from my examination of the report. They concern image, values, a certain coupling between rights and responsibilities, the security of people, the concept of human being, and the cultural constitution of the neighborhood.

The scope of the change sought by this report is beyond reach unless there are certain antecedent changes. One of those changes has to do with the image people have of themselves and the orientation they have toward the world in which they live. Social psychology, and certainly political psychology, suggests that before such major changes take place, we must replace the map which represents the collective image that people have in their minds of the world in which they live.

"What this report does, above and beyond all else, is elevate the security of people to a standing coequal with the security of states, and suggests that the former might even supersede the latter."

Today, the world in which many people live is one that is competitive, one made up of states that seek individual national goals and objectives, one that is semi-anarchic. The very title of the report, *Our Global Neighborhood,* seeks to effect a change in that image, that map. It suggests proximity, it suggests intimacy, it suggests common locality and, as Mr. Otunnu said this morning, aspirationally, it suggests the very character of the members of the neighborhood: neighborliness. Neighborliness, however, cannot be achieved unless it has as an associate principle some common blocks to link people together. I think that's part of the internal consistency of the report, that it seeks to establish a series of blocks through which the changes it seeks, especially the political and economic, can be effected. The emphasis on values must be seen in this light.

It is true that the human rights regime of the UN focuses to an extent on values, but these values are seen in terms of rights, and these rights are clothed in the rhetoric of legal discourse that sometimes appears aggressive and divisive. The regime also disregards certain responsibilities. Or, whenever they are mentioned, they are only mentioned faintly. What this report does is affirm rights while coupling them with responsibilities. That is a major contribution.

From this coupling, a number of possibilities emerge, among them what I call horizontal linkages. The people who elaborated the human rights regime, as the report suggests, saw the threat to human beings coming principally from government. As we know, threats to human beings and to human integrity come from many, many directions, so while the human rights regime envisions relationships and interactions between governments and individuals, the report envisions, in addition, the interaction between and among individuals and between and among non-governmental organizations. Therefore, it provides for the possibility of certain types of collective responses. It also does something else. It undermines a reigning philosophic outlook in international relations — something called moral skepticism.

Moral skepticism contends that moral judgments are not appropriately possible outside national borders. The basis on which this claim is made is that moral judgments spring from social interaction between and among people, especially in the realm of social cooperation, and since the international system is seen as principally conflictive, such judgments cannot be made at that level. However, the report contends that the world in which we live involves social cooperation that transcends the borders of states; that those borders are not the outer limits of cooperation at all; and that, indeed, if moral judgments are made on the basis of social cooperation, then perhaps decisions concerning activities beyond those borders ought to be morally grounded. This is also important in terms of economic considerations, because one of the reasons behind the recommendations in the report is that cooperative action between and among people makes for the possibility of a better material life than they would ordinarily enjoy if individuals were left to their own endeavors.

On a global scale, social cooperation makes possible a better life for nation states as well. But while it makes for a better life, there are few institutions that allow for a just distribution of that which is socially realized. Within the borders of states, institutions have sometimes been created to allow for what is called fairness — a certain form of distribution. We do not have these institutions in international relations, and, since social cooperation has become global, what one finds is a progressive deterioration in the distribution of that which is socially realized. Certain individuals and groups prefer and have been allowed to have a disproportionate allocation of the socially realized benefit as a means of pursuing self-chosen ends.

Unfortunately, the report does not establish a corrective here, although it makes room for one by focusing on the security of people. In doing so, it seeks to do something that the current UN system has done. Although the UN system initially focused on people's security, that area was largely consigned to what has come to be called "low politics." High politics deals with security of states. What this report does, above and beyond all else, is elevate the security of people to a standing coequal with the security of states, and suggests that the former might even supersede the latter. It also provides a generous definition of security, indeed — not only against hunger, disease and oppression, but also security against a hostile environment, and even against drastic changes that could be hurtful to one's manner of living. One can also look at security in terms of democratic entitlement, in terms of "the people's body" within the new structure, the Civil Forum, and in terms of putting women at the center.

Having said all of this, there are still some weaknesses that I hope Mr. Otunnu will help us address. Among them is the lack of emphasis on education. If people are going to make new, democratic choices, they need to have the education needed to make decisions. Secondly, there seems to be an emphasis on procedural democracy. I'd like to see something about substantive democracy and about the extent to which workers — the work of international labor organizations — might be more intimately integrated within the Economic Security Council.

This leaves me with two other areas to touch on: the concept of human beings and the kind of history that this report seems to reflect. Human beings are not just economic, or political, or social beings; they are that and more. The spiritual dimension of human beings has been emphasized in the report. It also suggests that human beings are capable of moral, spiritual, and intellectual solidarity, and that out of that form of solidarity, regardless of economic, political, or social divisions, they can indeed come together to address common problems. It also suggests that the nature of human history is such that one cannot divorce that history from the character of the individuals who make it. As such, it focuses on the idea that we ought to become individuals who ask, "Does what I do make for a better person — in the terms of the individual who is engaged in the doing and the parties who may in fact encounter the consequences of that doing?" It is out of such consciousness that individual and collective liberation might in fact take place.

My final comment is on the cultural constitution of the neighborhood. The neighborhood is not uniform. It is segmented, and these segments are principally cultural. I recently read an article by the Turkish humanist Yasar Kemal in which he notes the movement of business communities across borders and the disregard that governments seem to have for particular cultural expressions and identities. The loss of a particular cultural identity represents a loss of color, a loss of light. I think what the report does is acknowledge multiple expressions of human culture and the right of peoples to maintain and nurture their identity through the preservation of their culture. I hope that, as intellectuals who discuss these issues, we will follow the example of Antonio Gramsci, who suggests that we ought to assume organic links with the common problems of our community, of our neighborhood. Until we construct those organic links, questions of cultural preservation and of social and economic transformation will not be effectively addressed.

RESPONSE

By Mr. Otunnu

First of all, Professor Reardon: I have made note of all the criticisms that you have made of the report. Thank you for your kind words about the report; I shall convey your words to fellow members of the Commission. I will also explain to my colleagues the lack of elaboration, the lack of substantive development of the various perspectives that you correctly mentioned in your comments — the ecological, gender, culture, and learning perspectives.

Mr. Hauber, one central point emerged in your comments — the centrality of human values and how one may transform society in part by seeking to transform individual lives. You spoke of optimism. I am by nature less familiar with optimism. I want to learn more about it because I'm not so familiar with it. I'll tell you what I am familiar with. And there well may be points of intersection. I'm slightly more familiar with hope, and with faith, because hope posits faith in human capacity. It recognizes that within us there are many forces at play, some of them very dark and ugly, but despite that, there are also other elements that can be very powerfully beautiful and transforming. Ultimately, this is where faith and hope come together — in the belief that the capacity exists, in spite of present evidence, in spite of present realities, to transcend the ugly, the negative, and to achieve a measure of healing, reconciliation, acceptance, and embrace. That to me is hope, and hope meeting with faith. And there, I think, one finds a point of intersection between your notion of optimism and those of hope and faith.

Professor Langley put many points on the table, but let me just take up two very briefly. The completion of the continuum of rights: the rights of an individual, the rights of a group, but also responsibilities. In fact, in the Commission's discussions, some of us went so far as to say that it was fine to have the Universal Declaration of Human Rights but that perhaps we needed a sister declaration, a Universal

Declaration of Responsibilities. You're right in saying that when the Universal Declaration was drawn up — mainly through Western inspiration, given the experience of the West — the main villain was viewed as the oppressive, encroaching, intrusive state. There was a need to work on rolling back that power.

That still remains true, but what is also true is that there are many other villains who have emerged on the scene. After all, not just the state but insurgents, too, not just those seeking to retain power but those seeking to gain power have abused the rights of people. We've seen whole communities mobilized, whole communities regarding another community as the enemy and waging total war against that community — war that spares neither children, nor women, nor the old, nor crops, nor granary stores, nor animals — a total annihilation of an entire community as opposed to the notion found in many cultures and civilizations that distinguishes between those who are armed and those who are noncombatants. We see entire communities mobilized to neutralize, meaning eliminate altogether, other communities.

We are living in a very contradictory era. We see evidence of too much government as well as too little government. We need a state, a strong state, strong enough to be able to perform its functions. In Africa, Dr. Mubiru Musoke said, one must resist the state which has become too strong and oppressive. But equally bad is a state which cannot perform its functions, which has whittled away, eventually collapsing, as in places like Somalia and Liberia. All this is to say that the cast of actors who may impinge on rights has become wider and more complicated. This is all the more reason for a comprehensive view of both the issues of rights and of responsibilities.

Finally, Professor Langley, your point about procedural versus substantive democracy. I myself used to believe very strongly that procedural democracy was hogwash, and that what one really needed was substantive democracy. I have revised my views. I now believe that one needs both, and that achieving the one without the other is very difficult. You cannot achieve the substantive democracy of which we speak, by which I mean a more equitable allocation of power, resources, and opportunities — both social and economic — unless there are also procedural mechanisms in place — institutions which are strong and can mediate these kinds of relationships. And over time, the procedures, institutions, educational process, and socialization will contribute to a culture of democracy that can then ensure a more democratic society.

The lesson of the last several years, at least my personal lesson, is that we need institutions, we need procedural mechanisms. It's clear they aren't enough in themselves. But we'll also need to educate, socialize, and build a whole culture of democracy.

OPEN DISCUSSION
Following Panel #2

Mike Simpson: I'm from Harvard University's Center for International Affairs. I'd like to address a brief comment to Ambassador Otunnu and then a question to Professor Reardon. Ambassador, I am just an "ordinary people" like those Eric Hauber described, not an academic, but I would endorse the A-plus for this report. It offers a true vision of hope. As a good citizen of the neighborhood, I would say that we need both courage and patience to make that hope fruitful: courage to work for it but patience to know that it's a long journey.

Professor Reardon, my question has to do with what you said about gender perspectives. I entirely agree that any discourse or endeavor that excludes any perspective, be it gender, cultural, cosmological, or whatever, is poorer for that exclusion. With that in mind, and with respect to the upcoming conference in Beijing, my question is this: will the more traditional perspectives that derive from motherhood and parenting receive equal place at that conference with equity in the workplace and the opportunity for achievement in the professions?

Reardon: As you may know, the response to your question can only be speculative. Under any circumstance, it would be hard to say whether any one perspective will be given equal weight with other perspectives. However, if the question were, will those perspectives be part of the discourse?, I believe they will, because many of the people who come — both men and women — will be parents, and I hope they won't leave their perspective at the door when they pick up their credentials. But that's one of the problems we face — the disassociation of roles; when I put on this hat, I don't think about other things, and so forth. We have to think from multiple perspectives — as many perspectives as we can. Women who come who are mothers will bring that perspective. Clearly, the position, roles, and responsibilities of mothers are part of what is factored into such documents as the Convention that are meant to respect and protect people in particular roles.

Severyn Bruyn: I'm from Boston College. I would like to ask the panel to imagine with me some of the new directions for the United Nations that Mr. Otunnu sought. We could think of the United Nations in a capacity in which it cultivates the structural foundation of governance in ways that it hasn't before. For instance, in the area of religion, there are some world associations — the World Council of Churches and so on — but these associations are not linked or related to one another to my knowledge. In other words, Islam, Buddhism, and so on, at the world association level, are not in contact and dialogue in the same political sense that the members of the UN are.

On the economic level, we have world associations such as the International Chamber of Commerce, but they're not in dialogue with other business associations in ways that could create the foundation for this kind of civil society. The same is true of education and other areas. It seems to me that we need to think in terms of the structures as well as the values in which the norms and the procedures of fairness and justice can be pursued. Does the UN have a role in that?

Hauber: You ask about the interaction between world religions. I think that is something which is absolutely beginning to happen. There are national and international conversations taking place between different religions. It is just beginning. It has not happened to the degree that it needs to happen for the future to unfold the way the Commission sees it, but I think in many cases it doesn't happen because it's very difficult for us to put ourselves into situations in which we feel uncomfortable. We have avoided having the conversations with certain groups of people. Of course, the groups differ, depending on which other group is speaking. We have to get on and not wait for the structure. If we wait for the structure, whose structure will it be, and where will it come from?

I think that what we're really talking about is that if we are a member of a religious group, or if we are in a conference that involves a religious perspective, then we should guarantee that the conference contains within it the voices of the people with whom we normally don't dialogue. If we're talking about religions, then invite all religions. I think that what will happen if we start at the grass roots, is eventually that will take place at all levels, and the structure will build itself, based on individual actions on the lower levels.

Brian Aull: I'm from the Baha'i community of Cambridge. I want to amplify a bit on the theme of the culture of democracy which several speakers broached. I'm extremely heartened to see it being talked about here today because ten years ago, even five years ago, in peace and justice forums you would have been laughed out of court for trying to bring in such ideas. I am worried on the one hand, however, about the direction that democracy has been taking in the United States and in other countries of the world.

From the beginning, American democracy has been built in some measure on the exultation of individualism and on suspicion of government authority. Now that we live in this global neighborhood, both of those values are becoming obsolete in that we have to build political cultures in which there is a cooperative relationship between those who are governed and those who govern. There must also be a process of genuine dialogue between camps which, in the past, have been suspicious of each other's motives due to ideological zeal. So, I'd like to hear any comments about ways we can make progress domestically, in the United States, on building a political culture that supports genuine dialogue in search of unifying human values rather than adversarial and polemical debate, often of a superficial kind, such as that we see in Washington today.

Langley: I'll respond briefly to this and to the previous question. In 1993 there was a Parliament of World Religions commemorating the 100th anniversary of the first gathering, one that elaborated a tentative program of values that I believe could undergird almost any institutional matrix that the UN might wish to consider for the future. In response to the second question, I think that, in the US, we need to refocus on a word we have used here: values. Not that rights ought to be de-emphasized, but rights should be coupled with values — and not just individual rights. There is nothing wrong in focusing on the rights of groups. Don't forget, people point to Nazi Germany and the danger it represented because it glorified the state. Don't forget that part of what Nazi Germany did was try to kill a group of people merely on the basis of their membership in a particular group. Coupling rights and duties might begin to resolve the questions of the right to belong, the right to group identity, and the relationship between the community and the individual.

Reardon: I want to underline Professor Langley's response and add that it's important for us to understand that a lot of the contention in politics — much of which ends in violence — seems to be the consequence of believing that you are not heard, that you are not attended to. Much of that underlies the gender discourse: even when we say what we have to say, we are not attended to, so our message is not truly part of the conversation. As we look at restructuring or rearranging the democratic process, I think that's one of the issues we have to look to. How can we assure that voices are heard and attended to?

Otunnu: Mine is a smaller point. It has to do with where those who are called fundamentalists fit into the scheme of all this. Whether they are Christian fundamentalist, Jewish fundamentalist, Islamic fundamentalist, however they are defined, my view is we ignore those groups at our peril; we keep them outside the circle of dialogue at our peril. They represent not only fundamentally important groups and sentiments, they are also many in number. They are a force, and no major society today can proceed with an agenda which does not in some way engage them. I also think that within those groups there are nuances. There are some very serious, thoughtful, reflective people as well as fringe groups, and one must take account of all these nuances. I think it is the prophet Isaiah who said, "Come let us reason together." It is important to engage such groups in dialogue to the extent that it is possible.

Hauber: When we use the word dialogue it's almost like motherhood and apple pie. Who objects to dialogue? But it's important to remember that there are great dangers in dialogue. We have to approach it with the determination that if we enter into dialogue, true dialogue, we will dialogue to the end. The danger is that many times in the process of dialogue we discover that, even though we are both talking about the same thing, our motivations are completely different. That could fundamentally shake our willingness to continue to talk to the other person. And yet, true dialogue can begin at that point. Perseverance in the dialogue is essential.

Langley: This is related to something we have mentioned before about procedural democracy. In Algeria, in 1990, the Islamic group won about 189 seats out of approximately 231 and had the chance to form and shape the government through what may be regarded as the democratic principle. A number of other individuals decided that these victors were dangerous because they were going to cancel the very institutions which had made it possible for them to assume power. Very, very often there are groups that not only fail to share certain values that are elaborated by other groups in the community but feel that there is no reason to share them, because those other groups had paid no attention to them for a very long time. Indeed, part of what shapes the very idea of communities is that people believe they belong, that they are included and not systematically marginalized, whether on the basis of gender, race, or ethnicity, whatever. Dialogue and inclusion, rights and responsibilities are rather critical.

Sara Sue Koritz: I'm an activist and an officer of Community Church of Boston in Copley Square, the church that majors in social action policies. As such I also represent the church at Jobs with Justice, an umbrella group focused mainly on the problems of working people, trade unions etc. I want to address my question to Professor Langley. I know it's a very complicated world we live in. In our own country there are all kinds of people. We not only have a North and South in our country, economically, there's a north and south no matter where you live. Last Saturday I was involved with people who have been struggling against very big corporations in Illinois. They'd been locked out. In my view, there is a growing third world element in the most industrialized country in the world. Would you respond to that?

Langley: I couldn't agree with you more. I don't think the third world has anything to do with geography. It's a condition. It's a condition that has to do with health, with gender, with many things. One has only to go to certain areas of Boston, or Harlem, or other areas in other cities. It's not simply a question of housing, it's a question of health care, of life chances, etc.

There is something else in your question that I'd like to take the time to address. It relates to a question asked during the previous panel. I tend to think that part of what has happened is that business corporations have begun to dominate the political process. If we look at the evolution of the nation-state itself, we see that as early corporate society emerged, conflicts arose between businesses that had moved beyond the small cities and duchies and those that had confined themselves to local neighborhoods. We have the same problem today. We have competition between local (and national) businesses and those that trade and invest around the globe. The existing nation-states cannot control them, so we run the risk of having a form of global governance that is structured principally to deal with such trade and not with the more complicated social questions we ought to address.

As to the emphasis on values, to the extent that we take them seriously such emphasis is very encouraging. We also need to emphasize a little more of the social.

Seyom Brown: I would like to take the opportunity as moderator for the afternoon to share with you one observation of my own. As a political scientist, I usually greet official commission reports with a certain skepticism since I assume they are going to be filled with platitudes. This was not the case for this report. I found it to be extremely cogent and politically realistic in addition to offering a vision. If the other commissioners in any way approximate the range, depth, precision, and wisdom of the views of Ambassador Otunnu, we have the reason why this is such an excellent report.

CLOSING REMARKS

• • •

By Arvind Sharma

Arvind Sharma is Professor of Comparative Religion at McGill University, where he teaches Indian religions and comparative religion. He is the author of numerous books, and is currently exploring religions as positive resources for the affirmation of human rights and dignity, as well as compiling a source book of religious tolerance.

I've been told that the secret of good speaking is judicious plagiarism, so I sat this morning, paper and pen at the ready, as I listened with felonious intent to everything that was being said. Pretty soon I realized that the insights were coming so fast and thick that I was facing an embarrassment of riches and gave up. That confessed, I'll have to fall back upon my own meager resources. I'll try to present a conceptual framework along with my vision for dealing with, rather than resolving, the various issues that have surfaced here. And I would like to do that with four paired concepts. You might think of them as the blades of a scissors with which one might cut through the discussion, rearranging it according to one's heart's desire. These pairs are: morality and law, order and justice, government and gov-

"The basic problem of government is that the business of coming into political power and staying in political power consumes so much time, energy, and money that there is no time or energy left to do anything creative with that power."

ernance, and justice and equality.

I would like to think about the whole tradition of human rights as the fine moral product of the Enlightenment tradition, a tradition we can place alongside the tradition of morality developed in the world religions. To put it boldly, I want to observe and participate in the interface between the thirty articles of the Universal Declaration of Human Rights and the Ten Commandments, and see how they converse.

The first point I would like to make is that law represents a failure of morality. If there were no theft, there would be no need for laws against theft. Given this fact, and the fact that we have both morality and law, we have to accept the fact that there will always be ideas and that there will always be realities which differ from these ideas. There will be a gap, and we will continue trying to bridge this gap, either through morality, or law, or both. In today's remarks I could see that some were leaning on one side, some on the other, while some tried a judicious combination of the two.

The second point I would like to make is that, because we always have morality and law, when ideas move into action (as Commissioner Otunnu pointed out so effectively today) they do so only through embodiments — through persons, individuals. These persons may be good or bad, so morality is always mediated through individuals who in their own person represent both the radiant and less radiant dimension of our existence. This is also true of law, so you have a common issue here as well. But the contrast of morality and law at the level of practice is also a point of common interest.

This leads to my third point, one that emerges from the Indian experience with the NGOs, and that I would refer to as the move from idealism to ideology. Once an NGO becomes institutionalized, we see a movement from Gandhian idealism to the ideology of the Congress Party. The great danger in this movement — one that has relevance both for morality and law — is the phenomenon called "introjection": the reproduction in one's own work of all the pathologies and deformations of the system one is trying to correct. Democracies have this problem when facing dictatorships. If you look at the war record of the Allies, Britain was very much like Germany during World War II in terms of restrictions on freedoms. There was the War Measures Act in Canada and so on. The merit of the democratic system was that when the crisis was over, it could revert to the freedoms which it had voluntarily curtailed in order to combat totalitarianism, but in order to combat your enemy you must, to a certain extent, become like the enemy. This is a major problem we all have to face in the real world.

The final point I would like to make under the category of morality and law is on the need for common values. I'll begin with something quite obvious: if the violators of law outnumbered the upholders of law, laws could not work. If everybody was armed and started using their weapons against the police, the police could not enforce law. In other words, the remarks made by the Commissioner have a deeper ring to them: Law can only function when you have a bedrock of shared values. It [Law] can only deal with deviations. Morality can also only deal with deviations. If deviations become the law, then we are in a very different ball game. Although they are intangibles — common values, morality, law — they are very real in this sense.

Under the second category, order and justice, I would like to raise this question. Can we have order without justice? Please say yes, otherwise my whole presentation will collapse. But if it is possible to have order without justice, is it possible to have justice without order? I think that the answer is no. And there we find the logical explanation of why dictatorships, autocracies, and authoritarianism, though they are unpleasant, have been a feature of life on this planet. There is a reason for this. Given a choice between order and justice, people, at least in the past, have preferred order.

Now, the next point. By and large, the countries of the West, as functioning democracies, have had order for almost two centuries. But the rest of the world has just liberated itself from colonialism and has to pay more attention to order. This is a historical necessity, and, hence, we seem to be talking at cross purposes at times. That is why, when an Indian is told that Indian nuclear missiles can reach Europe, he feels excited. And, if the United States says there have been human rights violations in India, it does not faze him at all.

I'm sure that in a decade or two people in India will be quite ready to see things differently. It is adolescent rebellion, if you wish, and woe to the person who has not gone through it, and woe to the nation.

The other point I would like to make — and I hope that the last one wasn't too combative — relates to the idea of trusteeship, and the Trusteeship Council and its extension as recommended by the Commission. If it is coupled with the Gandhian view that those who possess more than they require should see themselves as trustees of society and should make the benefits of their wealth — whether intellectual or material — available to society free of charge as much as possible, we might have an extension of the idea of trusteeship beyond that found in the Commissioners' report. This might sound idealistic, but we should remember that ideals are sometimes realized, sometimes even in the course of a century, as in the case of the abolishment of slavery.

The final point I will pick up later, but I would like to make it here initially: order has a very problematical relationship with justice. Any attempt to achieve justice means that the prevailing order will have to be disturbed. So the ultimate question becomes, does society, or the polity, possesses sufficient Order (with a capital O) so as to handle the pressures of the disturbance of order (with a small o) and allow justice to be done? The ball is still rolling. Every justice leads to an injustice. As we are discovering with affirmative action, every attempt at justice leads to a perceived injustice. Kipling said that no question of social justice is ever settled. All we can ultimately aim to achieve is a declining amplitude in the swing of the pendulum from justice on the one side to justice on the other side — a space closer to the imaginary line that represents perfect justice (which will never be achieved) and around which the pendulum may forever hover.

Now, to move to the next two categories, government and governance. It is easy to see how government can exist without governance, but it follows from what I have just said that if you can't have justice without order, you can't have governance without government. If what we wish to achieve through governance is justice, equality etc., then against whom are we going to achieve it if there is no government? — government here representing order. This is the root of a sentiment expressed from the floor that I greatly appreciated: there is a genuine fear in the third world of another imperial regime in the name of internationalism and globalism. Have we thrown the colonial companies out so that other companies can come in from Europe again?

You might think this is a childish response given the interval and changes that have occurred, but if you said that to an Indian he would say that you are childish, that you don't know the realities we have faced. After all, it was the multinational which — in our perception — deprived us Indians of our freedom. That was a historical detour to emphasize the point made both by the panelists and by the audience — that there is a qualitative difference in awareness that has to be recognized first. I think it can be gotten beyond, but it has to be recognized. If not, there can be serious consequences.

I'll leave history now and return to the contemporary scene and the issue of the interplay between government and governance. What we see in India today is an explosion of volunteerism combined with the decay of public institutions. I find this upsetting in terms of the formulation I have just made, because you do need a strong government. I think the Commissioner made a very strong statement about how damaging a failed state can be. We have to be very careful about that. We say that the rights of the individual have to be protected against the state, but in what shape is the state? If the kind of incident that took place in Oklahoma took place in India, do you think that the Indian government could apprehend the culprit in two days? He'd probably be seeking political asylum in the United States by now.

This particular issue is highlighted by the fact that some of the problems pointed out in the report are problems of governments in general. Even the US government is struggling with problems of term limits and uniform codes. Admittedly, there is less problem with uniform criminal codes, but in India the issue of a uniform civil code is extremely divisive at the moment. These, then, are problems faced not just by the UN but by all governments and by anyone who tries to govern.

Now I come to what I believe is the most important point, and this is where I'd like to make whatever little claim I might to be putting something forward for the Commission's consideration. We have to address the basic problem of government. And what is it? In my opinion, the basic problem of government is that the business of coming into (political) power and staying in (political) power consumes so much time, energy, and money that there is no time or energy left to do anything creative with that power. Therefore, I would like to propose that the concept of governance embrace the following: along with a body, a political party, which comes to power, there should also be another body of people — people of good will such as the members of the Commission — who have programs in position which can be put in effect, and this body should be neutral in terms of its political affiliation. There are no Republican problems or Democratic problems;

only problems. I see this as the real function of governance.

The final distinction I would like to make is between justice and equality. And in that context I also want to make the point that equality is one form of justice, proportionality is another. If two people are hired and one works fewer hours than the other, then the one who works fewer hours should receive less money than the one who works longer hours. And the idea of proportionality will ultimately lead us to a justification of things like affirmative action when you factor in time. In terms of people working for a certain number of hours and being paid accordingly, if we regard that as a spatial expression of proportionality, a contemporaneous expression, it contributes to the question of the redressing of historical wrongs. I think this is going to come up. All dominant cultures will have to tackle this issue either on the global or on the national level. One of my colleagues thinks that one theological concept that will be extremely helpful in this context is forgiveness. I'll leave it at that.

From my point of view, a very significant development for our discussion of equality and its various manifestations is a distinction that has emerged in the Western experience of democracy: that is, the distinction between political and economic inequality. At the very time at which political equality was being affirmed (by political equality I mean equality before law and the right of individuals, first white men, then all men and then women, to vote) within the democratic system, economic equality was growing apace. One could further argue that the West won its human rights, its power, its sovereignty, its prosperity, by impoverishing the rest of the world. I know that this is an exaggerated statement, but I make it to make this further point, that there has been a trade-off within the West itself. One might even say that economic inequality is a congenital deformity within modern democracy.

Now, if this is the case, then all the issues which have been raised in connection with our discussion of an Economic Security Council acquire far greater relevance than would appear at first sight. In fact, one wonders if it is not in the interest of the West itself to create a level economic playing field all over the world, given its positive experience of this experiment in relationship to Europe.

Reforming the United Nations:
What is Ahead for
Our Global Neighborhood?

· · ·

MAY 25, 1995

Boston Research Center for the 21st Century
Cambridge, Massachusetts

PROGRAM OF THE DAY

• • •

Welcoming Remarks
   Virginia Straus, Boston Research Center for the 21st Century
   Daniel Cheever, United Nations Association (UNA) of
      Greater Boston

Overview of the Report, *Our Global Neighborhood*
   Barber Conable, Commission on Global Governance

"The United Nations in Trouble"
   Anthony Lewis, New York Times

Response Panel
   Daniel Partan (moderator), Boston University Law School,
      UNA-Greater Boston
   Richard Parker, Shorenstein Center for Press,
      Politics, and Public Policy, Kennedy School of Government
   Daniel Cheever, UNA-Greater Boston
   Virginia Straus, Boston Research Center for the 21st Century

Open Discussion

Closing Remarks
   Barber Conable

SUMMARY

. . .

At the evening forum on *Our Global Neighborhood,* Commission member Barber Conable examined the isolationist mood current in much of America characterized by the "Come home, America" attitude. "Disengagement is not an option for the United States," Mr. Conable indicated. There is no possible solution to the international challenges we face but to rely on the United Nations in some form.

"There's a great deal of potential and actual ethnic unrest today that has been exacerbated by migration — transnational migration, which is creating large and removed minorities in places where they weren't before, such as France and Germany, and rural/urban migration, which is mixing people that used to live in different ethnic enclaves within a country. There is a great deal of instability arising from these movements." Further, Mr. Conable stressed, "The developing world is growing very fast and becoming much more assertive."

In sum, he reflected, "It's a very good time to consider multinational reform and how to effectively use American influence." After all, he reminded conference participants, it's the fiftieth anniversary of the United Nations and the Bretton Woods institutions as well as being the end of the century and the end of a millennium.

Mr. Conable confided that "I was very critical of the UN when I was president of the World Bank. We had to pick up many of the messes created by the UN. I didn't like to go to UN meetings, even though we were a UN-associated group, because there was so much backbiting and fighting. Thus, when I was asked to become a member of this Commission, I felt obliged, as a critic of the UN, to participate fully, and to try to find ways of creating a UN we could support."

Following the summation of the major recommendations of *Our Global Neighborhood* by Mr. Conable, journalist Anthony Lewis castigated the United Nations for its failure as an instrument for peace in the world. He provided a moving account of the failures of the United Nations to protect citizens of the fomer Yugoslavia. The UN Protection

Force (UNPROFOR), he declared, did not accomplish the missions it defined for itself. It did not protect civilians in Sarajevo and other declared safe areas nor did it keep heavy weapons out of specified exclusion zones.

Mr. Lewis accused UN leaders of weakness and even of collaboration with the Bosnian Serbs. He chastised UN military and civilian leaders for failing to draw a distinction between aggressors and victims and for closing their eyes to violations of UN rules and to war crimes. He went on to say that "the fault lies not in them, but in ourselves. For, in failing to stop the worst aggression and genocide in Europe since World War II, the United Nations has merely reflected the policy of those members who dominated policy on Bosnia — the Western powers and Russia. They did not want to get involved."

Mr. Lewis concluded, however, by embracing the point that Mr. Conable had made earlier: the United Nations is as useful as we are prepared to make it. "For our own sake," he concluded, "we have to play a part in maintaining the world's peace and security and economic decency. That would be true even if the United States were not the richest and most powerful of nations, but it is. And so it would be folly — disastrous, self-defeating folly — for this country now to opt out of its obligations in and to the United Nations."

Richard Parker picked up on the theme of the meaningful survival of the United Nations and turned the focus to "a tragically broken world where poverty and violence are ever more visible," where the issues are "fundamental questions of democracy, equality, and liberty," where citizens have "grown increasingly frustrated and alienated." He urged that we find ways to reconcile the tensions between what he called the political equality we have achieved and the economic equality we have not.

Referring to the matter of the adequacy of the United Nations as a peacekeeper or enforcer, Dan Cheever responded to Tony Lewis's remarks by indicating that, to deal fully with the question, one should talk to people from all the areas where peacekeepers have actually done some good and where relief actually occurred, such as Namibia, Cambodia, Crete, and Haiti.

Mr. Cheever reminded participants of the history of the Security Council veto. "Fifty years ago this very month," he said, "the big problem was the veto. It led to an interminable delay and couldn't be resolved in San Francisco." He suggested that the lesson here was that if the unanimity rule had not been accepted, there would have been no United Nations. He suggested that it will be impossible to phase out the power of the veto until such time as "there is indeed a global civil society and a community of interests and shared values."

Boston Research Center director Virginia Straus praised *Our Global Neighborhood* for putting people at the center and for presenting a positive vision of the future where peace begins in the hearts and minds of people. Expressing a spirit of hope, she raised the following questions: Do we have any shared values? Will we stand up for them? Can civil society work together?

In open discussion, concern was expressed about the leadership gap we are experiencing. Daniel Partan was optimistic: "I would not put outside the limits of potential change any of the suggestions that are made in *Our Global Neighborhood*. It seems to me that what we need to do is to build a constituency for change and move beyond many of the suggestions made there."

Some debate ensued about a new movement stirring in public journalism. Mr. Lewis took strong exception to the notion that journalists "can serve the function of identifying what's good and running campaigns for the good. I don't think that's our job; I don't think we're capable of doing that," he declared firmly.

Richard Parker threw fresh light on the discussion by suggesting that "journalism is a form of preaching." He went so far as to say that American journalism is "about preaching as much as it is about informing" and that the public journalism movement may actually be on to something that ought to be pursued.

In a final reconsideration of the question of the UN's failure in Bosnia, Anthony Lewis was asked by an audience member to consider that "the UN is being pushed to do something it is neither prepared for, nor has the mandate for." Mr. Lewis responded that "What the best way of dealing with it might have been I don't know, but I will say that I agree with your statement at least to this extent: it need not have been the problem of the United Nations. I think it was fundamentally a problem for the Western powers and NATO."

Barber Conable brought the discussion to a close by citing former Deputy Secretary General of the UN Brian Urquhart: "The UN, for all its shortcomings, will be called on again and again because there is no other global institution, because there is a severe limit to what even the strongest powers wish to take on themselves, and because inaction and apathy toward human misery or about the future of the human race are unacceptable."

Overview of the Report
BARBER B. CONABLE, JR.

. . .

Barber B. Conable, Jr. is a member of the Commission on Global Governance. He served as a member of the US House of Representatives from 1965-1985 and was president of the World Bank from 1986-1991. Mr. Conable has served on the boards of four multinationational corporations and the Board of the New York Stock Exchange.

The words that are ringing through the halls of Congress these days are "Come home, America." I suppose that's an inevitable result of the end of the Cold War. The feeling is that somehow the risks are not so great any longer. But the risks are there. They are different, and they are very real. Actually, the Cold War represented order of a sort. It is in disorderliness in global affairs that peril lies. The world is an unstable place. I used to say that there are 1.2 billion people living in absolute poverty (poverty is defined by the World Bank as having less than a dollar a day), but nobody seemed to be impressed by that. People get numb in the face of all those digits. So now I say that five times the population of the United States lives in absolute poverty. That is a formula for instability in itself.

"I am sure there will be many who disagree with the suggestions in our proposal, but it's time for people to talk about this and to create the expectation that the powers of the world will get together and organize a UN they can support. We have no real alternative. "

There's a great deal of potential and actual ethnic unrest today that has been exacerbated by migration — transnational migration, which is creating large and removed minorities in places where they weren't before, such as France and Germany, and rural/urban migration, which is mixing people that used to live in different ethnic enclaves within a country. There is a great deal of instability arising from these movements. Pat Moynihan's latest book is called *Pandemonium*. In it he expresses intelligent concern about ethnic consciousness and conflicts and the perils they may bring to the world.

Another reality is that the developing world is growing very fast and becoming much more assertive. In 1993, the developing world grew at a real rate of over six percent while the developed world grew at a rate of a little less than two percent. This dramatic change is altering the power balances in the world. The tendency toward rather excessive American unilateralism produces more reaction than before. Back in the old Cold War days, people understood that they had to line up behind us and the Soviets. Now they don't see any reason for it, so they resent the bullying unilateralism characteristic of some of our national politicians.

Despite the "Come home, America" call, I believe disengagement is not an option for the United States. There are lots of reasons for this. First of all, we import fifty-five percent of our oil and much of our raw materials. Second, we are the world's largest exporting country. Our economic growth is affected by trade; much of the recent recovery in this country is attributable to the new jobs created by exports. Multinational investment is leaping. In 1992, the multinational corporations of the world invested four times as much in the Third World as they did in 1989, and since then the amount has continued to grow dramatically. There is now annually almost four times as much private investment in the Third World as there is official development aid. That represents a reality that Americans must take into consideration, since sixty percent of the multinational corporations of the world are American-based.

We have a commanding position in world money flows. A trillion dollars clears New York every day. That doesn't sound like the basis for an easy disengagement, does it? But most important, the American people are a sympathetic people. When they see starving babies or the results of mass terrorism on television, they want to send the Marines ashore right away. They say, "Don't let those people suffer out there, we care about people." So I repeat: disengagement is not really an option. It's a very good time to consider multinational reform and how to effectively use American influence.

After all, it is the fiftieth anniversary of the UN and the Bretton Woods institutions. It is also the end of the century and the end of a millennium. At times like that, you look back and you look forward. We know there will be a lot of reviewing of where we stand and where we're going. Also, the fiscal situation in the developed world, not just in the United States, but in other countries as well, requires the establishment of priorities of one sort or another. We have to figure out how we're going to do what we have to do as reasonably as possible, as inexpensively as possible. And so, from that point of view, too, it's a good time to review our priorities. And as I said, the unilateral Cold War leadership of the past is no longer possible. We've got to consider alternatives.

Now, I stand before you a Republican conservative, former Congressman, and I tell you there is no possible solution except to rely on the UN in some form. We may not support the UN now; as a matter of fact, lots of Americans do not. They're very suspicious of it. They see it as a threat to sovereignty. They look at it as an ineffective organization. But, if we can't support the UN as it is, we must have a UN we can support, because there is no alternative. Pax Americana won't work. The American public won't support the cost; neither will it accept the responsibilities. Therefore, as the only remaining major superpower, imposing our pattern in the world is not a possibility. Nor will the rest of the world let us; a reformed UN is the only chance we have.

I was very critical of the UN when I was president of the World Bank. We had to pick up many of the messes created by the UN. I didn't like to go to UN meetings, even though we were a UN-associated group, because there was so much backbiting and fighting. Thus when I was asked to become a member of this Commission, I felt obliged, as a critic of the UN, to participate fully, and to try to find ways of creating a UN we could support. Without US support, I am personally convinced that it is very unlikely that UN reform will happen. So, I believe we've got to start in this country and engage in a major dialogue about what kind of multilateral resolution of global problems we can support.

I hope that, starting with groups like this, you'll see this dialogue grow in the years to come. We in the Commission on Global Governance are not arrogant enough to believe that the leaders of the world will accept our recommendations in full. They won't. But if we can start a dialogue, if we can start along a path that will lead to some kind of ultimate negotiation, hopefully before the end of the century, perhaps we can salvage multilateral decision-making in a form that is acceptable to the world powers.

Now, I'm going to talk a little about the scope of the Commission's report, because I want to be sure you understand how broad it is. Some people think it's too broad. We worked for two years on it. We were a sophisticated and far-flung group, and we came up with a lot of interesting suggestions, perhaps too many. Perhaps we should have focused more than we did, but we believe that far-ranging reform is appropriate, starting with security. People look at security quite differently now than they did fifty years ago. Then, the only concern was the security of states. Now, we've got to worry about the security of peoples. And, given the internal problems that have the potential of boiling up into real world problems, we have to worry about the security of the globe, too. In fact, we all know that if the environment is not dealt with in a realistic way, that can ultimately affect our lives. And so security is a much broader concern than it was previously.

That is why we believe that there should be a right of petition to the Security Council and the Secretary General. People who see internal violations of human rights, serious environmental degradation, and so forth, should have the right to petition the UN. Special bodies should be set up to receive these petitions and to pass them on.

Obviously, in terms of the security of peoples, UN intervention in an internal problem within a country has to be handled very carefully. But nobody can doubt — looking at Yugoslavia, for instance — the potential for an internal matter in a locality like that to become a global problem. Of course, the Security Council must be changed. We suggest, for instance, that the number of temporary members be increased from ten to thirteen, and that there be five standing members, two from the industrial countries and one each from Asia, Africa, and Latin America.

We also believe that steps must be taken to try to phase out the veto, starting with some sort of concordat entered into by the members of the Security Council, an agreement that the veto will be used with great restraint — something that has not been the case in the past. Hopefully, soon after the beginning of the next century, a way will be found to phase it out completely. The veto of course is a serious problem.

As for peacekeeping, we believe that it is important that the Secretary General have a small volunteer force, perhaps 10,000 men, available to him for early intervention — to avoid problems boiling up and becoming intractable because of the tremendous delays involved in getting commitments of peacekeeping forces from the various constituent countries.

We favored the creation of an Economic Security Council. I have a particular interest in this. Although UNDP does a good job in tactical assistance, the only coordination of development activities that amounts to much goes on in the World Bank and in the IMF's Interim and Development Committees. After five years of struggling with those committees, I can assure you they do not function well. The coordination that is achieved is relatively modest and undemocratic. An Economic Security Council would be composed of many of the same people that make up the Interim and Development Committees: representatives from the finance ministries of the world. Why the finance ministries? They don't know a lot. All they do, generally, is say no. But finance ministers are people with real power, because they can say no. If you can sell them on a plan for security, something happens. Nothing happens if you just talk to the development ministers of the various countries. We think that an Economic Security Council should be a separate organization that would meet at least semiannually.

We believe that, if we get a functioning Economic Security Council, it will be possible to wind down some of the UN agencies that have outlived their usefulness or that have never been effective. For instance, the Commission put its finger on the UN Economic and Social Council (ECOSOC), the UN Conference on Trade and Development (UNCTAD), and the UN Industrial Development Organization (UNIDO) as possible agencies to be reviewed if· an Economic Security Council can be put together in addition to the World Trade Organization.

We believe in a democratization of the Bretton Woods institutions. I can tell you that it's very frustrating to the president of the World Bank to have a weighted majority go to the G7 on the board of the World Bank. They have fifty-two percent of the votes, even though they contribute nothing to the cost of running the Bank. Ninety-seven percent of the capital they contribute is uncallable capital. Therefore, they contribute very modest amounts to the financing of the World Bank, yet they have, as the major owners of the Bank, the power to vote down the developing world, which pays the cost of the administration, reserves, and profit of the World Bank.

While I was its president, the World Bank never made less than a billion dollars profit, which of course was used to reduce the cost of money on the loans; but all that was paid by the debt service of the poor countries. Nonetheless, they had very little to say about the actual running of the Bank. It's always fun to watch the Secretary of the Treasury go up to Congress and talk about how high the salaries are at the World Bank. The United States doesn't pay one cent of those salaries. It's all part of debt service.

We also believe there should be an effort to achieve compulsory jurisdiction for the World Court. As you know, countries can refuse to be bound by its decisions now. Further, we believe it important to establish an International Criminal Court, so we won't have the victors trying the losers in future war crimes trials.

We're talking about global governance, not global government. We believe that governance is a much broader term. It incorporates the NGOs, multinational corporations — all the various elements at work globally that make up our civil society. There should be some effort to bind these groups into the UN, to have them participate, since they have many ideas to give and are also major parts of the sinew that holds the world together. And so we believe a Forum for Civil Society should be established. Leadership is badly needed.

The US can, if it wants, influence multilateral decision-making. It has not wanted to do that very much. Much of the decision-making in multilateral institutions by the US has involved a trading of points, sometimes unrelated to the multilateral institution, because the US was hooked on program decisions that might have nothing to do with the welfare of the rest of the world.

We believe that this is a time for dialogue. I am sure there will be many who disagree with the suggestions in our proposal, but it's time for people to talk about this and to create the expectation that the powers of the world will get together and organize a UN they can support. We have no real alternative.

"The United Nations in Trouble"
by
ANTHONY LEWIS

• • •

Anthony Lewis, twice winner of the Pulitzer Prize, is a columnist for the New York Times. *Mr. Lewis joined the Washington Bureau of the* Times *in 1955, and has served as chief of its London Bureau. Mr. Lewis was a lecturer at Harvard Law School, and, since 1983, he has held the James Madison Visiting Professorship at Columbia University.*

Ladies and gentlemen, I'm afraid I'm going to be the Banquo at this feast — the ghost who reminds you of unhappy truths, one in particular. The United Nations, over the last several years, has had a defining test of its effectiveness as an instrument for peace in the world. It has failed that test: failed it miserably. The result has been to raise questions in many minds about the utility of the organization. Of course, I am talking about Bosnia. The United Nations peacekeeping mission there has become an exercise in self-humiliation. The UN Protection Force, UNPROFOR as it is called, was so feckless that its own leaders and spokesmen admitted their embarrassment.

The missions that UNPROFOR defined for itself were not performed: to protect civilians in

"For our own sake, we have to play a part in maintaining the world's peace and security and economic decency...And so it would be folly — disastrous, self-defeating folly — for this country now to opt out of its obligations in and to the United Nations."

Sarajevo and other declared safe areas, for instance, or to keep heavy weapons out of specified exclusion zones, as around Sarajevo. Civilians were killed by snipers. Bosnian Serb soldiers seized heavy weapons from sites where they had been impounded and fired them at Sarajevo right in front of United Nations troops. It was a dismal scene in terms of respect for the authority of the United Nations, not to mention in human terms. I put all that in the past tense because today there has been a change. For the first time in months, the United Nations command took action to enforce its authority in Bosnia. It called in NATO aircraft for a bombing strike at a Serbian military target near Pale, the capital of the so-called Bosnian Serb republic. Whether the action has any long-lasting meaning depends on whether it is just an isolated gesture or reflects a new determination. More of that in a moment.

How did the United Nations mission in which so many vested such large hopes come to so dismal a point? My answer is, through weakness. In military affairs, or for that matter in diplomacy or politics, weakness can never be expected to produce results. Yet that has been the stance of UNPROFOR from the start. Its leaders, military and civilian, decided to deal with the aggressors, the Bosnian Serbs, by wheedling instead of through firmness. Indeed, UNPROFOR took the position that it would draw no distinction between aggressor and victim. Thus, any effort by the Bosnian government forces to break the siege of Sarajevo was regarded with as much disapproval as actions by the besiegers — actions such as killing seven-year-old boys as they walked down the street, killing them not by accident, but by sighting them through a sniper scope and killing them in cold blood.

Indeed, the position was worse than an equating of aggressor and victim. UNPROFOR collaborated with the Bosnian Serbs in maintaining the siege of Sarajevo. It followed Serbian orders on who might fly in and out of the Sarajevo airport, a policy that reached some kind of peak when the planes were not allowed to take out the departing American ambassador because the Bosnian Serb leader, Radovan Karadzic, wanted to demonstrate his pique. But it was far worse than that. UNPROFOR actually patrolled the perimeter of the airport using search lights at night to pick out people trying to flee, some of whom were then killed by Serbian snipers. That and many other things had been agreed upon with the Serbian aggressors.

When journalists discovered that the Serbs were holding women in rape camps, UNPROFOR refused to act, on the grounds that helping the captive women was not part of its mandate. It refused for many months to investigate the notorious peddling of UNPROFOR fuel to the Serbs until finally the commander of a Ukrainian unit in the force was removed for that reason. UNPROFOR repeatedly allowed the Serbs to steal cargo from relief convoys, sometimes an entire cargo of medical supplies. The low point of the UNPROFOR record, in my opinion, occurred on January 8, 1993 when French officers taking the Bosnian Deputy Prime Minister, Dr. Hakija Turaljic, back to Sarajevo from a meeting at the airport allowed Serbian soldiers to stop the convoy and kill him in cold blood. An inquiry by the United Nations concluded that the Bosnian government was at fault for creating "an atmosphere of anxiety" among the Serbs.

I do not need to tell you that this shameful record of servility has also included repeated failure to punish violations of rules laid down by the United Nations Security Council, rules such as the inviolability of safe areas. The Serbs have attacked those areas with impunity. The former UNPROFOR commander in Bosnia, General Sir Michael Rose of Britain, steadfastly refused to do anything about massive Serbian attacks on the safe area of Gorazde in 1994. Then he visited Gorazde and, in brazen contempt of the truth, said it had not suffered much. Earlier this month, the UN military command asked for NATO air strikes on the Bosnian Serbs after a particularly flagrant violation. The request was vetoed by the UN's chief civilian representative, Yasushi Akashi. The reason for that and other examples of cringing that is given by UNPROFOR and Mr. Akashi is that the taking of a more robust posture might put UNPROFOR in danger of Serbian reprisals. That reasoning ignores the fact that the few times UNPROFOR has been strong, for example after the marketplace massacre in Sarajevo, the Serbs have stepped back. They understand strength, and they understand weakness all too well.

Many in the United Nations bear responsibility for the humiliation of this crucial peacekeeping effort: Mr. Akashi, Secretary General Boutros Ghali, and assorted military commanders. But the fault lies not in them, but in ourselves. For, in failing to stop the worst aggression and genocide in Europe since World War II, the United Nations has merely reflected the policy of those members who dominated policy on Bosnia — the Western powers and Russia. They did not want to get involved. They did not care enough about the horror to risk lives or treasure. A correspondent in the former Yugoslavia wrote with telling irony in a recent article on the deterioration of the UN role. I quote: "If the real mission of the United Nations is to be a fall guy for Western powers, including the United States, that are reluctant to commit the necessary forces, money, and brain power to solving Europe's worst conflict since World War II, then perhaps the UN mission has succeeded."

In short, the mission is what the key member governments want it to be. We can see that in today's air action, as in the long months of inaction in the face of insult and murder. Why did UNPROFOR finally call in NATO aircraft? Why did Mr. Akashi approve it this time when he had vetoed a bombing proposal under similar circumstances two weeks ago? The answer lies, I am sure, in the views of France, the United States, and Britain. France said out loud what many have understood, that a UN peacekeeping mission that kept no peace and did not enforce its own rules was worse than useless. Worse because UNPROFOR soldiers, especially French soldiers, were being killed. So the French said they would pull their troops out unless the UNPRO-FOR mission were made useful and feasible. This concentrated the minds of others wonderfully, as Dr. Johnson said, for without the French, all of UNPROFOR would have to be pulled out. The United States, and I believe even the weak British government, pressed for a firmer position — and it happened.

Alas, the firmness quickly evaporated. When the Bosnian Serbs took 400 UNPROFOR soldiers hostage, UNPROFOR said it would not negotiate with hostage-takers—and then secretly negotiated. It indicated that it would not again call in NATO aircraft, and the hostages were released. Emboldened by this display of weakness, the Bosnian Serbs attached and seized two of the supposed "safe areas," Srebrenica and Jepa, carrying out appalling atrocities. Only then did the West's humiliation become so flagrant, and damaging, that Western leaders said they would respond decisively to attacks on any of the remaining "safe areas."

So the moral of my story is that the United Nations is as useful as we are prepared to make it. Prepared, meaning that we commit the will and the resources. That is true generally, not just in Bosnia. The

Commission on Global Governance said as much in its admirable report. The greatest failings of the UN, it says, have not been structural. They have been collective failings of the member states. Thus it noted that some of the undoubted successes of the United Nations have been practical efforts that have reflected a substantial global consensus for action, such as UNICEF and the Office of the UN High Commissioner for Refugees.

The Commission also made some suggestions for reform that I found persuasively realistic. You've heard about some of them from Mr. Conable. They are the kinds of ideas one would expect from a body including such experienced, practical members as Mr. Conable and I.G. Patel of India, former foreign minister Dienstbier of the Czech Republic, Jacques Delors of France, the president of the European Commission, Oscar Arias of Costa Rica, Brian Urquhart of the United Kingdom, and so on. As you heard, one suggestion was for changes in the makeup of the Security Council. I will simply add that the ground given in the report was a very interesting one: such reforms would make it more fully legitimate in the eyes of nations and people.

Another point of particular interest to me was the creation of what the report called an international trusteeship over the global commons — the atmosphere, outer space, the oceans beyond national jurisdiction, and the related environment and life support systems. The report suggested vesting this enormous and crucial responsibility in the UN Trusteeship Council, whose task of overseeing the transition of trust territories to independence has been fulfilled.

We in this country live in a time of anger toward the United Nations and indeed toward all varieties of internationalism. Mr. Conable spoke of a mood in this country of "Come home, America." I want to add that there is a certain irony in that phrase, since it was the motto of George McGovern in his campaign for president. We've come full cycle in a sense. Left to right. But I believe it is a time not just of anger, but of suspicion, deep suspicion. A political figure as prominent as the Reverend Pat Robertson tells Americans that there is an international conspiracy dating back centuries that now wants the United Nations to take over the United States in the interest of international bankers. After the bombing in Oklahoma City, and what we have learned since about militias, one hardly needs to say this is a time of paranoia. But the inescapable fact is that we live interconnected lives today, all of us. The notion of Americans going back to some mythical time when each family could live on its own forty acres in a log cabin untroubled by government is just that. Mythical.

We all need each other in this country, and we cannot escape the world either. As Mr. Conable said, we have a world economy now with instant communication around the globe. For our own sake, we have to play a part in maintaining the world's peace and security and economic decency. That would be true even if the United States were not the richest and most powerful of nations, but it is. And so it would be folly — disastrous, self-defeating folly — for this country now to opt out of its obligations in and to the United Nations. I think, therefore, that the rallying cry that Mr. Conable put before you — the reform of the United Nations into an organization that will attract the kind of support that is so urgently in our self-interest and the world's — is crucial. With all its faults, even with all the failures which I feel so deeply in the former Yugoslavia, the UN is essential to Americans. To make us all understand that is the job not just of political leaders but of responsible individuals, which is to say, the people in this room.

Response Panel Presention by

RICHARD PARKER

• • •

Richard Parker is Lecturer and Senior Fellow at the Shorenstein Center on Press, Politics, and Public Policy at Harvard University's Kennedy School of Government, where he teaches courses on economics and the media. In addition to a long journalistic career (including cofounding and publishing of Mother Jones*), he has taught at Oxford, Stanford, and Berkeley. He is currently completing an intellectual biography of John Kenneth Galbraith.*

Following two such eloquent speakers, I hope I can add just a few words of some merit. Certainly following on Tony Lewis's calling upon Banquo as the ghost of the evening, I want to call up a ghost of my own, my great-grandfather, the Reverend Theodore Parker. He was a pre-Civil War abolitionist and Unitarian minister from Boston, an old friend of Frederick Douglass, Henry David Thoreau, and Emerson, of whom Emerson once said he never tired of chiding his fellow Bostonians. I will speak tonight in the tradition of my great-grandfather.

I note that we're celebrating the United Nations' fiftieth birthday this year, and I'm planning to celebrate mine next year. I'm always reminded by teaching the young how old I really am. Earlier last week while grading a paper, I

"I believe we live in a moment when, once again, it is not an issue of United Nations reform, but its meaningful survival."

found a student had spelled Lyndon Baines Johnson's first name "Linden," something of great concern, because this was a twenty-two-year-old graduate student at Harvard University. I could at least reassure myself that this was not the student I had had a number of years ago, not at Harvard, who, on a mid-term, had written that Karl Marx (spelled "Carl") once said, "workers of the world unite, you have nothing to lose but your claims." On the margin of that exam I wrote, "Dr. Marx was not an insurance adjuster."

I mention age in order to dwell on the ravages of time and the problems facing an otherwise commendable effort to revivify (or vivify) the United Nations, particularly as it was expressed by Barber Conable in his reflection on the work of the Commission on Global Governance. I believe we live in a moment when, once again, it is not an issue of United Nations reform, but its meaningful survival. The United Nations has always been a matter of mutinous suspicion to a branch of the Republican Party. Inclusion of the United States veto on the Security Council was the price Franklin Roosevelt paid for Senate approval to avoid repeating Woodrow Wilson's failure over the League of Nations. But I would argue that Republicans today oppose the United Nations not out of the traditional belief in isolationism, but instead out of a feeling of triumphalism which is perhaps even more dangerous.

Ebullient at the end of the Cold War, I believe they actually feel, in an arrogant way, that somehow the United Nations might impinge on America's right to unrestricted action wherever, whenever, and for whatever reasons we might choose. Having gone from a nation that in 1939 (as General Marshall warned Roosevelt) couldn't field one single battle-ready division on the eve of World War II, to one that spends more on its military than the rest of the world combined, I dare say the United States has come a great distance. But it is a distance which concerns me, and I hope concerns you as well. I dwell on the partisan Republican suspicion not to downplay the essential bipartisanship of our half-century-long arms race, but because Republicans right now control the Congress and, in my opinion, will for the foreseeable future. They also have a real chance to capture the White House as well. This, I submit, makes much of the *Global Neighborhood's* report on the United Nations tragically akin to the proverbial fussing about choice of deck chairs on the Titanic. Contestable seems a kind word for any argument that foresees US surrender of power to an organization it doesn't control or at least fully trust. Jesse Helms, not William Fulbright, chairs the Senate Foreign Relations Committee. I would invite anyone here to imagine viable hearings chaired by Senator Helms that would propose legislation that would, as the Commission suggests: 1) gradually surrender US veto power in the Security Council, 2) endorse General Assembly control over its own budget process, including the power to set contribution allocations, 3) approve a Trusteeship Council authority over what the Commission calls the "global commons," or 4) allow the removal of the United States from the General Assembly and Security Council for nonpayment of its bills.

At a moment when conservative passion is running full throttle to downsize American government, what can we reasonably expect to do when faced with the claims of a group on global governance? It seems to me, by the way, that many of the suggestions made by Conable and by the Commission are sound: closing ECOSOC, merging the Second and Third Committees, downsizing or abolishing UNCTAD or UNIDO. All of these have some merit, even the formation of an Economic Security Council—which I believe has a great deal of merit, having served as an economist with the United Nations Development Program and having seen the problems therein.

But with all due respect, these are bureaucratic and policy solutions to bureaucratic and policy problems, modest steps by measured men and women. By contrast, the opponents to the United Nations are anything but measured or modest. Disciplined to think and act politically and not bureaucratically, they possess the uncommon power of true believers. The crisis we face isn't about United Nations administration but about a tragically broken world where poverty and violence are ever more visible, and where there is an ever-diminishing willingness to help those in need. Many of those who sought a strong United Nations in 1945 finally accepted a weakened United Nations structure because it seemed stronger than its predecessor. They — and, in some sense, we — stopped short of pressing for a document equal even to America's old and quite weak Articles of Confederation.

At issue, not simply in the United Nations but in the global future that we would seek for ourselves and for each other, I hope, are fundamental questions of democracy, equality, and liberty. In the bipolar era of the Cold War, America learned to sacrifice all of these in the name of anti-Communism. Today, without a Communist conspiracy to oppose, we fill the void with an inchoate fear of the dangers of ethnic tensions — Samuel Huntington's thesis, one that holds tractable power with any number of policy makers and editorial writers around the country. When James Woolsey, giving testimony at the hearings on his nomination as head of the Central Intelligence Agency, sought to justify a 30-billion-dollar spying budget for the United States, no one drew attention to the fact that the sum was twice what America spends on Aid to Families with Dependent Children. Instead, Senators listened with rapt attention as he warned that it's "a dangerous world out there," thereby implying the necessity for the 30 billion a year spent on intelligence.

It seems to me that what Tony Lewis has done very well—as did Barber Conable in his presentation of the values that this Commission espouses—is emphasize the need in America today for progressive values and progressive visions as the only possible foundations for addressing what I think the American people really want in the years ahead. I believe, in fact, that contrary to the talk about America as a pinched and mean society, we are in fact a people of great generosity and even greater vision. But we live in perilous times. We have become what Toqueville warned we might: anxious men of little property, most of us poised between modest possession of a home, an education, a job—and a deeply disturbing future in which we may have none. For the last twenty years, we have used strong language, indictments really, to chastise our fellow Americans. This is not merely the political language of extreme partisanship, it is more, and includes an economic indictment: we have somehow failed as a nation, failed to produce, failed to save, failed to compete.

While listening to that language, we have, as a nation, grown increasingly frustrated and alienated, not only from one another, but from the potential and dream that America represents. We have grown more competitive, more prosperous — and more indelibly unequal — than at any point since income distribution figures were first gathered by the US government. In the endless quest to be "Number 1," America has become "Number 1" in the industrial world in its inequality of wealth and income. According to MIT economist Paul Krugman, seventy percent of the income gains achieved during the incredibly wealth-oriented 1980s went to less than one percent of the population. It seems to me that the language we are missing is not the language of competition, of ambition, productivity and savings, but language we haven't used for a long time, language we ought to get back to, language the Commission itself draws upon in an important way and which we ought to listen closely to. It involves terms like "the respect for life," "liberty," "justice and equality," "integrity," "caring," and "mutual respect."

Oklahoma City represents more than the madness of a fringe part of American life; it represents a toxin in our body politic, a flame that could permanently destroy our dream of America as a city on a hill. What lies unreconciled at the end of the twentieth century, here and abroad, are the tensions that live between the political equality we have achieved and the economic equality which we have not. That, it seems to me, is at the heart of what we ought to care about — not only around the globe, but here at home.

Let me close by sharing with you a favorite phrase drawn from Max Weber. "We shall not succeed in banishing that which besets us — the sorrow of being born too late for a great political era — unless we understand how to become the forerunner of an even greater one."

Response Panel Presentation by

DANIEL S. CHEEVER

• • •

Daniel S. Cheever, Professor Emeritus of Political Science at Boston University, is chairperson of the Board of the United Nations Association of Greater Boston. His service to the United Nations began with his assignment to the Department of State for duty on the Secretariat as Special Assistant to the Secretary General of the UN Conference at San Francisco in 1945.

I n view of of what has been said already I will say only a very few things. To Tony Lewis I would say: I trust I'm correct that your portrayal of the United Nations in the former Yugoslavia, if not one-sided, is at least an incomplete measure of the adequacy of the United Nations either in peace-keeping or enforcement. Before I could agree total-ly with what I understood you to say, I would want to talk with people from Namibia, maybe even from Cambodia, certainly from Crete and from another fourteen or more areas where peacekeep-ers have actually done some good and where relief actually has relieved suffering. Perhaps we can even speak of Haiti. Our friend Jonathan Moore, who has represented the US at ECOSOC, goes there tomorrow as does Mr. Conable himself. I ask myself, and I would ask some critics of the UN,

"Abolition of the veto will only be possible after we have achieved a global civil society of shared values, interest, and conception of right and wrong."

would we really like to have the Marines go back there again rather than UN representatives? These are just random thoughts inspired by what I heard from the previous speakers.

On UNIDO, the United Nations Industrial Development Organization: I trust the panel members did not miss the irony that Senator Helms also agrees with them. UNIDO is to be cut out of the bill he favors for US participation in international organizations. Now that doesn't damn it; I think UNIDO is unnecessary, and I certainly agree also that the necessity for UNCTAD has passed. There is a better way to deal with development and the relations between rich and poor. In my prepared remarks, I was going to say the more things change, the more they stay the same.

Fifty years ago this very month the big problem was the veto. It led to an interminable delay and couldn't be resolved in San Francisco. The issue involved more than Roosevelt's concession to Republican leaders; it had to do with an argument between the United States and the Soviet Union as well. How was it solved? Mr. Harry Hopkins, ill and in his declining years, made a special trip to Moscow to speak to Secretary Stalin in person. He came away convinced that a matter could be brought up and discussed in the Security Council under Chapter 6 and that the veto would not prevent such a matter from being discussed. With that understood, the conference proceeded on to the glorious, successful conclusion of June 26.

The lesson? If the unanimity rule had not been accepted, I'll be so bold as to say, there would have been no United Nations. Which gives me a little pause with the Commission's veto recommendation. The *Global Neighborhood* has a very cautious, rather coy phrase: the power of the veto is to be "phased out" after the turn of the century. I hope so. But for that to happen, a global civil society will indeed have to be developed, with a general consensus on what is right and what is wrong in human affairs. There must be a community of interests and shared values. I will not go into these. But veto there will have to be to keep the US in the UN until that work has been done. A big power has vital interests which it is not going to entrust to other powers.

I'm proud of the United Nations Association of Greater Boston, by the way. The Association foreshadowed one of the recommendations of the Commission — the revised, increased size of the Security Council. We called the big powers that were to be added something other than "standing members," but whatever the designation, Germany and Japan must be there. We also wondered (and I don't think the Commission mentioned this) about the European Union and Germany. Is it possible to organize power realistically, militarily, or economically, without making the European Union a Security Council member? That is a backhanded way of asking whether France and Britain should give up their veto. This matter concerned us in our work in the UN Association of Greater Boston. We expressed the view that the European Union which includes Germany should be a permanent member of the Security Council.

One more point, since I want to offer an upbeat ending. This document, the UN Charter, is very flexible. Unlike the Law of the Sea Convention, it's brief. It isn't full of particulars about every possible problem in the world, and it has been remarkably successful. It needs very few changes. The Commission, for example, urges us to amend the Charter so as to permit intervention in domestic affairs. A laudable objective, and one I sympathize with. However, as I reread the Charter I'm not sure it's necessary. If you read the Articles containing the principles of the Charter, you will note that Article 2, Paragraph 7 — which stops the organization from interfering in matters that are essentially domestic — seems to allow an exception to this hallowed principle of sovereignty. If the revamped Security Council finds there's a threat to the peace, it has the legal right — if it has the political will — to intervene and stop an internal conflict that threatens international peace.

If the Charter needs to be amended, it can be done. It has been done before. And it will take amendment to bring in India, some Latin American power, and, I hope, a European Union and an African country, perhaps the Republic of South Africa.

Response Panel Presention by

VIRGINIA STRAUS

• • •

Virginia Straus is Executive Director of the Boston Research Center for the 21st Century. As a public policy specialist, she formerly directed and helped found Pioneer Institute, a state and local policy institute. Ms. Straus served as an urban policy aide in the Carter White House and as a financial policy analyst at the US Treasury Department.

The Boston Research Center for the 21st Century is not your usual think tank. We do not undertake research, arrive at solutions, and then go out and try to persuade everybody of the rightness of those solutions. Instead, we create opportunities for dialogue, bringing together people with different points of view, and helping them to pool their wisdom. A certain human solidarity grows through such exchanges. We also seek out ideas for discussion that can bring hope and happiness to people in the coming century.

Because of our unique mission, we were delighted when the report, *Our Global Neighborhood*, was released in January. It seemed to us that, unlike many earlier reports on the UN, this report puts people at the center. Moreover, it presents a positive vision of the future at a time

"When the report calls for shared values, and includes the mass media in civil society, perhaps it's saying the media could think about serving the long-term interests of humanity, could look for what might build hope in people and what might help people mobilize for social progress."

when people reading newspaper accounts of the fighting in Rwanda, Somalia, and Bosnia feel very discouraged about the UN and its peace-keeping mission. And it conveys a sense of urgency about the changes that need to be made as we enter the twenty-first century. In my presentation, I will focus on some specific aspects of the report that contributed to our enthusiasm and made us decide to sponsor a series of forums highlighting its conclusions.

First of all, the report gets the source and direction of social change right. It says, in many different ways, that peace in the world begins in the hearts and minds of people: changes in people's consciousness and values are really what transforms institutions. As a think tank established by an international Buddhist organization, we found this approach to social change compatible with the Buddhist belief in the infinite potential of the human being. Human potential goes by different names in the various religions; in Buddhism we call it one's "Buddha nature." We believe not only that every person has it, but that a single human being can change the destiny of the world. That is why we found a fundamental appeal in the report's suggestion that change comes from inside people and radiates outward towards society.

We also were intrigued by the process through which the Commission reached consensus on its recommendations, given the variety of people on the Commission. It was made up of people from many parts of the world and different walks of life, women and men with divergent experience and distinct points of view. I learned from one member of the Commission that when they first got together, they almost despaired: how could such a diverse group possibly create a report they would all endorse? They finally realized that, if a global neighborhood or a greater sense of community is needed in the world, the Commission members would have to create that sense first among themselves. They stopped then and took the time to talk heart to heart about their lives and how they viewed the world.

As a result of this sort of thoughtful dialogue, they initially agreed that an ethical vacuum exists in the international arena. Yet, they also realized that before a more humanistic global order can be created, people must first agree on shared values. This is why they put a whole chapter on values at the beginning of the report, thus providing the basis for a broad vision of global governance they could all share.

Another major attraction of the report is that it attempts to make the UN live up to the phrase, "We, the peoples" in the Charter. Of course, we know the UN, in reality, is just "We, the states;" there is no room now for the voice of the people in the UN. The report makes room for that voice. The founder of our research center, SGI President Daisaku Ikeda, includes recommendations for changes in the UN each year in his peace proposals. In a recent proposal, he said that the UN cannot be properly reformed until the voice of the people is heard and empowered there. The report sounds a similar theme when it offers an expanded definition to civil society.

Today, civil society — at least in UN terms — is made up solely of the NGOs that report to ECOSOC within the UN. Furthermore, these NGOs have only limited influence. The report, on the other hand, asserts that there is more to civil society than these NGOs; there are also the mass media, academia, transnational corporations, and citizen movements. We need to enlarge our conception of civil society and make room in the UN for all these other actors. That is a powerful notion.

The Commission also proposes that a forum of civil society organizations meet each year before the General Assembly convenes. This Forum of Civil Society would bring out the best in civil society by helping it become the conscience of the UN. Rather than lobbying for narrow interests and along separate tracks, civil society organizations gathering at this forum could discuss ideas to be considered in the General Assembly, thereby bringing the people's advice to the UN in a remarkably sensible way.

The report also outlines a role for civil society in protecting people. Civil society representatives would serve on the Council for Petitions through which non-state actors could seek action to redress wrongs that imperil people's security within states. In essence, the Commission decided that, on their own, states would never move against other states to protect people. The initiative would have to come from representatives of the people. So, the Commission proposed that the Council for Petitions be composed of distinguished global citizens who could recommend nonviolent action by the UN prior to the point in an escalating conflict when the choices narrow to the use of force.

These are just a few of the reasons this report appealed to us. Now, as we think together and discuss *Our Global Neighborhood*, I would like to raise some further questions for us to ponder. Most importantly: Do we have any shared values? The Commission hopes that we do, but is it clear what they are? And will we stand up for them? For example, one principle mentioned in the report is nonviolence. The Center's newsletter recently carried an interview with Robert Thurman, a Professor of Religion at Columbia University. In it he says, "For there to be world peace, more people have to be willing to die not to do violence than are already willing to die to do violence." In the report, there are many references to the violent cultures in which we live. Are there enough committed people around to create a nonviolent culture?

Another question: can civil society (as broadly defined here) work together, or do we have too much suspicion of one another? For example, can citizen movements get along with transnational corporations? Can the mass media work with NGOs? And how can we, with all our mutual distrust, engage in dialogue that arrives at a common vision, as the Commission did?

Those are my questions. I would like to conclude by expressing a hope. Today, more than ever, we experience "long-distance suffering." We are inundated with media accounts of events such as the bombing in Oklahoma, the earthquake in Japan, the continuing tragedy in Bosnia. These accounts evoke empathy in all of us and a desire to respond. I read a story in the *Boston Globe* recently about a young man, 18 years of age, who is now a paraplegic living in a hospital in Sarajevo. He was maimed by a sniper bullet which hit him as he walked across an intersection. A cameraman, waiting there for a possible news story, shot a video of the whole thing. The young man fell to the ground and lay there helpless, unable to move, while the camera continued to roll. Nearby, a UN officer just stood, staring at him. Apparently, he felt he didn't have the authority to do anything. Then, a Sarajevan man ran up and started yelling at the UN officer: "Move your van." He got the peacekeeper to move his van, and, using the van for cover, he went on to save what's left of this young man's life.

I believe that story and many like it are slowly kindling within people around the world the collective will to fundamentally reshape the global order that tolerates such suffering and inhumanity. This is the same collective will that motivated the Commission on Global Governance to envision a people-centered UN for the twenty-first century, an organization that would, in essence, strengthen the hand of that lone Sarajevan man who realized it was in his power to help.

OPEN DISCUSSION

• • •

Daniel Partan: In order to legitimize these proceedings, we're going to put the people at the center. It's now up to you to offer comments and questions for our distinguished speakers. The ground rules are that you be brief, whether it be a question or a comment. Then we'll turn to the panel and see who would like to respond.

Janice Broadwin: I'm Director of the Center for Innovative Action and Training Technology. One thing that you talked about a lot was a common set of objectives. Now, if we actually asked the Republicans and the Democrats, or people on the left and right, what their objectives were, they would talk about similar things. Everyone wants bipartisanship, but there's an incredible divergence of opinion about achieving these objectives, and what the underlying values are. I don't see anyone taking a leadership role in saying you cannot get me from here to there — to peace, etc. — by building more jails, by cutting back assistance to developing countries. Do you have a sense of where this new kind of leadership is going to come from, and whether it actually can be effective?

Straus: In the Commission report, the commissioners came up with another prime conclusion. Besides the ethical vacuum that exists in the world, they saw that there is a poverty of leadership at all levels, precisely the kind of leadership you mention. So, they call for new leadership based on shared values. This requires standing up at the local level, too. Having the courage to reflect upon and support the values that we hold in our daily lives is an action they hope will lead to change.

Lewis: I'd like to ask Richard Parker a question that follows from what was just said. Richard, if we really are still a people of generosity and vision, why is it that there is so little of it coming from our leaders?

117

The questioner is right. Why is it that, in fact, nobody ever hears generous answers from our leaders?

Parker: In some very real sense, we've lost contact with what it means to be a nation. We have instead accepted our role as being the world's largest shopping mall. I believe it was Clemenceau of France who said that America had gone from barbarism to decadence without once stopping to be a civilization. I want to reserve my judgment about whether that is premature, but I share Prime Minister Clemenceau's concerns.

I think that we live in a period, born after the Second World War, when the combination of a Keynesian emphasis on aggregate growth — rather than on growth with democratic redistribution — plus the paralyzing conformity of anti-communism, starved or leached out of American political life the diversity that once made this such a rich and voluble grassroots democracy. Our leaders fail us because we've been caught in a poisonous downward spiral which neither leader nor populace seems able to escape. I think that with the end of the Cold War, for the first time in my life at least, the possibility exists for us to emerge as a diverse and civilized nation. Whether or not a combination of leaders and vocal people will themselves call us back to that opportunity and possibility, I don't know.

Conable: The process of reform usually starts with identifying the flaws in the way society is organized, but our tendency on television and elsewhere is never to go beyond the negative. In other words, we have a tendency to identify what's wrong and never to suggest the correctives. That's why, in this report, so much emphasis was put on values. What do we have in common? If a group like the Commission on Global Governance could find common values, then it should also be possible within a country like the United States which has a great activating principle, the principle of democracy and freedom.

The problem is that we are a distracted people and frequently accept the negatives without then asking what we can do about it. As has been said several times today, questions can be raised in a conference like this, where caring people decide that they have heard enough of the negative and are willing to take the next step. I regret that what makes news so often about Congress, about the government, about all our public institutions, is what's gone wrong with them. But don't forget there is a second step.

Louise Damoree: I'm a former NGO representative to the UN. I think core values are very good to strive for. I want to add that caring is not a noun. Everything else is a noun. I would suggest using "loving care" instead of caring. To counteract the hate in the world that exists on an individual and group level, "loving" might help. I also want to say that when I served on a committee on world hunger, as we talked about assistance through organizations, it struck us that everything can be individual as well as organizational. Don't cross out the individual. We're all striving for the same thing here.

Dylan Parker: I'm President of the Greater Boston Chapter of World Federalists. Has any thought been given to a parliamentary assembly that would be elected by people? The General Assembly is undemocratic. The small countries have a vote that, theoretically, has the same weight as that of the large countries. The Security Council, too, is very undemocratic.

Conable: It's interesting that many of the invitations I've had to talk about this report have come from the World Federalists. And I have a message for them: don't let the best be the enemy of the better. I think that we're going to have to take steps that are possible. I worry about world federalism. In a world in which it's possible, you really don't need it. I believe that a formal procedure of the sort that you're suggesting, a parliamentary group, would frighten a lot of politicians. We'd hear a lot about sovereignty again.

I acknowledge that this is a very modest report, but I'd like to think that it's possible to achieve some of the goals it sets out. I want to repeat one thing, though. If the United States does not take an interest in this process, it is very unlikely that it will be successful. As a former president of the World Bank, I am distressed to report to you that everybody waits for the US to commit itself and then tailors their commitment to that of the US. So, if we can't start the process with something that's acceptable here — and I think this is a modest proposal — we're very likely to not get anything going at all. Burden-sharing is a concept that seems to have taken everybody by the lapels and held them in thrall. And the US, having the largest economy and, in many ways, a high degree of moral leadership in the view of others, has to take the first steps.

Cheever: Would you care to comment, Mr. Moderator, on the proposal for the Council of Petitions, composed of individuals independent of government?

Partan: We are caught up in the throes of change, and to see just where that change will take us is a very difficult, perhaps impossible task. I would not put outside the limits of potential change any of the suggestions that are made in *Our Global Neighborhood*. It seems to me that what we need to do is to build a constituency for change and move beyond many of the suggestions made there.

When you look, sector by sector, at the willingness of serious, thoughtful people, both inside and outside government, to contemplate multilateral decision-making, it seems the world is prepared to move well beyond what we now have. Perhaps we recognize that what has existed for the past fifty years is insufficient for the needs of humanity. Once we have that recognition, the boundaries are open with respect to change. The Council for Petitions is one such idea. Another that astonished me is the willingness of the American Bar Association to support a renewed commitment by the United States to the jurisdiction of the International Court. Several years ago, had you asked me if that was possible, I would have said no.

Lachlan Forrow: I'm the chairman for an organization named International Physicians for the Prevention of Nuclear War. The three principles I've been hearing are: 1) we have to operate from shared values; 2) as Anthony Lewis pointed out in discussing the former Yugoslavia, the rhetoric of shared values is not enough when actions are radically different. We have to be able to look at people in the former Yugoslavia and say, "some of you may say you share values, but you're not behaving that way;" and 3) we need to demand very concrete actions that show people are adhering to those values. The first category of recommendations from the Commission deals with promoting security and says, "Weapons of mass destruction are not legitimate instruments of national defense."

There are 700 NGOs around the world, including ours, that have worked for a couple of years on something called the World Court Project, through the World Health Assembly. We requested an advisory opinion by the International Court of Justice on whether the explosion of nuclear weapons would violate international law, given the indiscriminate effects on civilians and other things. Petitions and samples of signatures from 110 million citizens worldwide supporting the view that use of these weapons would violate civil conscience were accepted by the International Court of Justice. The United States government, among others, has filed briefs arguing that there is nothing in international law that says that the use of nuclear weapons would be a violation. The United States government, through its delegation at the Nuclear Non-proliferation Treaty conference, joined others refusing to put any teeth whatsoever into a commitment to abolish nuclear weapons. The people of the United States and the United States media are virtually silent about that.

At the end of World War II, most people were in absolute terror that weapons of mass destruction might destroy the world. Fifty years later, on the rhetorical level, all of us say weapons of mass destruction are not legitimate instruments of national defense, but the United States government is opposed to that position in practice, and the United States people are silent about it. I'd like to hear from Mr. Lewis, representing the media, or from others about what concrete steps we can take, either in relation to weapons of mass destruction or something such as world hunger, to have a victory that's very concrete and not rhetorical?

Lewis: I'm not familiar with the legal proceeding that you've just described. My own instinct on these matters, though I entirely share your view of the inadmissibility of the use of nuclear weapons, is that we, in the world that we have, deal with the problem in two ways. First, through public education and an arousal of conscience (an area in which the International Physicians have been singularly successful over the last many years) and, in the diplomatic world, through the often unsatisfactory, but still helpful, incremental process of negotiating reductions in weaponry. That has gone on with a good deal of success and, given where we were a few years ago, we're better off than we were. Everybody is concerned about limiting the acquisition by still further countries. I think that's correct, and although it's a long, hard slog, I don't know any other way to do it.

Straus: I don't want to put Anthony Lewis on the spot, but I do want to say something about the media. I read recently that there's a new movement stirring in public journalism. Previously, the idea has been that the media should view themselves as the watchdogs of society, ferreting out corruption and evil in human nature and bringing it to light. This is very important since, as Mr. Conable said, we can then ask the next question: what to do about it?

On the other hand, how do people develop knowledge about what's happening? Take the example that Lachlan Forrow gave. The media could ferret out the good things that people are doing and, with an equal vigor, could create hope in addition to serving as watchdogs. When the report calls for shared values, and includes the mass media in civil society, perhaps it's saying the media could think about serving the long-term interests of humanity, could look for what might build hope in people and what might help people mobilize for social progress. We hear that kind of story when we come to conferences like this, but it doesn't attract enough attention in the media for people to mobilize into a broad-based movement.

Lewis: I have to respond to that, and I'm not just going to play Banquo, but the absolute devil. I'm entirely against what you just said, Ginny, entirely against it. I think it's a terrible idea. I do not think journalists can serve the function of identifying what's good and running campaigns for the good. I don't think that's our job, I don't think we're capable of doing that. My colleague, Max Frankl, had a column in *The New York Times Magazine* a short while ago examining the very proposition you've gracefully made. I'm sure many would call me cynical, but I don't think it's at all cynical to say that's not what we do; it's not what we know how to do. If you want to be a preacher...

Conable: Well, I think somebody has to carry a burden of explanation. I think politicians can do that much more than they do. Politicians make the arbiter of their careers getting reelected, and that means frequently appealing to the simplistic. I do believe that somebody has to worry about the breadth of the education our people have. For instance, I hear a lot of people saying we shouldn't give any more money to the Hottentots until we've taken care of our own poor people. Nobody worries about the difference between relative poverty and absolute poverty. Our homeless people, if they're willing to buck the bureaucracy set up to try to take care of them, can have per capita incomes far above that for eligibility for World Bank loans. Still, a lot of Americans will fall back on a mantra of the sort, "Let's not do anything for those foreigners until we've taken care of ourselves," as if it were a great truth.

The fact is, people have to be educated if we are going to have a stable world. We've got to have a balanced relationship with the world, not one that's entirely introspective — one that focuses on the flaws in our own society while ignoring our responsibility to humankind as a whole. I worry about how we get the burden of explanation out there so people will see things as they are. Bill Fulbright said there's an inevitable divergence — attributable to the imperfections of the human mind — between the world as it is and the world as men perceive it. And that's one of our great problems. We have a perception of the world that is very, very parochial.

Parker: I want to respond briefly to my dear friend Tony Lewis's comments about public journalism. I am the former managing editor of a magazine called *Ramparts,* and I cofounded another magazine called *Mother Jones,* of which I was editor and publisher for a number of years in its early days. I actually believe that journalism is a form of preaching. I think that anyone who followed the *Times* or *The Washington Post* coverage of the NAFTA debates, for example, or who can think back to the early days of the American news coverage of the Vietnam War, understands full well that American journalism is about preaching as much as it is about informing. And I think that Jay Rosen and the public journalism movement actually are on to something that ought to be pursued. The argument is that we live in a triangular relationship between our leaders, our journalists, and the people themselves, but it is the people who have been excluded from that relationship, and that part of the relationship needs to be restored.

Lewis: Mr. Moderator, may I have a brief word? I'm being unfair to the question, but I want to say I agree with you. Certainly someone who writes an Op-Ed column would not be against preachers in journalism, but that's different from what I understand public journalism to be — something in which you try to make yourself a higher thing. I don't think we can do that.

Joseph Barratta: I work with the Coalition for a Strong United Nations which is also a member of the United Nations Association. I wished to ask a question of Mr. Conable, but before I do, just to follow up the last bit, I must say I'm a fan of the *Encyclopedia Britannica.* If you ever open up the Britannica, you'll discover not a single murder, not a rape; what you'll discover is nice little accounts of scientists who have, over the years, discovered new properties of chemicals or made new compounds — real triumphs of human ingenuity. If you want an example of positive journalism, I highly recommend you open the *Britannica.* The section under Leda and the Swan actually touches on the rape issue quite effectively.

I wouldn't want to pass up an opportunity to address a specific economic question to Mr. Conable, the former president of the World Bank. I'm really troubled by the proposal to establish an Economic Security Council. I do not understand the practical politics of it. I do remember a little bit of the history of the founding of ECOSOC. Another analogy that seems instructive is the founding of the European Community and the Council of Ministers. ECOSOC, in the Dumbarton Oaks draft, was almost nonexistent. It was the Latin American countries and other small, poorer countries that demanded greater economic development power in the United Nations. Is there such a politics today?

In the case of the European Community, France and Germany had fought almost to the death, but after the Second World War, a number of visionaries, including Jean Monnet, argued that there should be some kind of council of finance ministers to prevent such a thing in the future. I'm asking you a question through these historical analogies: are "we the peoples" supposed to play the part of the Latin American countries, or are we to anticipate a general war? How can we possibly transform ECOSOC in the Charter to an Economic Security Council?

Conable: My impression is that ECOSOC is largely an ineffectual group. I would prefer to see ECOSOC very much reduced and phased out. As for the Economic Security Council, my support for that is much influenced by my experience at the World Bank: there is a great deal of development work going on and very little coordination of it. There's a tremendous amount of waste and duplication; every bilateral aid program has a parliament directing it to do something — to study the effects of DDT on black flies in the rivers of Mali and Burkina Faso, or something like that. You'll find four or five such programs going on at any given time instead of using resources to ensure that high quality work is done and coordinated among the various agencies that are providing official development aid.

There's a lot of sentiment that Official Development Assistance (ODA) is no longer necessary because of the tremendous amount of transfer in the private sector, or because trade is so much more important than aid in terms of resource exchange. But the fact is, we're going to have to have aid anyway. The private sector depends very heavily on the existence of an adequate infrastructure in a country to provide support. To assure schools, roads, port facilities, an electrical grid that will provide adequate energy and so forth, ODA will have to continue to function even though it is now relatively small compared to the amount of private sector investment that is going on. Since it seems to be a shrinking part of the relation of nations, it must be carefully coordinated to avoid waste, duplication, and tremendous gaps in the human resource development necessary for it to be truly sustainable. So, I look at the Economic Security Council as a far preferable way to coordinate ODA in comparison with the kind of makeshift arrangement we now have now with the Development Committee — the regional groups that are trying to coordinate aid — and bilateral aid, which so often is simply an expression of domestic political concerns. Certainly, our US Agency for International Development is remarkable in this respect. We give three billion to Israel (which isn't even a poor country) and two billion to Egypt (as long as it speaks to Israel), thus making it impossible for us to get any economic reforms in Egypt; and 450 million to Turkey (as long as we have bases there), and 350 million to Greece (as long as we're giving 450 million to Turkey), and so forth. Really, we need much better coordination than we're getting.

Unidentified: I'm from Boston College. Getting back to the bleak picture of the United Nations as a failed organization, I would like to remind all of us of their successful missions. I remember my uncle packing and going to the Sinai when the UN stood between the troops of Israel and Egypt. And let's remember the successes in Cyprus, Cambodia, and so on. I don't think we should leave the impression that the UN has failed just because there has been a failure in Bosnia. The UN can only keep peace if there is a peace to keep. What happened in Sinai? Until Israel overran the UN positions, there was a peace.

Now, back to what Mr. Lewis said. I appreciate your writing, sir, but I respectfully disagree with your picture of the UN failing in Bosnia. I think someone else is failing, and I think someone else's organization is failing to act through the UN. The UN is being pushed to do something it is neither prepared for, nor has the mandate for. You said in the beginning that today there has been a change. What kind of change is that, sir? The Serbs kept fighting. They have not turned in their weapons. In your picture, the Serbs are bad guys and everybody else are good guys. You have spoken so eloquently, so sharply, and so vividly that you almost made them look good. Can you comment on this, Mr. Lewis?

Lewis: I don't think I'm going to persuade you, because you have a different view of rights and wrongs. To me, it's fairly clear that a people who have killed many thousands of others solely because of their religion, caused the flight of two million people from their country, and held women in rape camps, etc., are the aggressors, and in a particularly horrifying way. I don't know what else I can say to persuade you of, what seems to me, the obvious truth.

What the best way of dealing with it might have been I don't know, but I will say that I agree with your statement at least to this extent: it need not have been the problem of the United Nations. I think it was fundamentally a problem for the Western powers, and NATO, and I think, to put it very simply, that if Margaret Thatcher had been Prime Minister of the United Kingdom when the Serbs began shelling Dubrovnik and Vukovar in the fall of 1991, none of this would have happened. She would not have hesitated to say, "You can't do that in this world. Sorry. One more shell, we bomb you." It would have stopped right there.

Unidentified: Let's turn to public journalism again. Tony, in terms of journalism, I remember taking a bus ride from Vojvodina to Zagreb. I was riding with students from their national university and being mocked in 1979 and in 1980 for our journalism here. I think the entire civilized world, without exception, realizes that our journalism is skewed. And while it's alert and aware, in many cases I think it's very destructive. I think that we can, as Virginia Straus says, take a more positive view.

Daniel Cheever, all of us would be delighted if the nations of Africa had a more appropriate voice within the United Nations, especially South Africa. I am delighted with the change in the economic picture with United Nations, and with the idea of strengthening the economic councils there.

Mr. Conable, I have a question for you. What kind of impact do the United Nations countries have on the decisions about who gets your money and who doesn't? And, does international business — never mind the United Nations — have an effect on the decisions that you make?

And Mr. Lewis, can we change some of the reporting that we do? What is it going to take to change that? All of us observed what happened in Yugoslavia: the control of the television and the media by a very destructive group was part of what precipitated the events in Yugoslavia. All of us here in the United States have been irritated by all the negative reporting. What can we do to change that?

Conable: Well, I take it you're asking who gets money from the World Bank. All the members of all the countries in the world are owners of the World Bank, and they all participate in programs if they qualify. They have to be below a certain per capita income. This means they are sorted out as to whether they are either the poorest of the poor countries — in which case they get concessional aid — or whether they are middle income countries, those going up to 3,800 dollars per capita. Then they receive aid at commercial rates, which are lower than bank rates, because the World Bank can borrow much more cheaply than commercial banks can. Each country that qualifies for loans has a country director who meets with the government and talks about their priorities. Sometimes we have to shut countries off because their priorities were not acceptable. For instance, if they're spending more on the military than on education and health put together. A program based on their capacity to absorb the loans that we make to them is established for each country. Provided they live up to the conditions of such programs — international competitive bidding to avoid corruption, projects that will be broadly distributed among the poor, and so forth — they get the money they need.

Lewis: I'll just enter a plea of *nolo contendere* on the quality of the American press. I do agree that it leaves a great deal to be desired. And those of you who want more good news in newspapers, I want to remind you who the person was who wanted a good-news newspaper. His name was Spiro Agnew.

CLOSING REMARKS

• • •

By Barber Conable

It's very late and everything's been said that should be. I want to end with a quote from Brian Urquhart, who for many years was the Deputy Secretary General of the UN and is a member of the Commission — a man of grace and understanding. He said:

> *In the great uncertainties and disorders that lie ahead, the UN, for all its shortcomings, will be called on again and again because there is no other global institution, because there is a severe limit to what even the strongest powers wish to take on themselves, and because inaction and apathy toward human misery or about the future of the human race are unacceptable.*

If you start with that premise, then you must be in favor of the reform of the UN, because an institution incapable of reform is incapable of survival. And we, as a human race, are incapable of survival unless we can reform our institutions to bring them into conformity with the tremendous changes going on around us. It is not enough simply to wish things well. We must encourage procedures to meet the current needs of humanity.

A Women's Response to Our Global Neighborhood

• • •

JULY 10, 1995

Boston Research Center for the 21st Century
Cambridge, Massachusetts

Jerilyn Huskins

Panelists, left to right: Barbara Sundberg Baudot, Betty Reardon, Virginia Straus, Helen Caldicott, and Sayre Sheldon.

Barbara Sundberg Baudot is an Associate Professor at Saint Anselm College in Manchester, New Hampshire. Previously, she was a Fulbright Scholar in Norway, an International Relations Fellow with the Rockefeller Foundation, and an economist with the United Nations. Dr. Baudot has been an advisor and consultant to various international bodies concerned with problems of development and the environment.

Helen Caldicott is cofounder of the Physicians for Social Responsibility, an organization with over 22,000 members which was awarded the Nobel Peace Prize in 1985. She is the author of best sellers titled *Missile Envy* and *Nuclear Madness*. Her book, *If You Love This Planet*, was published in 1992, and she was the subject of an Academy Award-winning documentary called *If You Love This Planet*, the same year. In 1994, Dr. Caldicott received the Distinguished Peace Leadership Award from the Nuclear Age Peace Foundation.

Betty A. Reardon is the founder and director of the Peace Education Program at Teachers College, Columbia University, and of the International Institutes on Peace Education. She is a peace educator who has taught at all levels, from elementary to graduate, and has published widely in various fields related to peace education.

Sayre Sheldon teaches Literature and Women's Studies at Boston University and was founding president of Women's Action for New Directions (WAND) where she served as national president until 1987, and is now President Emerita and National Board member. Presently, Sheldon is working on an anthology of women's war writing in the twentieth century, entitled, *Her War Story* (publication date 1996).

SUMMARY

• • •

The luncheon seminar began with a discussion of the world view that informed and is represented in the report of the Commission on Global Governance. "The report," Barbara Sundberg Baudot commented, "objectifies the environment without seeing the metaphysics of it." In addition to lacking an ecological perspective, seminar participants said of the report, it also left out fundamental perspectives about women.

It is *not* a question of transferring power to women who would keep doing the same things that men have been doing, Sayre Sheldon suggested, but that we must have a transformation that comes from *seeing things differently.* The Commission has recognized the issue insofar as it has brought the question of individual security to the micro level but, she said, "they haven't really talked about the women's revolution that is already taking place today in the world at the grassroots level, or how to give political attention to it."

Helen Caldicott reminded participants that in India, Japan, and elsewhere, it is generally women who lead environmental movements, who are very powerful. The question, she posited, is how do we get these women to represent the planet? The United Nations, she observed, is male-run, debt-ridden, and bureaucratized to a degree that it's almost paralyzed. In addition, she said, the transnationals now have a lot of control in the United Nations. "I don't," she said, "see any leadership in this country."

Barbara Sundberg Baudot reminded her colleagues that the United Nations "is an intergovernmental organization that's only as good as the members that make it up. It's only as good as the top leaders of the organization and what they permit. And they each have different styles of leadership." What we lack today, participants suggested, is leaders who have imagination, who dream, who bring out the best in people.

But the crux of the issue with respect to individual action, seminar participants agreed, is to disseminate information about how the UN functions, what it is, and what it represents; we must do something regarding the terrible ignorance that exists about this critically important organization.

The women expressed grave concern about the greed that propels so much behavior today to the detriment of people and the planet. Further, they decried the fact that ideas from our militaristic society have been transferred to the economic arena where we now see terms like "economic cold war" and "fight for domination" when we speak of world markets.

Keying in on the idea of dialogue, Betty Reardon suggested that women must not depend solely on the media for the communication of fundamental information, that women must find other modes of dialogue. "I think," she cautioned, we must get information out in a way "that enables people to reflect on the implications of the information they receive. That's one of the things women do; they reflect on the implications of information for themselves and those they care about."

Professor Baudot shared her experiences from the Slovenia conference with participants. "We set out," she said, "to look at what was meant by civil society, at the mindset that underlies social progress, and at the cult of money and how you get around it. It really came down to a question of the nature of mankind." She spoke of the fact that inherent human dignity is what enables people to survive and overcome the most untoward material conditions. "You're not," she said, "going to change anything unless you awaken in everyone the recognition that women have dignity and nobility."

Participants agreed that a different conception of power must be promoted, perhaps one that espouses a different relation to material possessions, a different relationship with the environment, nature, and the universe, a sense of being one with it, a spiritual sense. There was unanimity on the view that *Our Global Neighborhood* should have made reverence for life a more central issue.

The concern with breaking the hold of rampant materialism was a consistent theme among participants, generating expressions of anger about the influence of large corporations and the media in "brainwashing" citizens about the value of goods. Virginia Straus suggested that to break the hold of the transnationals you'd have to have something stronger than they have. The NGO movement, the human connections, and the emergence of the so-called civil society all say that human beings are starting to bond across borders, have compassion, and give others dignity.

Dr. Caldicott sounded an optimistic note when she observed that if America could set the example, that would help to save the planet.

"I think that," she concluded, "at the moment, we're seeing a battle between good and evil that may be the final battle. You see it clearly in this country. I don't think it's a gender-related thing. I think that each of us has to make a decision. Each of us could lead a revolution if we wanted to, so I think it's an entirely personal decision."

A Women's Response to

OUR GLOBAL NEIGHBORHOOD

• • •

The third meeting in response to Our Global Neighborhood *was a luncheon dialogue among women, several of whom have been involved in other response meetings. At the beginning of the seminar, Virginia Straus recapped key points surrounding the Commission's report and emphasized the purpose of the gathering — to explore and consider the response of women to the report. As a means of focus, Straus outlined several questions to be considered:*

1) The Commission report suggests that in order for global governance to succeed, there needs to be a broad acceptance of a global civic ethic to "guide action within the global neighborhood." Betty Reardon, in her May 13th presentation, talked about the need to give more social value to the lessons and courage we derive from intimate sources. *How can women find their voice — elevate the social value of the contributions made by them on an intimate, but profoundly influential level of human society?*

2) *The Commission report proposes an Annual Forum of Civil Society Organizations and a Council of Petitions. Are these viable ideas, and how can they be implemented?*

3) The Commission report points to a leadership vacuum "over a wide spectrum of human affairs." Professor Dessima Williams, in her May 13th presentation, spoke of her enthusiasm about sisterhood and solidarity and asserted the "women can and must exercise leadership." *What leadership roles do you foresee women taking in this decade and into the next century?*

A People's Response to Our Global Neighborhood

In a lively, earnest, and honest exchange, the women dealt with both the strong and weak points of the Commission's report, ranging in topics from perspectives of gender to the problems of a consumer-oriented society. In these excerpts, we highlight critical points of the discussion, particularly those issues that were not covered by these speakers at one of the other UN Renaissance events.

Betty Reardon praised the report on several grounds, citing its "authentic global perspective" in that it takes all "actors in the system" into account. She also lauded its emphasis on human values as well as its futuristic aspect. Reardon also noted the report's shortcomings, such as the omission of certain perspectives of gender, culture, ecology, and learning.

The discussion began with a closer look at how the report covers the environment. Reardon stated that "the problem is seen as what happens in the environment, not in the behavior of people." Caldicott added that the report describes the symptoms, not the cause, of environmental difficulties. This conversation ensued:

Betty Reardon: We define problems in simplistic terms, focusing on symptoms rather than on causes. People speak about the problem of the "homeless" when the problem, in fact, is "homelessness." The problem is not the condition of the environment as such; it is the behaviors that produce it. This evidences the lack of an ecological perspective — a concern with the planet as a living system, not just as the host for the human endeavor.

Barbara Sundberg Baudot: I think another way of expressing the same idea is to say that the report has a very materialistic perspective on the environment: it objectifies the environment and ignores the metaphysics while, in fact, it is the mind-set that creates or envisages the environment which you have to attack in order to do something about it. I think Lynton Caldwell characterizes the distinction very well when he contrasts the earth view and the world view of the environment. The former is objective reality and the latter human perspective of reality.

We are all constrained by a world view because our minds cannot empirically perceive the truth. The temporal world is always in motion. Our views have to be subjective. And views about the environment have usually come from people pretending to perceive the earth view — and offering as scientific reality what is in fact their educated world view.

Sayre Sheldon: I think everything you said could apply to population too, since the report presents it as a scientific problem. Left out is the whole question of why women have children — why they have the number of children they have and what they need to change if they do need to change. It's all applied very much from the outside rather than by looking at it from a cultural or gender point of view. That's the problem with most discussions of overpopulation — they're always based on statistics. But how can you lower the population without talking about the lives men and women lead, and the causes behind the number of children they have?

A lot of this is a question of whether ideas and information move from the top down or from the bottom up, and that's one of the things I found missing in the report to some extent. Even though it speaks about and gives wonderful support for grassroots movements and NGOs and so on, it still doesn't really look at how certain things will come about. If women are going to have a full role in all of these things, it will not just be by giving women power — by putting them in the UN in higher positions, by...

Baudot: Tokenism.

Sheldon: Right. We have to change our attitudes about where change really comes from. That means looking at issues that are not considered politically interesting today but that are really the basis for how women and families operate. In other words, it's not just a question of transferring power to women who would keep doing the same things that men have been doing all this time. It's got to be a transformation that comes from seeing things differently. It is so important that we don't just fall into that trap of saying, "Let's give more power to women," without changing the whole way that society operates. I think the Commission has done some of this, because they've said that security is not just a question of national security. It's individual security. If you can't feed your family, you're not secure. So they have, in a sense, brought it down to the micro level, and that's really important. But they haven't really talked about the woman's revolution that is already taking place today in the world at the grassroots level, or how to give political attention to it.

Straus reintroduced the first question here, regarding ways in which women can elevate the social value of their contributions.

Sheldon: We have to "elevate the social value" of women's contributions. Women have a tremendous importance in all the small economic movements that are going on around the world, but we don't acknowledge them because we don't see the things they do. They're not transnational corporations. They're people bringing things they make to the market and feeding their children.

Helen Caldicott emphasized the importance of looking at the issues "from a grander scale" and with the understanding that "time is of the essence." She cited numerous instances around the world that bear out her caveats, and urged that the broader issues be attended to. A more complete expression of her views can be found in Caldicott's address at the United Nations Renaissance Conference held on July 22, 1995. She began the following dis-cussion on the issue of women in particular:

Caldicott: Now, let's bring women back into the discussion. If you look at the environmental movements in India, Japan, and elsewhere, they're usually led by women. They work to save the forests, the trees, to stop dams from being built. And they're very powerful. But how do we get these women representatives to represent the planet? After all, we are the majority on the planet, fifty-three percent, and we've done most of the work! I'm not sure how to do it; the UN is almost archaic in a way. I support it totally, but it's male-run. It's bureaucratized to a degree that it's almost paralyzed. It's in debt up to its eyeballs, mostly because the United States owes huge amounts of money and will not pay, particularly with this Republican Congress — even though the UN was started in the United States with the United States' blessing and initiative.

The transnationals now have a lot of control in the United Nations I've heard, and I'm sure that's true. I've been at the United Nations, and it takes ages to get anything done because of the bureaucracy. That's not the way women function. The Commission was chaired by two men. Why wasn't it chaired by a man and a woman? And I don't mean a male-type woman; I mean a woman in touch with what's actually happening.

What the solutions are, I don't really know. I think some of the suggestions are good. The Security Council is obsolete, and there should be more nations on it, but that's putting icing on the cake. What we've got to look at is the cake, and we don't have a lot of time.

The report addresses leadership and that, I think, is the key. I don't see any leadership in this country. I see that Peres is acting as a leader, and Arafat to a degree. I see that John Major is. He's helped to initiate the peace process in Ireland. What happened in South Africa was excellent. There's leadership there, but in very few other places. But even that is not leadership in the direction to save the earth for the children or for all future generations of all other species.

Straus: Barbara, since you worked in the UN, do you have any comments?

Baudot: I've worked in it, and I'm married to it. My husband was the former controller, so I have some familiarity with the functioning of the organization. First of all, people forget what the UN is, what it represents. It is an intergovernmental organization that is only as effective at any point in time as the members that make it up. It is only as useful, at any point in time, as the top leaders of the world permit it to be. Also, each Secretary-General has his own style and personality which permeate the organization.

Dag Hammarskjold, for example, had vision, a dream; he had imagination and brought out the best in people. He saw the best in people. Under him the United Nations was criticized but respected for its intellectual and moral leadership.

The United Nations, however is not an entity that acts on its own in such a way that one can simply sit back and just criticize it. Criticize your country's behavior within the UN — that would be more effective. And I think if responsible citizens in every country had a knowledge and an interest in how international fora function, they would become more involved with them. But there's a terrific ignorance of the UN, of what it is, and what it represents. And there's a lack of good books about how it operates.

Caldicott: And the vision it could have.

Baudot: And the vision the United Nations has had. I worked in the Economic Commission for Europe back in the 1960s, and there was tremendous creative activity. I had been hired by the United Nations in New York, originally to be one of the junior professionals at the creation of the UN Conference on Trade and Development (UNCTAD). Philippe de Seynes, then the Under Secretary-General for Economic and Social Affairs, and his team had a vision of the UN playing an active role in filling the void at the end of the colonial era and needed a lot of people for the task. The need was in part for basic researchers as I was at the time coming out of graduate school. I also witnessed the creation of UN Industrial Development Organization (UNIDO).

Now there are suggestions that both UNCTAD and UNIDO be done away with. I just can not believe it — because they were spawned to respond to a need which still exists. Get rid of them, consolidate their former functions into one big entity, and you end up putting too much in one central organization. By spawning these different groups, more people were able to get into the act and get more things done. All this talk about efficiency is very superficial. I say, give more people roles. The political elites talk about employing everybody and yet they pride themselves on firing people as they strip down organizations. In light of the world's problems and the needs of people, it is like "straining at gnats and swallowing camels."

Caldicott: But where does that come from? Let's talk about the cause. Where does that thinking come from?

Baudot: It's coming from materialism and profit.

Caldicott: Yes — and who spawned it?

Sheldon: Patriarchy.

Caldicott: Yes, but it's not just that. It's coming from corporations. Corporations have been at this since they developed in the late '20s, and they've spent literally billions of dollars brainwashing people, conducting social engineering. We even use their terms: "marketing," "product," "efficiency," etc. They're really at their zenith now, because they've got the whole Congress with them.

Baudot: It's the Republican message.

Caldicott: Well, it's not the Republicans. In fact, it's the corporations themselves who are writing the legislation. They're sitting in on the committees as the regulations and laws are being written, so we're at the zenith of corporate power, capitalism, greed, selfishness. And no one gives a damn about people, let alone species.

Baudot: Well, at the initiative of Philippe de Seynes, whom I mentioned earlier, and later under the leadership of Peter Hansen, now head of Humanitarian Affairs at Headquarters in New York, the UN took a prominent role in trying to bring the multinational corporations within the international community. With these corporations, the UN, through its Centre on Transnational Corporations, attempted to elaborate rules of the game, a Code of Conduct, that would guide big business and bring to all nations the benefits of their activity while controlling the excesses of wild capitalism. A few year ago, under the pressure of the most conservative groups in the US, this Centre was suppressed.

Later in my career, I worked at UNCTAD in Geneva. UNCTAD, at its conception, was the UN's response to the power and limited membership of GATT. UNCTAD was successful in getting through guidelines about restrictive businesses practices. As I said earlier, UNCTAD is now on the hit list.

Caldicott interjected that in fact little was done and discusses the shortcomings of the World Trade Organization (see presentation, July 22). She then turned to her views on the World Bank:

Caldicott: What the World Bank has been doing in the Third World has been obscene. Tighten your belt, be efficient, sorry we don't like your health care programs, your education, sorry about the children. Yes, you'll have to starve a bit, but we have to have our debts paid back.

Baudot: And we have to streamline all your public services and industries.

Straus cited a chapter in the report where it is stated that the Economic Security Council would elevate questions of economic interdependence and environment to the level of importance of security questions.

Baudot: For years — until the last five years or so, since the end of the Cold War — the primary activity of the United Nations and its primary concern has been in economic and social areas. The Security Council was hardly operational and was involved in minor issues. In economic matters, UNCTAD conferences, for example, were major venues for negotiations on economic cooperation and for helping developing countries to help themselves. There was also significant work on social issues, such as the situation of children or of persons with disabilities.

Sheldon: All during the Cold War, as we looked ahead to its end, we said the next competition in the world would be economic. Well, the end of military competition is over because we have deterrence — although I don't know how true that is. But lately it seems we've taken over all the ideas from our militaristic society in our economic society. In fact, people are now talking about a "cold peace" and an "economic cold war." The same value system has just moved on to fighting for world markets.

We're having a war with Japan. "Trade war" is the expression for it. So we haven't succeeded in moving from the Cold War mind-set to a new post-Cold War mentality, even though economic is better than military — I hope. It could kill just as many people, I suppose, given the World Bank and some of the ways in which it has been operating.

Caldicott: It could destroy the world quicker than a war could.

Straus referred to an earlier comment about the effect of leadership by women at the grassroots level on value-based change. She asked Reardon to respond.

Reardon: Well, I am interested in leadership issues and values in terms of something that you said about Daisaku Ikeda's views on dialogue at the opening of this conversation. It seems to me that everything we have been saying is not generally communicated to the broad public via the media. But it is known. We know it. Most people in our circles know it. So the question is in large part one of communication and the form, mode, and purpose of the communication by any agent or actor who can communicate, whether it's media, groups, individuals, whatever. The public in general depends on the media for fundamental information, so much information is not known to the public. Those of us who have that information have to find modes of dialogue with the public that don't just depend on the media. After all, the media are controlled by the same general systems as the nation-states, the transnational corporations, and all the other institutions.

The transnationals are probably the most powerful actors in the system, and I don't think the report takes a critical enough stance toward them. I think women have everything to gain by calling them to responsibility. I think we need to be called to responsibility — to this dialogue — so we can find the areas in which we can talk to others, and try to get this information out in a way that enables people to reflect on the implications of the information they receive. That's one of the things women do; they reflect on the implications of information for themselves and those they care about.

I don't think women need to be empowered. Women are powerful. What women need is to recognize their power and use it. We have been conditioned by these frames of references, by ways of thinking that are reinforced by the media. There are gradations in our perceptions of power, and if you don't have the power to get attention, it seems that you don't have much power. Women have not been attended to. We need to get attention.

I think we need to be involved in intentional dialogue with various other sectors that might support these kinds of changes; we need to demand more attention from people such as those who write these reports and formulate the various policies that determine what happens in the short term. Even though we do have to take a longer range view, as Helen said, very much depends on what we do on a daily basis.

Baudot: I agree with everything you said except this demand for attention. I think we should just take it.

Caldicott: It's like the Equal Rights Amendment. Women made a terrible mistake. They said, "Please, give us equal rights." The answer was, "No." You don't ask. You just do it. And the media are the key. I want a talk show. I want to take on Rush Limbaugh — full frontal, and be as provocative as he is, but in the other direction. How do I get it?

Baudot: Find other women who can raise money, pool it, and let's do it.

Caldicott: Yes! I'm investigating the possibility now, it's what we should be demanding. We should be going to ABC, CBS, and NBC, saying, "Okay, we want equal time — thank you very much." That's the ethics of journalism: Rush Limbaugh has that time, we want this time. It's got to be a woman who'll say things as they are and speak the truth that has to be spoken.

Caldicott discussed two key points elaborated in her July 22 presentation concerning paranoia about the United Nations since the end of the Cold War, and the obsolescence of the Pentagon and suggestions for redirecting its expertise. She stated that the trade war is "just another form of war, but with the same players."

Sheldon: Returning to my concern about adhering to a military orientation, I believe it is very bad for women. In the military model, women don't have decision-making power. If you take that same model and transfer it to economics, then women aren't going to have any power in the economic realm either — they're at the low end. In military situations, they're usually the victims, and there are victims all over the world now. We have all the figures to show that civilians now are the major victims and that soldiers are safer. Then, if you look at women economically, they're at the low end there, too. And they're down there doing ninety percent of the world's work.

Caldicott: We don't have to accept it, Sayre.

Baudot: Yes, and you cannot play victim.

Sheldon: I think that some women are doing things. There are women from Pakistan who are saying, "We're not going to spend that money on those airplanes." As you said before, Helen, there are women all over the world who are doing these things, but attention isn't being paid. We have to be like Greenpeace and get out there.

Baudot: Well, it is a start.

Reardon: I'm very concerned about whether what we're talking about now will develop into an effective confrontational mode — I'm not sure, given what happened to Greenpeace, and given what I saw happen in Paris last week. People are just cowed into accepting. At one point there was a fairly vigorous disarmament movement there, and large demonstrations against the testing. But there weren't more than 5,000 people at either of the recent demonstrations. It seems to me that we need to do some learning, too, about inventing some other ways.

Straus noted that the women have discussed how leadership isn't just a matter of transferring power to women, and how it is necessary to look at problems in terms of causes. She asks about the ways in which this can be done.

Baudot: I've been doing a lot of thinking about that in connection with what we did in Slovenia. I just finished a booklet on population and the environment.

Straus: Do you want to explain a little bit about the Slovenia conference?

Baudot: This was a meeting organized by the United Nations in the context of the preparation of the Social Summit (March 1995 – Copenhagen). It was a seminar conceived by the secretariat responsible for coordinating the World Social Summit. Three governments, the French, the Swiss, and the Austrian, put up the funds and the Slovenian government invited the group to meet in Bled, Slovenia. My husband, who was the coordinator for the Social Summit, was responsible for the seminar and I, behind the scenes, was the woman pushing for a spiritual perspective.

We pulled together thinkers with hearts. We had journalists: the former editor in chief of the *Christian Science Monitor* and the foreign editor of *The Financial Times*. We had scholars of various religions and philosophies. There was a Jesuit and a monsignor from the Vatican. We had professors of business, the environment, ethics, culture and language, physics, and political science; representatives of human rights interest groups. There were diplomats and national politicians.

We set out to look at what was meant by civil society, the mind-set that underlies social progress, and at the cult of money and how you get around it. It really came down to a question of the nature of humankind. We stated that all of us share a common spirit, and that at the core of that spirit is human dignity. However, when one looks at a textbook on Third World politics today, one reads that dignity is attached to material gain — a home and creature comforts make a person dignified. That idea is very sad indeed, and fails to recognize that human dignity and nobility are inherent in the person.

Nonetheless, that inherent human dignity is what enables people to survive and overcome the most untoward material conditions. It's that which enabled Elie Wiesel to survive the concentration camps. It's what many a tribesman has. It's what you see in the bearing of American Indians when you look at photos of them from the nineteenth century. You don't see it today on the reservations.

I think the same awareness, the same idea on universal spiritual roots and dignity, then flows from there into how you look at future leadership roles for women. You're not going to change anything unless you awaken in everyone the recognition that women have dignity and nobility.

Caldicott: Their spiritual essence. That's the key.

Baudot: It's there, and you find it in the first chapter of Genesis, where women are created; male and female are created in the image and likeness of God. That's what underlies the mind-set that, in the past, envisioned women with that kind of dignity. If you begin there and then turn toward her leadership roles, you will find an empowerment that comes of itself. Women's leadership role should be in the promotion of the values of equity and equality, promoting them through their own expectations and dignity, by acting as if they enjoyed these values because they have them. With that consciousness, one has charisma, a charisma that others respect.

The next point is to promote a different conception of power. What kind of power are we talking about? Are we talking about material power? Or do we have a power which is inspired by a sense of wisdom and love?

Caldicott: Which is spirit.

Baudot: Yes. Someone exercises and reflects compassion. The power is in the compassion and the comfort you can offer. At that point, women's leadership role could be in the promotion of a different relation to material possessions. We live in an infinite world of ideas, and the best things in life are free — the music, the poetry. We need all of these things and less greed — less interest in money and more in the quality of life. Helen, you've so beautifully expressed it, as has Betty: the promotion of a different relationship with the environment, nature and the universe, the sense of being one with it. And finally, there's leadership as the heart of a family. I have seen, in many women today, something that just turns me off. I see the kids thrown to the tides of the world. A woman would rather fight the man and have an equal role with him than be concerned with the child. The children are the biggest losers in this whole thing.

Caldicott: I think the woman's movement has promoted that, I really do. I live in New York City, where children are being walked around by nannies. Their mothers aren't there.

Baudot: Neither are their fathers.

Sheldon: If they're lucky enough to have one.

Caldicott: Their mothers and their fathers aren't there. I have to say, I had three babies and it was the most wonderful thing I ever did. Let's be frank, kids need their mother, need her breast, need her love, need her smell, need everything about her. I left mine when my youngest was three, and it was too early. Yes, fathers, too, can take a very important role, but we've gotten away from the fact that a baby needs its mother. I think that's why a lot of families are disintegrating now. The mother has to rush out and work.

Sheldon: She's not doing it because of the woman's movement; she's doing it because she's responding to the economic needs of her society. She can't live without that money now.

Caldicott: No, it's not just that.

Baudot: The problem is really who's going to take care of those kids. I think that's a person's first obligation. And I think women should consider themselves persons, not something else. Women are a people and men are a people. We should not be out confronting, we should be cooperating. That's where it starts. The kids should be the starting place for leadership.

Caldicott: The kids should be number one.

Baudot: They should be number one. And women can take the leadership role in that area. If the husband doesn't do it, well, too bad. We brought them to life, we've got the instinct to nurture and to love — and somebody's got to do it. We just can't let it go. If we do, the world will go to hell in a basket.

Caldicott: You sound like Dan Quayle.

Baudot: I'm not talking about family values. I read something absolutely beautiful recently. It was about the idea of great humility. Leadership should not be of the sort that one exercises in order to get into *People* magazine, to be famous and have your name in lights. All of us have a calling, and I think every person's calling is equally important. George Eliot describes a wonderful woman in *Middlemarch:* Dorothea. The kind of leadership that she represents is just extraordinary, the charisma that she has. I'll read you one little paragraph.

> *Her finely touched spirit had still its fine issues, though they were not widely visible. Her full nature, like that river of which Cyrus broke the strength, spent itself in channels which had no great name on the Earth. But the effect of her being on those around her was incalculably diffusive: for the growing good of the world is partly dependent on unhistoric acts; and that things are not so ill with you and me as they might have been, is half owing to the number who lived faithfully a hidden life, and rest in unvisited tombs.*

This may be one of the greatest glories and the most fulfilling mission.

Caldicott: Amen, George Eliot, a woman.

Straus: Actually, this reminds me of Betty's comment at our May 13th event. You talked about how the section of the report on human values and ethics should have made human dignity and reverence for life more central.

Reardon: Well, what I referred to as "reverence" is an element of awe and love that is not comprehended in the word "respect," a word that has a context external to the person. We respect behaviorally. Reverence is something that comes from within and can manifest itself in behavior. But it comes from within. It's also the source of the courage I talked about as the main thing that we need now — because people are afraid, for example, that their children will have no future.

Caldicott: It's up to them to make sure their children do, so what's holding them back? Why are they inhibited in doing that?

Reardon: Because they have a sense of powerlessness.

Caldicott: Why?

Reardon: Because we have not been able to convince them of what we were discussing before. I think people do not realize that they do have power.

Caldicott: People are asleep because they've been hypnotized by television. And all of that is partly orchestrated by social engineering, by the corporations. I think we've got to really get down to the cause of all of this, and really think carefully.

In Australia people are much less passive than here. In America I'll give a lecture and people whine, "You've made me feel awful." It's not American to feel awful, is it? You mustn't feel awful.

Baudot: That's an American thing?

Caldicott: Oh yes, they're truly, truly hypnotized.

Straus: But not in Australia? You're saying that you wouldn't hear that in Australia?

Caldicott: Much less. I'm generalizing, of course. But it's a reaction I get a lot here. And I think, why? What's happened? Why are people scared? And people, girls come up to me and they say, "You've just said everything I've ever believed." And I said, "Why don't you say it?" People are inhibited about speaking the truth. "How are you?" "Fine." [I'm really not fine at all, I feel awful.] "Have a nice day." [I don't want to have a nice day.] "Thank you for calling AT&T." [I don't want to call AT&T.] All of this crap that goes on, the euphemism. We've got to bust through and speak the plain, stark truth. Political correctness is crap, too. Everyone's mesmerized, brainwashed to behave like a puppet. That's how I see it.

Sheldon: I really like what Barbara said earlier about breaking the links to materialism. The values that you described are, in part, women's values, or at least values that seem important to a lot of women. One of them was to break this dependency on material goods. We're lumped together in this country as one big person, the consumer. Every day I read *The Wall Street Journal,* and every day it discusses what the consumer is doing: is the consumer nervous, is the consumer buying cars, is the consumer afraid to buy a house this week? Everything is based on…

Caldicott: The market.

Sheldon: Which is all of us put together. How do we defeat that?

Caldicott: The market? Stop buying.

Sheldon: I think women should be in charge of budgets. Women would never spend money on some stupid thing that doesn't work, like a huge nuclear submarine that you can't use. I think women are practical. How can we break that material slavery that we're all in, and that America's spreading around the world? If it's not as bad in Australia, it's going to be by next week. People are going to start killing each other for the right kind of sneakers.

Straus raised the subject of the importance of the Civil Society Organization Forum in bringing the NGO voice into the daily work of the United Nations to reinvigorate the UN from the bottom up. She also stressed the importance of the Council on Petitions as empowering citizens — including women — to address cases of oppression that lead to violence before the violence begins. She asked the participants to comment on the potential for these forums to serve as a global outlet for women's leadership.

Baudot: I think that is emerging through these exchanges between the NGOs.

Reardon: I think women's organizations as we know them would probably have quite a significant role if this truly were an assembly of civil society as it's conceptualized here. But I fear that it would still exclude those who are most in need of being heard. What percent of our fifty-three percent of the population is not represented in any of this?

Caldicott: Eighty percent of the fifty-three.

Reardon: Who never get to see a television, who have no will or capacity to be heard beyond their own immediate community?

Sheldon: I'm going to Beijing, so I'm really interested in how NGO influence will develop. One idea I had was that NGOs could adopt sister NGOs. If you're working on the same thing, say, an American NGO like mine, working on militarism, could connect with a sister organization in Burma or Pakistan, and really work together with it. I thought that was a good idea.

In America we tend to feel we have to give to other organizations that are less privileged than organizations in our society, but when I meet these women at the UN, they're just doing incredible things that American women aren't even thinking about. We've got a lot to learn from other countries.

Maybe it's because there are so many women in so many societies that are really in grave trouble. And they're not afraid. They're so hard up that they're willing to take these risks. I keep thinking of these women at the UN from Pakistan who talked about the military budget. They get their agenda into their newspapers. They just do it.

Caldicott: We don't try hard enough, Sayre.

Reardon: I have a point related to my concerns about the way we are speaking for women. Particularly because there are not only cultural differences among women but great disparities in material possibility. Although we want to move from a material revolution of *having* to a revolution of *being*, many women of the world are poor and illiterate, so in our thinking about the process of dialogue, we have to ask how we enter into a dialogue in which we really hear them.

Caldicott: There needs to be global redistribution of wealth, period. It's not right that twenty percent possess eighty percent of the world's wealth. That's the problem. Every woman should have access to free contraceptives. She should be educated about the population cycle, and her standard of living must be elevated. That's the only way the overpopulation problem will be addressed.

Reardon: But they're not going to get access so long as we're consuming the way we are today. There has to be a drastic change in the patterns of consumption — we have to be willing to take the bus.

Sheldon: The first thing we have to do is be willing to criticize ourselves. When you're talking with women from other parts of the world, as soon as you do that, they respect you, they listen to you, they hear you. As soon as you say, "We've got this problem in the United States; our military sends more weapons to the rest of the world than any other country, and we're ashamed of it; we're trying to work on it, and this is how we're doing it," it's okay, because you haven't come in as a condescending person insisting they do things our way.

Straus: It seems to me that to break the hold of the transnationals you'd have to have something stronger than they have, and I think the NGO movement, the human connections that Sayre is talking about, and the emergence of the so-called Civil Society is another way of saying that human beings are starting to bond across borders, to have compassion, and to give others dignity.

Caldicott: The strength is in the spiritual bond that Barbara talked about.

Straus: I believe it is. It's much stronger than the transnationals.

Caldicott: And I think we have to start talking overtly about it. I'm starting to. I've been on a spiritual journey the last five years, and I've learned a huge amount. And I'm only just starting to come out and talk about it; it's sort of scary in a scientific world, but I think we have to be prepared to actually address it.

Baudot: One has to be very careful because people can dismiss the spiritual dimension as "New Age." But to address it as dignity or nobility, there is spirit in those. And to build from there, saying there's a spirit in the person. Humankind is not mere matter in motion, or a little particle in a torrent driven by passions. Actually, what mankind is doing with this materiality business is becoming less than an animal.

Caldicott: Oh, much less. The other thing I want to say is that this country is determining the fate of the earth. If America could set the example, which means a big turnover in consciousness, then that would help to save the planet. To be totally practical, those are the things that we have to achieve. And we'll only achieve them by making a hell of a lot of noise and by educating.

Baudot: Yes! We're not going to achieve that by cutting taxes.

Caldicott: We need to pay more taxes. How dare they cut taxes?

Straus: It may seem like the long way, but the way to achieve it is to talk about the meaning of human life, the purpose of life.

Caldicott: Not just human. All life. Those trees up there. They're all life. In Scandinavia there's a movement called "The Natural Step," started by a physician who said that every cell — be it dolphin cell or leaf cell or human cell — is basically the same, with the same enzymatic systems. If dolphins die and fish are getting cancer, etc., that will happen to us, too. Biologically, that's the model. We mustn't do anything that damages living cells, that's the whole thing. The whole business community has taken it up in Sweden, and the farmers have taken it up, the King's endorsed it, the physicians are supporting it, and it's spreading like wildfire. They're just setting it up in Australia now. And there are people in Boston who are starting to organize it. That's not spirit, but in a way it is spirit.

Baudot: It is and it's not, since people are being careful because of themselves; it's self-interest. One would want them to have the mindset to be that way because that's the way life is, and because it's the duty of the person, not just because it's going to save us.

Caldicott: Not just us, the elephants. There is no separation.

Reardon: Separation is part of the materialism that you've been talking about.

Baudot: I think you can go beyond that, though. You can say we're all really one thought. If you break down those cells, you get down to energy and pluses and minuses and quarks. And in the end all life really starts in that. So we're all one thought or energy force without even a self beyond that.

Sheldon: I think there's a real reaction going on against bigness. A lot of what's happening politically in America these days is a response to the idea that everything's gotten too big, that the government's gotten too big, and the UN has gotten too big. Huge institutions no longer seem to be working, and people know it. And some of the criticism is being used in absolutely the wrong way — to destroy government rather than get it to do the things it should do. But there's an energy there. The Republicans have used it.

We should be able to use it, too, because breaking down big structures and making small structures more powerful ties in with what I was saying earlier — women tend to work in small-scale ways that are truly powerful, even if they're not recognized or are unable to immediately overcome the forces of these enormous bureaucracies. But something is happening, and if we could get individuals to make changes in their daily lives, women could be the leaders in that. They have to be leaders on their blocks, leaders in their families.

Caldicott: But it has to happen nationally, Sayre.

Sheldon: No, it doesn't.

Straus: In fact, some academics have begun to wonder why the powerful growth of the NGO movement hasn't led to a focus on political leadership by women.

Sheldon: But leaders do a lot of damage.

Sheldon: Many leaders just cause a lot of trouble. We do have some great leaders, people who have that spiritual dimension, but we also have leaders who are just trouble for everybody.

Baudot: Woman leaders.

Sheldon: Mary Catherine Bateson talked a lot about how women do many things at the same time because their roles involve them in doing all those things. Then she said that most of the harm in the world is perpetrated by people who only do one thing. That's a wonderful way of rethinking how society rewards men for doing one thing all the time. Women try to take care of ten things at once; they are just amazingly flexible. But because of that they don't get the big prize or have one blockbuster achievement. I think our definition of leadership has to change too.

Caldicott: I'm looking for inspirational leadership.

Sheldon: Why is it important?

Caldicott: I'll have to speak for myself. When I stand before an audience of one or two thousand, I can go on and on about a lot of things, and they get informed. But when I drop down into where I really live and speak soul to soul — to their spirit — and talk about the beauty within a single cell and the beauty of the rose and the meaning of that beauty, getting down to the way people who are dying talk — because that's what I deal with, dying people and children — at that level, you can crack open their psychic shell, and they'll follow you over a cliff.

That's the sort of leadership I'm talking about. That's the inspiration that people are hungry for. They stand up when I finish speaking, they cry, tears rolling down their cheeks, because they don't hear it elsewhere because the feeling's gone out of life. Often, they don't even get it in their intimate relationships. They're hungry for it.

Caldicott outlined her view of four aspects of the human being elaborated in her July 22 talk. She ends by noting that we must get back to a spiritual aspect.

Baudot: I want to sneak in some comments on the UN here. Sayre just made a comment I've heard before. There's this mind-set that the UN is just a US toy. We have an ethnocentric view of the UN because we happen to have been in on the founding of it. And since it's in our country, we think we own it. But we despise it when we do not seem to wield the dominant power; that is when other groups of countries compete with us. Furthermore, whatever changes we the Americans think are needed in our government, we think they have to be applied to the United Nations, too. Today, because we say the US government is too big, we are also saying the UN is too big. If you look at the budget of the UN and compare it to the budget of the US government, you are talking billions in difference. The UN budget is peanuts.

Caldicott: They do a lot with it, don't they?

Baudot: They do tons with it. And if you look at the agenda, if you look at how much is being done by so few people, it is mind-boggling. That Social Summit was put together by ten people in the Secretariat. They organized all the NGOs and did everything. That is phenomenal. I've seen how we put together the World Economic Survey, how we put together meetings on restrictive business practice. Five people. Three people.

Caldicott: It's always the way to get things done.

Baudot: Always. But it's so little understood. You can't measure the impact of ideas, and once you start to put price tags on them and try to measure them as material quantities and output, you lose the whole spirit of the system.

Caldicott: Like the GNP.

Baudot: Exactly. The UN is a small organization. Tiny for its mandate.

Caldicott: But in terms of what we've been talking about, you know, women's work is not measured in the GNP. It should be. We should be valued and paid for it or something. That's terribly important, globally.

Sheldon: Yes. It should be part of every budget.

Caldicott: I remember Margaret Mead spoke after me once in 1978. I said, "Women are the civilizers." She stood up and said, "Yes. When we were troglodytes, it was the women who nurtured and cared for the children and the men. They went out and caught the saber toothed tigers and came back, but the women were the civilizers." That's not valued in this present economic model, but it should be.

Sheldon: Because there's only the market, only goods and services.

Straus here asks the women to conclude their discussion with a final statement.

Sheldon: We obviously need much greater women's input, in terms of leadership, in every aspect of life. But we have to redefine power and the uses of power rather than simply say that the only way women can do anything is to do them as they've been done. We have to change the way people operate, incorporating those values we've been talking about here today. I don't even see it as male or female in a sense. I believe that men's roles have been enormously denigrated in our culture. This revolution has to involve every single human being. But it's also true that women are underrepresented and that they are moving towards a new phase in human life. Because of that, we also live in a time when there's a huge backlash against women around the world. In other words, it's a crucial, exciting time. Doors are opening, and at the same time some want to slam them shut.

Caldicott: I think that, at the moment, we're seeing a battle between good and evil that may be the final battle. You see it very clearly in this country. I don't think it's a gender-related thing. I think that each of us has to make a decision. Each of us could lead a revolution if we wanted to, so I think it's an entirely personal decision.

Reardon: I think Helen's quite right in saying it's largely a question of what the individual person does, the decisions we make. There is something rather important about women's roles right now in that we are the vast majority of the performers of human activities. This entails responsibility. Everything that we have been talking about — value structures, ways of looking at the living world, ways of relating to people — can be profoundly influenced by how women bring out the persons in their children. That gives women the power and ability to positively influence the transformation of the world. I think that's very, very important.

Baudot: I would focus mostly on the new look of woman, the heroine, and the secret of the heroine. You can find it in the virtuous woman in *Proverbs*, you can find it in the description of love in *Corinthians*. I'm reminded of a song that Placido Domingo sings called "The Great Hero." I'd change that to "The Great Heroine." Simply acting with love in everything you do — that's the bottom line.

United Nations Renaissance Conference: Creating a Civil Society in Our Global Neighborhood

. . .

JULY 22, 1995

Columbia University
Kellogg Center
New York, New York

PROGRAM OF THE DAY

• • •

Welcoming Remarks
Eric Hauber, Soka Gakkai International
James M. Olson, United Nations Association

Musical Presentation

Overview of the Report, *Our Global Neighborhood*
Shridath Ramphal, Commission on Global Governance

Response
Helen Caldicott, MD, Physicians for Social Responsibility

Response Panel
Stephen P. Marks, School of International and Public Affairs,
Columbia University
Nancy B. Roof, Center for Psychology and Social Change

Open Discussion

Response Panel
Gururaj (Raj) Mutalik, MD, International Physicians for
the Prevention of Nuclear War (IPPNW)
Virginia Straus, Boston Research Center for the 21st Century

Open Discussion

Closing Remarks
Shridath Ramphal

SUMMARY

· · ·

Shridath Ramphal, co-chair of the Commission on Global Governance, opened the conference with an invitation to participants, "Let's look ahead to what lies beyond today." Addressing values and vision, Ramphal cited Jean-Paul Sartre: "When one day our humankind becomes full grown, we will not think of the world as the totality of its people, but as the infinite unity of their mutual needs." That, said Ramphal, is the spirit of *Our Global Neighborhood*. We are neighbors, and we must find ways to cooperate and to move together into the twenty-first century.

"The first realization which we must seize upon," Mr. Ramphal said, "is the sense that we can make a difference." Until we develop a collective vision of the neighborhood, of the goals toward which we are striving, we cannot change our institutions.

"We talk about governance that makes space and accommodates new players alongside of nations and governments. The world is enriched by diversity, not made more difficult." We must recognize, he went on to say, "that we are part of the instruments of change and that a part of the process of change is changing ourselves."

Mr. Ramphal reviewed some of the structural changes recommended by the Commission and summarized the need for new mechanisms to respond to the crises of our times by saying, "When the security of the people within a country is outrageously ravished, when people are facing genocide and mass violence, a line has been crossed which makes what is going on there no longer the concern of the people of that country alone but the concern of the neighborhood."

In her response to the morning remarks, Dr. Helen Caldicott noted that "What we need to do is live with integrity every second of our lives, and that's darn hard work." The planet is not in good shape, she indicated. The causes of the mess besetting our planet, she said, are science, overpopulation, transnational corporations, and capitalism. "We're the curators of life on earth now; we hold it in the palm of our hand." Dr. Caldicott berated the selfishness in our thinking and lamented our lack of indignation and anger over what is occurring around us and to us. Like Mr. Ramphal, she exhorted the audience: "There has to be a change within our hearts and souls." She urged conferees to have courage and to love and care for each other.

While noting that *Our Global Neighborhood* is effective as a call to action, Stephen Marks observed that "I don't think the document as it is written is designed to serve as an instrument of popular education." The concept of governance, he asserted, is a somewhat ambiguous notion, and he speculated that its use instead of *government* was politically motivated. On the other hand, he suggested that the report provided one of the best recent redefinitions of security and contributed to the redefinition of the international community by its focus on the importance of civil society. Marks found *Our Global Neighborhood* wholly deficient in its treatment of human rights, asserting, for example, that other documents such as the Universal Declaration had already treated the issue and that documents like the Declaration of Bogota of 1948 had, in fact, already linked responsibilities to rights. With respect to newly articulated "rights," such as the right to equal access to the global commons, Dr. Marks suggested that "this is a very interesting concept, and its significance as an addition to human rights thinking might well be further developed, but it's lost within a reformulation of already existing human rights."

While Nancy Roof indicated that "I feel refreshed by the spirit of innovation, truth, and integrity that permeates this report," she also had criticisms. "The areas of deficiency are in not fully recognizing the need for deterrence and limits on the destructive tendencies of individuals and groups. I think we need to understand what human nature is, and what our capacity for being either helpful or harmful in the world is." Dr. Roof elaborated her concerns: "I now feel strongly that we have to create deterrence, restraints, and limitations given the flagrant, destructive actions that abound in the world."

Dr. Roof suggested that many forums should occur where the values that provide a base for the report are discussed. "Are there," she asked, "intrinsic values that are good in their own right, values we don't have to justify?" She posed a number of questions: What of the instances where two important values clash? What of gender differences in values? How do we prioritize our values? She suggested that we must find ways to incorporate our values into the behavior of nations.

In the open discussion, concern was expressed about a number of areas, including the following: (1) as access to the UN by NGOs increases, it will be the developed world that gains access so that we will continue to pit North against South; (2) we need to pay more attention to what we know about conflict resolution, employing reconciliation, for example, as an integral part of the conflict process; (3) instilling respect in our children for other human beings is the most immediate action we can take; change will begin within families; (4) the gap in access to information is going to create enormous increases in destructiveness; (5) the level of education must be raised so that those who should be reading the report will be able to understand it.

"These are the issues," Dr. Raj Mutalik suggested, "that need to be addressed: national security versus common security; the widening gap between haves and have nots; and the deteriorating environment and quality of life — population growth, increasing poverty, growing violence, the persistence of hegemonies in the world that pit those who have the power, those who have the means, those who have the technology against those few countries who hold the vast majority of the persons living in this world."

Virginia Straus discussed the need to engage in true and meaningful dialogue to achieve the goal of civil society. She shared with conferees David Bohm's notion that "To have true dialogue, people have to trust each other enough to reveal the deeply held beliefs that lie behind their surface opinions. Then, they can question each other's assumptions and begin to establish a context for shared thinking and action." She drew a connection between the ideal form of dialogue and the work of the Commission. "They state their values," she said, and "invite us to share the values and the vision." In practice, she suggested, we must trust ourselves, we must engage in true dialogue among NGOs, and then NGOs will have the power to challenge the authority structure that now resists change.

In open discussion, Mr. Ramphal decried the military culture and, near the end of the conference, addressed the issue of the Commission's agreement on the Nuclear Non-proliferation Treaty (NPT): "The countries that had their arms twisted to agree to the indefinite extension of the NPT feel that they were duped. They no longer feel morally bound. And can you blame them? The Security Council has five permanent members; all five are nuclear powers. When two of them — within weeks of that agreement — announce a program of nuclear testing, and when France (one of those five and, unlike China, right up front in the nuclear race) announces a program of testing in somebody else's backyard...what kind of global governance can be expected?"

Enlarging on the moral issues, Mr. Ramphal went on to ask, "What is the difference between poor countries sending drugs to rich countries...and rich countries sending arms that kill people to the countries of the developing world?"

As the gathering drew to a close, Mr. Ramphal exhorted members of the conference: "I ask you to believe that you do matter. Human survival is too important to be left to governments."

Overview of the Report
SHRIDATH RAMPHAL

• • •

Shridath Ramphal is Co-Chairman of the Commission on Global Governance. He was Secretary-General of the Commonwealth from 1975 to 1990, and Minister of Foreign Affairs and Justice of Guyana from 1972 to 1975. He is currently Chairman of the International Steering Committee of LEAD International — the International Leadership in Environment Program. He was a member of each of the five independent international commissions of the 1980s, and the chairman of the West Indian Commission-IUCN from 1991 to 1993. He is the author of Our Country, The Planet, *written for the Earth Summit.*

L et me begin by thanking the Boston Research Center for having, unsolicited by the Commission, identified our Report as the basis for their intensive effort — through lectures and conferences such as this — to open up discussion and, on a much wider level, involve people in the issues that we tried to present in our work. And, of course, I also want to thank the other organizations that have made today's events possible.

Let's look ahead to what lies beyond today. The commemorative session of the United Nations takes place in October, and then will come the period leading to the end of the century — the end of the millennium — a time when

"Neighborhoods are people whose fates depend on each other, people who, most of all, can recognize that the neighborhood can't be good for anyone unless it is good for everyone...We have to develop a vision of and values for the world of our inseparable humanity."

we're going to have to look our children and grandchildren in the eye and say, "This is what we're leaving to you for the twenty-first century." I'm not confident that I can rise to that challenge now. I'm not sure if any of you are confident about that. We have very little time, but we should at least be able to say to them that we used that time trying to move governments and people to change institutions and structures.

That was the kind of urging that led to the establishment of this Commission. Why another commission? We've had the Brandt Commission on development, Brundtland on environment, Palme on Security, we've had the South Commission, we've had a commission on humanitarian issues. Why another? Well, its origins lay in the mind of a great man, Willy Brandt, who had given his life to an *Ostpolitik* from which would come Glasnost and Perestroika — to opening a window that could lead to the end of the Cold War and to a new era, hopefully of prosperity for all people — Willy Brandt felt that beyond the single-issue commissions that had looked at development, security, the environment, the South, and humanitarian issues, there was need for us to look at them all together — to look at how we can get to the point through better management of world affairs, where we can do something serious about development and the environment and all the rest, do something about the unimplemented, virtuous recommendations of those other groups.

That's how it began: "Let's seize this moment in history." We weren't thinking about the fiftieth anniversary; it wasn't on our minds at the time. Actually, it wasn't until the first meeting of the Commission that someone said, "You know, when this report comes out three years from now, it's going to be the fiftieth anniversary of the UN. It's going to be a marvelous time when the world is going to be looking for something like what we're trying to do. Perhaps we should keep that in mind." And we did; we've made it very much a part of the presentation of the report. But that is not its only purpose. It's a happy conjuncture that can serve its purpose, but we must, for reasons I will come to later, look beyond October, beyond this year, and further down the road. I will start with another, more general observation, because in these overview remarks I don't want to be preoccupied with structures. I want to talk a bit about values and vision. Without them, nothing we say about structures, changes, and institutions will really make sense or matter.

For all of us there are little pieces of writing that stick in the mind and turn us on to the point that we say, "My God, isn't that true." One of those little pieces of writing, for me, is something that Jean-Paul Sartre wrote thirty years ago in his introduction to Frantz Fanon's book, *The Wretched of the Earth.* Sartre wrote, "When one day our humankind becomes full grown, it will not define itself as the sum total of the world's inhabitants, but as the infinite unity of their mutual needs." What a marvelous capturing of the unity of human requirements! I recalled it in San Francisco when Maya Angelou spoke those marvelous words she had written especially for the Charter ceremony. You remember, her poem spoke of a wonder that she likened to the great wonders of the world — the wonder of our human capacity to acknowledge the eternal unity of the needs of the world's people and our generation's potential to respond to those needs. She longed for the day when we would reach that point.

And that is what this report is about. We called it *Our Global Neighborhood.* The title, in a sense, is the message of the report. We were under no illusions about neighborhoods. This university, this wonderful seat of learning and culture, rests in a very rough neighborhood. And there are neighborhoods like it all around our world. Some are just nasty, some are horribly deprived. Neighborhoods are not just places with white picket fences. Neighborhoods are people living together in a great variety of conditions. There are neighborhoods filled with people who don't even like each other, but they're still neighborhoods. They are people living together, like it or not. Neighborhoods are people whose fates depend on each other, people who, most of all, can recognize that the neighborhood can't be good for anyone unless it is good for everyone.

We were trying to say that the world had become that kind of neighborhood, brought about by a great many things, including globalization and the reality of "interdependence," which used to be used as a code word but has become the reality of our human existence (whether we are talking of security, of health, disease, war, peace, whatever) in the context of the worldwide transformation that has taken place since 1945. Nothing was more forcibly evident to any of us who were in San Francisco than that we were in the same hall, but we were very different people from those present at the founding of the UN. Governments were different. In 1945, governments — not just the governments who fought and won the war, but all governments — had the perception that the world was a world of states, of nations. It was a world of so many sovereign countries, the repositories of the sovereignty, and the power that governments wielded.

Very few who speak for governments in the capitals of the world today — if they speak honestly — will tell you that they have a sense of power. They have, in truth, a sense of powerlessness. Powerlessness for the best of reasons: power is dispersed. The transformations about which I have been talking have made it impossible for any country, including this country which represents the world's largest reservoir of wealth and power, to go it alone. No country can manage its destiny alone. We must, therefore, have global dialogue on a variety of issues. Why? Because, and perhaps this is the foremost of the effects of the way the world has changed, there is now not just the option of cooperation in the world, there is a compulsion for cooperation.

That is why we have conventions on climate change and biodiversity. No one country could respond to the challenges to the environment by itself. That is why issues like drugs and terrorism and migration have ceased to be national issues and become global issues. That is why we have to have a conference on non-proliferation. I hope we'll find a few minutes to talk about what that conference has *not* succeeded in doing. But it was necessary for all to agree on where we were going, or thought we were going, in relation to the nuclear threat. It couldn't be done by anyone alone. That is why the General Agreement on Tariffs and Trade evolved into the World Trade Organization. If we were going to bring sanity into the marketplace, it had to be on the basis that all would play by rules to which all had agreed. That is why fishing in the North Atlantic by a Spanish trawler could bring Canada and Europe to a point of conflict. That is why a rogue trader gambling on the value of the yen could bring down a major bank in Britain and devalue major currencies around the world.

We are no longer separable. Nation states are not about to disappear. We are not talking about world government, but something has happened on the way to the twenty-first century. And what has happened means that you — people — are part of the process of the dispersal of power, that you have become rather more important than you used to be. Or thought you were. All the great changes that have taken place on the national level have been sustained by the people.

Whether it was civil rights, the environmental movement, the women's movement, or the anti-nuclear movement, these movements were all led by people and the government eventually came on board. But there hasn't been the same realization that international issues could be determined by people until now. Until Rio. Until Cairo. Alas, I cannot say until Copenhagen. And I doubt whether I will later be able to say, "Until Beijing."

But people are on the move globally: people in professional organizations like Physicians for Social Responsibility, and people across the board in non-governmental organizations and in international civil society. Governments will have to take note. That, I believe, is the first realization which we must seize upon — the sense that we can make a difference, that people can make a difference. Indeed, after a career spent in intergovernmental affairs, I profoundly believe that only people can make a difference. There was a time when I definitely believed that what the world needed was at least a nucleus of enlightened leaders who could make the decisions that needed to be made. But that's not enough. We need enlightened leaders, but enlightened leaders need you. And no amount of enlightened leadership will be a substitute for people-action.

This report speaks a lot about people-action. That is why it is not just a report about the reform of the UN. It's about that, because the UN has to play a central role in the management of the affairs of the world. But it is also about the world beyond the UN. It's about that neighborhood. It's about civil society. It's about non-governmental organizations. It's about the universities in a very special way. It's about professional people. It's about the business community. It's about a whole range of new actors in that neighborhood.

Every neighborhood has an authority of some kind. Each has its governance arrangements — municipalities, councils, whatever — but it also has its people. And you know that at the neighborhood level, at the sidewalk level, people matter. Governments need to understand that at the national level and respect it at the global level.

So how do we begin to translate all this into something we can do? How do we respond to the transformations that have taken place in the world? How do we change institutions to make them more responsive to these larger transformations? When the Commission came to that, it didn't take us long to recognize that we couldn't even begin to talk about the reform of the Security Council or the future of ECOSOC or the Bretton Woods Institutions or how to tackle the issues of poverty. We couldn't begin to talk about them until we talked and agreed among ourselves about values. Until we developed a collective vision of the neighborhood, of the goals towards which we were reaching.

Without those values, without a global civic ethic, without a vision of the world, how are we going to begin the building process? What architect sits down and just begins to doodle? He has to have a vision before he can develop the architecture. And that, you know, was there in 1945. When Roosevelt talked about freedom from fear and freedom from want, he was talking about values. When he talked about a world in which there would be enforcement of peace under the law, he was talking about values. And Truman said at San Francisco that if we pay lip service to these principles and later abandon them, we will incur the wrath of generations still unborn. He was prophetic. We did pay lip service to them. And we have abandoned them. And we have incurred the wrath of generations not then born. We have to return to values. We have to develop a vision of and values for the world of our inseparable humanity.

We came to the early conclusion, which you will see permeating the report, that we had to offer suggestions for a world of diversity, not of uniformity. That is why we don't talk about global government. We don't talk about centralization into supranational authority. We talk about governance that makes space and accommodates new players alongside of nations and governments. That is fundamentally important because, you know, there will be few audiences in the world's capitals that will not agree that *their* world conforms to values, or that our instincts are the source of our values. *My* values. That can't be what we're talking about. That can't be the prescription for a world of diversity. But first we have to recognize that the world is *enriched* by diversity, not made more difficult; that variety is not a problem, but a resource.

In a global setting — and you Americans in the audience will understand — this cannot mean a suffusion of diversity into a melting pot. There has to be a harmonization of variety as in a bouquet of flowers — variety made more glorious by being assembled harmoniously. It is for that kind of world that we have to be reaching. And once we can get that in our minds, we can begin to develop a system of values, of tolerance, of mutual respect, of equity, of justice — of the things they paid lip service to after San Francisco, like the rule of law in the world. Then can come enlightenment and leadership. It means, too, that we have to begin to adjust our minds to trimming the edges of some of those sacred creeds that were part of the different world, like sovereignty and self-determination, which will still retain their core meaning, of course. But they have to be trimmed at the edges.

Furthermore, change for the future is not going to involve merely changing the structures at the center, it will involve changing ourselves. If we remain a part of the old world, the new world cannot be born. So we can't just condemn governments. We can't simply condemn the United Nations. We must not condemn the institutions, whether national or international, without at the same time recognizing that they are what we allow them to be, that we are part of the instruments of change and that a part of the process of change is changing ourselves. I suspect that when we do, a great many things will become a lot easier.

Now let me turn to the third dimension of the report, which is the hard stuff, the practical stuff, the stuff that you really have to do something about. I was recently in Halifax. I am not part of G7, so I wasn't at the G7 meeting. I was at the alternative G7 in Halifax, with you. And one of the things I said at Halifax was that the problem is that this is not a meeting of the G7, this is a meeting of the G13. I don't know how many Canadians are among you, but in the pecking order by which they have assembled the G7, Canada is number thirteen. So, at best, it was a meeting of the G13 with six members left uninvited. China wasn't invited. India wasn't invited. Brazil wasn't invited. Indonesia wasn't invited. Russia was…well, invited to tea. And the day after, *The Washington Post* hailed the G7 as the directorate of the world? The directorate! Even in terms of economic standing — by which the G7 identifies itself — it is now anachronistic. And because it is anachronistic, it is powerless. The G7 cannot function as a directorate because it does not represent all of the major economic players of the world. This is serious, because the world needs something in the nature of an apex economic body to take account of the implications of globalization.

What are we going to do about the financial markets that, left to themselves, can plunge us all into chaos? What are we going to do about the policies of the Bretton Woods institutions and their relationship to the other economic issues that are being faced in other parts of the global system? Issues such as poverty. The Commission has proposed an Economic Security Council to be that coordinating body. And you know, on the Commission we're not just a bunch of non-economists not knowing what we are doing. There are people like Jacques Delors who has seen the G7 function from the inside, as president of the European Commission. There's Barber Conable, your Barber Conable, who has been both a congressman of long standing and a president of the World Bank. And I.G. Patel, one of the most respected economists in the developing world, who's been the director of the London School of Economics. They were serious people, talking about serious needs. And yet I suspect the whole notion of an Economic Security Council is one that will not be received with enthusiasm by some of the world's leading treasuries, because they want to cling to the fantasy that global decisions can be made in the capitals of a handful of countries. It can't happen.

Security. We thought of security — and certainly in San Francisco they thought of security — as the security of countries, the security of states: freedom from aggression, freedom from interstate conflicts. What is the reality today? Interstate conflicts are not extinct. Iraq's invasion of Kuwait is a reminder that they're not extinct. I'm not sure I agree about every method by which we responded to that aggression, but the aggression was very real and needed a response. So aggression hasn't gone away, but the conflicts that the world is confronting, and I suspect will continue for decades to confront, are primarily intrastate conflicts. What is Somalia? What is Rwanda? What, above all, is the former Yugoslavia? What is Chechnya? When we talk of freedom from fear today, it is the fear of people within countries about the conduct of other people within those same countries. It's neighborhood fear in a very real sense. And the Charter does not provide for it.

So the Charter has been stretched and strained. The Security Council has never been more active than it's been in the last year. But it's been active under a whole lot of pretenses, because the Charter sets its face squarely against United Nations action in those situations. We are at the crossroads in this area of law, because what the international community can do and cannot do is a matter of law. The issues that are being discussed have been in discussion longer than since yesterday. The question of what to do in Bosnia was, of course, substantially political, but it was also about the rule of law in the global neighborhood. What does NATO mean? Is it a freewheeling NATO with decisions taken by a few countries? Is it a NATO that is responsive to the will of the international community as expressed through the United Nations? It came down to arguing whether the UN element of the dual key arrangement was going to belong to the representative of the Secretary-General or the commander of the UN Forces. This is how we are slipping and sliding. We are into a new time and we are not acknowledging the need to respond to it.

The Commission does acknowledge this. The Commission calls for the amendment of Article 2.7 of the Charter. It says, let us recognize change. Let us give effect to the consensus that we in the Commission believe exists in the world, that when the security of the people within a country is outrageously ravished, when people are facing genocide and mass violence, a line has been crossed which makes what is going on there no longer the concern of the people of that country alone but the concern of the neighborhood. And there is then legitimacy in neighborhood action. I can tell you that there are not many governments in the world that are willing to agree to that amendment because, "There but for the grace of God go I." That is true of the countries in my world, the Third World, and it is true of countries in the developed world.

There is also another dimension to this new understanding of security. Let me illustrate it with a story. In March this year, the International Peace Academy (its president Olara Otunnu is a member of the Commission) and the government of Austria cosponsored a symposium on the future of the United Nations. The Secretary-General was in Vienna, and was invited to open the Conference. He did, in a very eloquent, forthright, important speech, in which he talked about the United Nations and the new priorities. Very prominent among those priorities was the universalization of democracy and why the United Nations has to be so effective in this new area, and why it is democracy that is going to be the key to peace and development. Then he did a rather unusual thing for a UN Secretary-General: he said he would take questions.

It was a semi-open meeting, and from the back of the hall the first questioner rose, a young woman. She said, "Mr. Secretary-General, I have applauded all you have just said about the centrality of democracy in the universal order and the commitment of the United Nations to it. But my name is Abiola. I am from Nigeria. My father is in prison. He is in prison because he won the elections. Now what is the United Nations doing about Nigeria? What is the Security Council doing about the setting aside of those elections and the imprisonment of my father? What, Mr. Secretary-General, are you doing?"

Well, there was of course a hush and the Secretary-General said, and this is the point I want to make about the need for change, he said, "My dear" (and I suppose once you've started with "my dear" you know there are going to be problems), "I sympathize with all your concerns, and I am truly sorry about the plight of your father, and, of course, I know all about the situation in Nigeria. But, you know, we must understand the *realpolitik* of international life. Nigeria is a very big country. It is perhaps the most significant country in Africa. And, you know, unless vital national interests are at stake, governments really do not like to be critical of other governments. And in any event, the Charter precludes us from interfering in internal affairs. So, I'm afraid I cannot hold out to you the hope that the United Nations, the Security Council, or I, myself, will be able to do very much about your father."

Some of us in the room thought, "What a dreadful commentary on where we are in the world." Because he was right again, in one sense. Governments do not take on other governments. No government in the Security Council is about to raise the issue of Nigeria. Today it is worse. Now they are about to execute a former prime minister. They have confirmed a sentence of life imprisonment on General Obasanjo, a former head of state who brought Nigeria back to civilian rule and has been an active champion of justice and democracy. Many of us have raised our voices. Many governments have sent quiet petitions. Not one has raised the issue in the Security Council. They won't.

Why am I telling you this? Because in the report, we have sought to provide an opportunity for you to raise such issues. We have called for a Right of Petition by which people could go to the Security Council — by means of a sifting process which we have described as a Council for Petitions — and say that this is happening. And it is happening not only in Nigeria, but in Zaire, in Myanmar. It is happening in any number of places today, and more tomorrow. One should be able to say when something is happening which threatens the security of people and must be brought to the agenda of the Security Council. Nothing we do will ensure how the Security Council responds, but the fact that such problems can be brought to the Security Council will be very important, since the reason they are not being brought there now is that governments don't want to take a position. What we have to do, what you have to make them do, is amend the Charter to give you the right, give Civil Society the right to bring the issues to them and make the world face up to the need to respond to these dreadful crimes.

I want to end by reminding you just a bit of those wonderful words of Maya Angelou:

> *We, this people, on a small and lonely planet*
> *Traveling through casual space*
> *Past aloof stars, across the way to indifferent suns*
> *To a destination where all signs tell us*
> *It is impossible and imperative that we learn*
> *A brave and startling truth.*
> *...*
>
> *When we come to it*
> *We, this people, on this wayward floating body*
> *Created on this Earth, of this Earth*
> *Have the power to fashion for this Earth*
> *A climate where every man and every woman*
> *Can live freely without sanctimonious piety*
> *Without crippling fear*
> *...*
>
> *That is when, and only when*
> *We come to it.*

OPEN DISCUSSION

• • •

Lucy Webster: I want to speak as someone who has been active in the World Federalist movement for forty-eight years. The idea of world federation draws inherently on the idea of decentralization — of bunches of chrysanthemums and roses all maintaining their cultural integrity and their historic reality. This implies a decentralization beginning with and proceeding down from nation-states. It implies the dignity of ethnic units within historic nation states as well as the transfer of sovereignty to a global government system. The global system of government that is suggested in the report is exactly what, as far as I know, all world government supporters are in favor of, so one should not try to create dichotomy there. World government is the decentralized system that is so evident at this time of history.

I also want to make one substantive point. The idea of amending Article 2.7 is very important, as is the idea of a Council for Petition. We could make that happen *de facto* without waiting for any charter changes. But the idea of an international criminal court, which the report endorses, is of utmost importance today and could be made a reality within the next couple of years. Even if these criminals in different countries are only indicted, if it kept them from ever leaving their own territory, there would be incentive to behave properly.

Steve Brant: I represent a profession that you probably don't hear about often, the quality management profession. It's a profession that thinks about and deals with systems. I'm in a small wing of the profession that is trying to get involved in social concerns and problems. We have looked at this question using the pioneering material in Dr. Demming's philosophy of the system of the UN. One of the things which we saw was that in 1945, the year the UN was established, the world was a product of two basic concepts: Darwinian theory and Malthusian economics. Despite all religious and moral desire, they were the operative paradigms. Two other systems theorists, Buckminster Fuller, a man who would have been a hundred years old last week, and Gerard Piel, wrote that around 1955 humanity's technical ability to sustain itself altered for the first time in history. It no longer had to operate on the basis of the paradigms of scarcity and the survival of the fittest because the technical ability was there to act otherwise. They wrote about it but didn't get a whole lot of publicity.

We in the profession are now trying to get the word out that a technical change has taken place in addition to the various moral changes that have occurred throughout history. We're trying to get people to see that we have to start altering the structures of society based on that technical change as well as on the basis of all these other desires. One of the things we have spoken about is the vision that it takes to guide people. What I've been inspired by recently is the movie, *Apollo 13*. I've been thinking that someday the UN could have a department that encourages the peaceful exploration of space as a way to unify people around a cooperative activity.

Ramphal: I'd like to respond briefly to each of those questions, because each of you represent something very dear to me and yet each of you represents for me an area of doubt. I am, I suspect, an undeclared world federalist, but I worry about labels, and you know the World Federalist Movement has a problem with labels. The World Federalists have been very prominent in their support of the report, and we value that. But you have a wing that is in favor of world government. That's not a good wing. That's not what we want. We don't want to scrap the UN Charter. We don't want to create a constitution for the earth. We don't want to create a global government. The two groups in the United States that have been most vocal against the report have been that wing of the World Federalists — the world government people — and who else? The Montana militia. I don't need to say more. We need to work closely to fulfill the vision of the World Federalists, but I think you need to work on that label.

I worry a little about this gentleman. You are concerned about the global neighborhood, but I'm not at all sure that you're right in promoting the idea that technology has opened up human capacity to cope with consumption or offer resources of an unlimited scale. And I'm not sure if space exploration produces those resources. I believe, on the contrary, that the world scientific community is telling us, "Hold on, we cannot consume at the level of the largest and highest consumer." The population crisis is a crisis of consumption. Of course, it's a hard issue for politicians because changing rates of consumption means changing lifestyles. Changing it for the better, I believe, but how do you get the message across? How do you convey the message that China cannot consume at the level of the average person in the United States if the world is to stay viable? We face massive problems of human extinction because photosynthesis, the touchstone of life, will not support that kind of consumption. So I believe there is a danger in telling the world not to worry, that technology is going to solve it all.

Response to the Report by

HELEN CALDICOTT

• • •

Helen Caldicott is co-founder of the Physicians for Social Responsibility, an organization with over 22,000 members which was awarded the Nobel Peace Prize in 1985. She is the author of best sellers titled Missile Envy *and* Nuclear Madness. *Her book,* If You Love This Planet, *was published in 1992, and she was the subject of an Academy Award-winning documentary called* If You Love This Planet, *the same year. In 1994, Dr. Caldicott received the Distinguished Peace Leadership Award from the Nuclear Age Peace Foundation.*

What Buddha taught and what Jesus taught are the ethics by which we need to live. We never have. We have decided that we will worship or believe in them or that if we have faith we will end up in the right place when we die. What we need to do is live with integrity every second of our lives and that's darn hard work. We need to be honest to ourselves, and most of us are not. We need not to lie, ever. We need to tell the truth to other people. We need to live in integrity within the cities, within our country, and within the world, and that's a big job now — because the world is dying. I speak as a scientist, and I speak as a pediatrician and a physician and a mother and a grandmother: the world is dying. When I wrote my book, *If You Love this Planet*, four years ago, I had researched the scientific literature and found that

> **"We've lost a sense of the mystic. We've lost the sense that within our own souls we have the wisdom to save the earth."**

most scientific observers would give us to the year 2000 before the changes that are occurring on the planet become irreversible: ozone depletion, greenhouse warming, toxic pollution, radioactive pollution, nuclear proliferation, overpopulation of one species, deforestation, and species extinction.

I don't mean to say that the planet will be dead by the year 2000. But when you have a patient who's got serious cardiac failure, say from viral cardiomyopathy, you put them in the intensive care unit. Their heart hardly beats, the kidneys then tend to fail because they don't get a decent blood supply, and then the liver starts to fail and you get what's called total organ flex, which becomes irreversible. Then there's nothing you can do to fix it. That's what's happening to the planet. Recently, it was 124 degrees Fahrenheit for two weeks in India. What play did that get in the *New York Times* except a tiny little article? Who owns half the cars on the planet? People in the United States. Seven percent of the world's population owns 250 million or more cars, and every night on the television you see ads for more cars. But we're driving cars in the light of clear evidence that global warming is actually occurring. We've just had more than 400 heat-related deaths in the United States, which is nothing compared to the floods in northern China recently where thousands died. But that doesn't get much play either.

As physicians, we need to look at the causes of the mess besetting our planet. The causes include science, overpopulation, transnational corporations, and capitalism. Let's be frank. Communism did a dreadful thing by polluting terribly the environments of the Soviet Union and of China, but capitalism does it more subtly. If you go out to Silicon Valley, you see huge corporations in stainless steel buildings, all totally hygienic. There are people in them designing the ways to destroy the world, but there is no scent of blood or decaying bodies. It's done at a distance. Most transnational corporations emanate from the United States. Japan learned how to be capitalistic from the United States, after the Second World War.

Just look outside. Look at the air. It's a hot day. There's an inversion system, and the smog and the pollution hang heavily over New York. I looked out the windows just now, and I wondered how many people living in those buildings out there have the faintest notion of what we're talking about. Do they know that the Earth is heating up?

Do they know the oceans will rise perhaps five feet in the next fifty years? Do they know that this country may not be able to grow its own food, let alone export to the rest of the world? Do they know that Australia may become rich and verdant because we may have rainfall in the desert? Currently Australia is one big desert, that's all, but we may be growing pineapples and bananas in the desert. Do they know that the futures market speculates on this now? That's wicked. Do they know that in Australia the incidence of skin cancer has tripled in the last ten years? Do they know the incidence of malignant melanoma has doubled?

Do they know and understand what the world will be like for our children fifty years hence? All the corporations are interested in this. But we have to look 500 generations from now, because that's our responsibility. Humans have only been here for three million years. That's a tiny, tiny little tick in the expanse of time during which the earth has been around and life has developed. Yet look at the damage we've done. And today, do you notice that all we've talked about is ourselves? We are anthropocentric. We are so selfish. Read this one sentence at the end of this report: "Selfishness will make genius the instrument of self-destruction." But we're not very important. There are too many of us. It's like in bacteriology. If you take a plate of agar enriched with blood and add some bacteria from the throat, a few colonies will develop. If you keep it warm, they grow and eventually they cover the agar plate, and then they die. They use up all the nutrients. And that's exactly what we're doing. In the year 1800, there were only one billion human beings. Now there are probably 5.7 billion. And we're proliferating like bacteria on an agar plate.

Of course, it's our privilege to have as many babies as we want. I know that feeling; I loved having babies myself. Reproduction is the strongest biological drive we have. It's stronger than eating. Do we have the courage to take ourselves on and stop reproducing? As we prolifically reproduce and consume, we destroy other species, a hundred of which are becoming extinct every day. Then what do the scientists say, "Oh, don't worry. We'll put their genes in a gene bank, and one day we'll rediscover the elephant when the elephant's extinct." That's wicked. We're the curators of life on earth now; we hold it in the palm of our hand.

We are currently destroying the tropical rain forest at the rate of one football field per second. I've been to the Amazon. I've seen it. Go before it disappears. It's happening in New Guinea, where wonderful people have lived forever in harmony with nature. Malaysians and Japanese have gone in to "log." Log is a euphemism for chopping down all the trees in New Guinea. It's happening in Malaysia. It's happening in Indonesia. It's happening everywhere. Go to Japan and see how the Japanese use timber. They love it. They throw away the equivalent of one forest per day in disposable chopsticks. We can't do that anymore.

I had some coffee here. I have to be frank. You're using plastic cups. Look at the rubbish tin and see what's disposed of. Wooden stirrers to stir the coffee. We can't do that anymore. We have to be cognizant of what we're doing. We're in the process of destroying pockets of multifarious life forms in the tropical rain forest, and the coral reefs are dying from pollution and ocean warming. We're filling in the wetlands for expansion and growth. We call it "development," which is a euphemism for destruction. We're destroying the possibility that, even if we do kill ourselves, evolution can continue. We have to think more broadly about what we're doing. And I think we have to get off the subject of ourselves somewhat. I don't like the way we think. It's selfish. Never did I think as a child that the elephants would become extinct.

When we started understanding the laws of nature — or God's laws — in a scientific sense, we suddenly decided we were God, and we lost our sense of humility before nature and before photosynthesis — before the wonders of life. Have you ever gone diving and looked at the fish in the sea? It's a whole universe down there. How did that develop? We, at the moment, are the curators of that. We've lost a sense of the mystic. We've lost the sense that within our own souls we have the wisdom to save the earth. We fill our lives up with noise. We have the television on from the moment we get up in the morning till the time we go to bed, or else the radio. The time when wisdom and intuition come is when we're quiet, scrubbing the floor, doing the ironing — God is in the laundry. Or walking in a forest; or in a garden getting dirt under our fingernails as we used to do before the industrial revolution occurred.

Now what are we going to do about this? How will we rein in the transnationals? I don't happen to think that GATT was a good idea. I don't happen to think that the World Trade Organization is a good idea. It's run by three men who are trade representatives, who have no scientific background, or probably don't, but who can enact trade barriers against any country that violates the right of the transnationals. They call and say, "my country, Indonesia," or "my country, Japan," but it's actually transnationals speaking because the transnationals run governments now. Look at this government. This government is run entirely by transnationals. They sit on the regulatory panels, they write the legislation, and Newt Gingrich is their prostitute — excuse the word, but that's the truth. Japan is run by transnationals with tremendous power. The prime minister of Japan: he's a nice man, but he has no power.

My government is run by the Australian transnationals. McDonald's is metastasizing across my country. What does that mean? They put advertisements on television, with kids dressed in back-to-front hats, long baggy pants — American culture that we don't need in Australia. Kids don't speak English. They say, "like but wow, like." There are no verbs or pronouns or sentences. We don't need deculturalization via television, via McDonald's hamburgers, or via the kindness and generosity of Rupert Murdoch — who is one of the most dangerous people in the world today. And I say that advisedly because he's my fellow countryman. He comes from the town I grew up in, Adelaide, and he used to print my articles in editorials on the front page of the national newspaper, *The Australian*. But when I started to move against uranium mining he blackballed me and has ever since. That's a personal thing; but in the interview Dennis Potter gave three weeks before he died of pancreatic cancer — that wonderful man who wrote *The Singing Detective* — he compared Murdoch to his cancer. It was the most lucid, truthful, honest, profound interview that I've ever seen. I don't often see things on television today that I can't drag myself away from. Television is full of banal trivialities meant to sell.

When I was a child, I spoke as a child. I read things. There was no plastic. There was no packaging. Packaging is the third largest business in the United States today — all about destroying a planet. Making aluminum cans for Coke is destroying the planet. Making aluminum is exorbitantly energy-consuming, which adds to global warming. Cardboard comes from trees. Look at the way they package things these days — in cardboard and aluminum foil. When you make plastic from oil, you make massive quantities of toxic products which the First World tends to dump in the Third World if they possibly can.

They're carcinogenic, almost all of them. Those polystyrene cups that we used are made of two chemicals, styrene and benzene, both of which are carcinogenic. We had very hot coffee. In those cups you can taste it. You can taste the chemical. They're fat-soluble. They're carcinogenic. Why is the incidence of cancer rising now? Partly because we live longer, but also because we have super-toxic chemicals sprayed on our vegetables, and we use them every day as plastic. I go to a shop, and the people are really destroyed if they can't put my batteries, already packaged, in plastic and cardboard and aluminum, in *another* plastic bag. I don't want anymore bags. No more packaging.

You see, it's true. If China adopts the way we live, the earth has had it. One billion people in China, and guess why they want to live like us? They're getting our television now, via Rupert Murdoch and the corporations in the world that now control the national media. And we sit idly by, watching it. Psychically numbed. I've just revised my book, *Nuclear Madness*. This country wants to build 175 more nuclear reactors here in order to burn up the plutonium and uranium that is coming out of decommissioned Russian bombs. It's good that it's been taken out of the bombs, but do you want to have nuclear waste all over the country — and in breeder reactors? I talk about this and how radioactive isotopes produce cancer in the latent period of carcinogenisis, and how it takes a single mutation in a single gene and single cell to produce cancer. I talked at the University of Seattle — a lot of young people — and at the end they just sat there, like lumps. I felt like doing a strip. "Get some feeling, get some emotion. Don't you care? Where's your anger? Where's your sense of indignation? Don't you want to live?"

I think television anesthetizes people. It transmits at a hypnotic frequency which goes right through the left brain — without giving you time to think — and sends very quick images into the right brain, which become feeling. And then we walk into the supermarket, even though we're cynical about advertising, and the thing that's just been advertised is what we buy. It's called impulse buying. People are numbed out and anesthetized. The electronic babysitter is destroying families.

I could go on and on. You could talk all day and all night about this, couldn't you? But the corporations who have produced the products that are destroying the earth also own the media — and they own the governments of the world, and to a degree run the United Nations. I know that because they have a very powerful influence in the United Nations. Why hasn't America paid its huge debt? How dare they not pay their debt. Who do they think they are? America, who doesn't have an enemy anymore, has focused its paranoia on the United Nations instead. Now, most Americans are nice people, and they're kind, but most Americans are fairly ignorant, and they've been kept ignorant by the media. As one Russian said years ago during the Cold War when he came here, "Americans have a curiosity a mile wide and an inch deep." And that's true. You don't have to be well informed about the rest of the world when you are the most powerful country on earth. But there's no Cold War. There's no Enemy. The Pentagon is obsolete.

Now let me talk about the militias that were referred to. Those people are clinically sick. They need therapy. They're going to be shooting people. The poor government employees are so threatened; their families are threatened now — their children. This is like Nazi Germany. It's like the Brownshirts. It's scary. And now, there are organizations of government leaders who put off their conferences because they've been so intimidated because the United Nations is supposedly flying around in black helicopters. This is clinical paranoia. I've met Ronald Reagan. I've read his history, and I spent an hour and a quarter at the White House holding his hand talking about nuclear weapons — about which he knew nothing. He had a history of clinical paranoia.

It's important to analyze what is happening from a clinical perspective, but no one seems to be doing that. The *New York Times* writes a lot about the militias, but I don't see any really good, hard, analytical thinking about why it's happening. These people, they're being betrayed by their society. Why doesn't this country, the richest in the world, have free medical care? Why doesn't it have free education? Where is all the money going? Why do people feel ostracized and outcast? Because it's going to the Pentagon. And it's spending almost as much money this year, although there's no enemy, as Reagan spent during the years of the Cold War — and he spent more money than all past presidents combined. He converted America from the greatest credit nation to the greatest debtor nation in history — from which it will never recover. It's really Japan that's now the most powerful country in the world, because she supports the debt of the United States of

America. But let's wait! In ten years, watch China. That is why I'm talking like this. There is enough money in this country for National Public Radio, for the National Endowment for the Arts, for free medical care for everyone — for what everyone has in Australia, in France and Great Britain, in New Zealand and Canada, etc. The doctors need to be pulled into line. When you talked about nations being afraid to criticize each other, it reminded me of my colleagues, some of whom practice very bad medicine. We don't pull them into line, so we *all* get sued. That's a similar situation. But the money is there to provide everything that this country needs. The expertise of the Pentagon needs to be transferred to the United Nations. America has to give up its need for patriarchal sovereignty, for nationalism and patriotism — which are dangerous now. We are a global community and America, in its goodness and generosity and goodwill, could become one of the mentors of the planet by providing that expertise to the United Nations.

Bosnia. I first read about Bosnia when I first read about AIDS. I thought AIDS would become an exponential epidemic and there would be nothing we could do about it. The virus is sensitive and mutates all the time; we'll never develop an immune vaccine. Eventually it will mutate itself out of existence. Bosnia: nothing you can do. Send forces in; see more people get killed. More guns? More people get killed. The arms trade has to be looked at seriously by the world community. True, the Security Council needs people involved much more. France should be out of it. Who does France think it is? Chirac blowing up bombs in the Pacific. You know, it's so serious in Australia the video stores have thrown out all the French videos; they've closed down the French restaurants. The French consulate in Perth was burned down the other day. It's very big time. England should be out of it. England's had it's day. No English in the British Empire anymore. Who do they think they are? They're in a terrible mess anyway. Thatcher was the end of them.

This country [America] reminds me of the Roman Empire. It's really going downhill big time. They are no morals; children don't have any morals. There are no leaders. There aren't any Martin Luther Kings. There aren't any Roosevelts. Roosevelt was the last great president of this country. He loved his people. He had compassion, he had dignity. He was manipulative, but he did everything for the people. And they loved him. There are no leaders. So the children have no sense of hope. If I were an adolescent now, I'd be taking drugs and drinking. And the incidence of suicide in Australia is extremely high. Why? I probably would kill myself too. I lit up on the beach when I was 15 — that was enough for me. I was never the same again. I never felt protected. That's how I got into anti-nuclear work — one day I woke up and I'd had a baby, and I thought, oh my god, I'm now an adult, and that means I have to take responsibility. And it's true, there has to be a change within our hearts and souls. The truth is we all know it. The truth is we all have enough courage. The truth is that this generation is determining the fate of life upon the planet. The creation. And if we tap into our spirit, which is an extension of something higher, we can save the earth.

I never thought — when I was the anti-nuclear bag lady trudging around this country — that the Cold War would ever come to an end. Never did I think. But I did learn that if you speak the truth with a clarity, it does resonate down time like a bell; but more than that, there's help from somewhere else. I thought it would be an American who would stop the Cold War. No, it was a Russian. Probably, I'd have to say, the greatest man of the century. Prophets are never recognized in their homeland. As Jung said, leaders are always betrayed or destroyed. And if you decide to be a leader, know that people won't love you. Don't do it for approval, like Clinton does, or you'll lose everything. You have to be courageous, and you have to speak your inner truth. And there's always guidance, and there's always help. Not from other people, although you'll make lots of wonderful friends. It's within yourself, and it's up there, and it's out there, in nature, which is where I get my strength and joy from. And as you're doing this work to save the planet, if it's not joyful, you're on the wrong track. It should never be, "Oh my god, this nation's full of victims."

I swim at the YMCA, and I sometimes accidentally bang into a woman. In Australia you'd both jump up and say, "Sorry, I'm sorry." But the woman rolls her eyes up like you've done it on purpose. Well, we have to stop being victims. We have to love each other and care for each other, and hold our joy up to each other. Our energy affects other people. If you walk around in a cloud of negativity and anger, you'll swear at the guy who pumps petrol into your car, and he'll go home and swear at his wife, and she'll smack her children, etc. But if you go around with real joy and love and caring, that ricochets off to other people and has profound effects. I think that's what we mean by changing. It is a spiritual change.

I'll just end by saying there are four parts to the human being. There's the intellectual part — we're so bound up with information, we've got enough information to last us for the next 500 years. Our left brains are so hard pushed, we walk around sort of with our heads hanging down. We don't need any more information. We need wisdom.

Then there's the psyche: we don't all lie on couches, but some of us do — talking about our childhood. That's finished! We're adults. We need to leave that behind, grow up and move on.

And there's the physical body. Have you had your breasts lifted or your buttocks fixed or your nose straightened or a face lift? We don't need to lift our faces. We need to lift our souls. Bodies have nothing to do with anything except for light shining out of the eyes. That's all that matters. That's the beauty.

And then there's the spirit, which we have ignored for a long, long, time. I don't believe in organized religion — though the Buddhists do it all right — it's patriarchal, it's controlling, and it's got nothing to do with individual spiritual journey. There's a sense of community in churches, but I think on the whole they're not going the right way. I used to go to churches often and say to them, "You should be preaching about the impending state of nuclear war." and they'd say, "well, if I do that my contributions would drop, and I wouldn't be able to fix the roof on my church." And I'd say, "Well, what would Jesus do?" And they were silent.

Jesus hung on the cross, and we have to be prepared to give up our lives to save our children and life on earth. There's nothing to be scared of. We're going to die anyway. But we won't be killed, if we surround ourselves with positive energy and light, because we're doing it for the right reason. There are two energies in the world: there's love and there's power and control. If you operate from love, you'll be protected and will prevail. Get into power and control, and we'll lose the lot. It's like Tolkien's *Ring* trilogy: good and evil. We're right here, right now at the crossroads of time. And I think this report is excellent, but must be taken out into the world. You'll know if you're succeeding if everyone in all those apartments up there is talking about what we've been talking about today.

RESPONSE
By Mr. Ramphal

I want to say how profoundly complementary I thought every word Helen Caldicott spoke was to the inner feelings of the membership of the Commission. We may not have expressed it all eloquently enough, we may not even have gotten all the recommendations right, but the inner driving forces were those to which she responded.

I wrote a book a little while ago which I called *Our Country, the Planet*. It was written for Rio and expressed many of the sentiments Helen has mentioned, in particular that the world is dying. I asked myself a question. I came to that point that I felt I had to ask the question, So what? What is dying? The first thing that will die is us. Humans. And in the process we will bring many other species down. But you then have to ask a further question. Might the planet be a better place because of our going? We have made ourselves the greediest of predators and, in the process, have destroyed life. But life, like after the age of the dinosaurs, was also without us. Flora and fauna may be the better for us going. But we also have to ask if there is a higher purpose and obligation for us as humans, an obligation, obviously, to future generations, but also to our humanity — to preserve life. To live by an ethic of survival. Survival, of course, in a sustainable way. Survival in the way that Helen talked. The way the world used to be, the world in which some of us grew up.

In the report we have made one functional proposal that responds to these needs, and I will mention it in this context. We have proposed that the Trusteeship Council, which has exhausted its mandate since there are no longer any trust territories to administer, be given a new mandate, a mandate to be trustees for the global commons. By that we mean the atmosphere as well as Antarctica — trustees for the life-giving and life-sustaining properties of the planet. To blow the whistle, to do what Helen has been doing in a global context, at the highest level with the best hope of capturing the attention of governments. And to do it as an official mandate within the global system. It's never too late. It's five minutes to midnight, but it's not too late.

The global system now has no mechanism by which it can blow that whistle. Rio didn't produce it. It produced the Commission on Sustainable Development. We can't just wait for another rain, so in the recommendations there is a proposal about the new mandate for the Trusteeship Council. We present it in terms of the security of the planet against all the disasters and elements of disasters that are causing the world to die. That is not melodramatic, not apocalyptic. It's reality and, as I said earlier, it's all about looking our children in the eye sometime down the road.

Response Panel #1
STEPHEN P. MARKS

• • •

Stephen P. Marks holds academic degrees from Stanford University, the Universities of Paris, Strasbourg, Besançon, and Nice, as well as the University of Damascus. His principal fields are international law, international organizations, international politics, peace and conflict, and human rights. He is currently a Senior Lecturer at the School of Public and International Affairs of Columbia University. Recently he served as head of human rights education, training, and information for the United Nations Transitional Authority in Cambodia (UNTAC).

I have the particular pleasure of welcoming you on behalf of Dean John Ruggie, the Dean of the School of International and Public Affairs. As a member of the faculty, I'm delighted that an event acknowledging the significance of this report and looking towards its popularization and political recognition in the United Nations this fall is taking place at this institution. This conference is on "United Nations Renaissance." It arrives in this building at a time when the School of International and Public Affairs has embarked on its own renaissance in United Nations studies. We have recently added courses on UN peacekeeping, and law and politics in the United Nations. We have

"I welcome very much the effort to stress the role of civil society and especially global civil society at a time of growing tension between a sense of empowerment and a sense of disenchantment with the political process. They're of course not incompatible because the synthesis of these two forces resides in more actual exercise of political power"

courses taught around the University in various aspects of the UN, but the time has come to reinvigorate these studies. Hosting this conference in our building will contribute a lot to that longer term objective.

In preparing for this conference I assumed that it was going to offer an opportunity for the authors of the report and the Secretariat promoting the report to prepare a credible political strategy for October so the right mix of proposals could be adopted by the political decision-makers. But after attending this morning's session, I realize that is really not what is happening here. Something different and perhaps much more important and much more profound is taking place. This conference is really challenging us to look within ourselves, to examine whether or not such proposals for a reform of the United Nations and for tackling global problems will help us conceptualize at the personal level what we genuinely believe should be the evolution of the international system.

This makes it a bit difficult for me to deal with the proposals in an academic way, since the approach is basically not an academic one. I will, nevertheless, attempt to sketch some of the international law and international organization dimensions of the report, with a particular focus on human rights and international peace and security.

The report is not and does not purport to be a thorough academic analysis of the international system. It is designed to be a mobilizing document, a call to action, and an agenda for change. I think, though, that one of the defects of the report as an agenda for change and as a call for action is that, if *Our Global Neighborhood* were placed in all of the apartments that Helen Caldicott pointed to earlier in the neighborhood around Columbia University, it would probably not be very well understood. The fault does not lie with the authors, for the book is a model of clarity and lucidity. The fault lies with our educational system, which has not prepared the youth of this country, with the exception of a small elite, to reflect and act on a study of such scope. It is to the Commission's credit that it has also produced a popularized version of it. The shorter version is going to be extremely important in reaching out to non-elites.

The value of the document as a call to action resides in the fact that it is roughly divided into chapters that deal first with what the problem is (i.e., what is wrong with the world, what the structures of the world today are, what should be done) and, secondly, how to go about doing what must be done so that results can be achieved commensurate with the challenges raised in the first section.

First of all, as was suggested this morning, the concept of governance is a somewhat ambiguous notion because of the subtle distinction that is made between government and governance, and because of the emphasis on the fact that the report offers not a prescription for global government, but global governance. I think one of the reasons for this lies not with the Michigan Militia or a branch of the World Federalists, but is politically motivated. It is written in a way that won't scare away the member states of the United Nations, represented by their governments, to whom it is addressed, in part. The authors excluded "global government" so that governments would take it seriously when examining what can be done for the fiftieth anniversary and beyond. It is, nevertheless, a subtle distinction and probably one that those of us engaged in international organization studies need to devote more attention to.

My second observation on the general issues raised and the underlying philosophy is that it provides one of the best recent redefinitions of security. It is extremely important in examining international relations to pull together the various efforts at rethinking of security concepts, including the security of peoples and of the planet. The latter dimension needs to be more broadly understood and the report does a magnificent job of it.

It also contributes to the redefinition of the international community by stressing the importance of civil society at a time when new patterns of empowerment are emerging and, as the report says, when disenchantment with the political process itself is growing. Of course, this process reaches pathological proportions in this country. I welcome very much the effort to stress the role of civil society and especially global civil society at a time of growing tension between a sense of empowerment and a sense of disenchantment with the political process. They are by no means incompatible. A synthesis of these two forces can be found in greater exercise of political power. The report does not go very far in enhancing the effective exercise of political power by civil society, but it certainly acknowledges a greater participation of civil society in the state-run global system.

My fourth point about the general philosophy of the report has to do with values, the focus of the next speaker's comments. I will offer what I hope will be some constructive criticism regarding the way human rights is treated or perhaps neglected in the document. I think it is only appropriate to cite the Universal Declaration of Human Rights and human rights texts as my starting point. The report finds the human rights regime as it exists today to be deficient in two respects, which it proposes to remedy. First, individuals should accept the obligation to recognize and protect the rights of others. The premise here is that "human rights" as developed in the UN Charter and the Universal Declaration and subsequent documents and procedures conceives such rights exclusively in terms of limitations on government abuses of people. But in fact, human rights thinking, back even before the Universal Declaration of Human Rights, did not place this limitation on the norms of human rights. The application of human rights to relations between individuals has always been part of human rights thinking. There is even a word for it: *Drittwirkung* is the expression that is used for the obligations that individuals have towards each other to respect human rights.

The Universal Declaration itself was proclaimed as a standard of achievement "to the end that every individual and every organ of society, keeping this Declaration constantly in mind, shall strive to promote the respects for these rights and freedoms." Furthermore, among these human rights are the right to an effective remedy and the right to a social and international order in which the rights set forth in the Declaration can be fully realized. These ideas are based on the premise that a well-ordered society ensures that individuals and not just organs of society must respect human rights. So I think the authors of the report are barking up the wrong tree.

The second defect of the existing human rights regime that the report proposes to remedy resides in the idea that rights need to be joined by responsibilities. Again, the Universal Declaration of Human Rights and other human rights thinking, going way back, already incorporate this notion. The Universal Declaration itself says that everyone has duties to the community only through which the free and full development of his personality is possible. One basic human rights text, the Declaration of Bogota of 1948, even has the word "duties" in its title.

The report proposes a set of "common rights and responsibilities" that should constitute the global ethic, and most enumerated rights and responsibilities that constitute this ethic are already reflected in well-established human rights standards. Indeed, with all due respect, I would say that they are probably articulated in a more useful form for international action in international texts than in *Our Global Neighborhood*. Further, the list for this global ethic is a little bit misleading because it includes not only what I would call a weaker formulation of preexisting and well-articulated human rights, but tosses in a few other concepts that should be flagged as requiring new normative developments since they're not already part of human rights. A rationale for their inclusion in the human rights panoply should be added.

For example, among the rights listed is the right to equal access to the global commons. This is a very interesting concept, and its significance as an addition to human rights thinking might well be further developed, but it's lost within a reformulation of already existing human rights. Also under the list of responsibilities is the responsibility to protect the interest of future generations by promoting sustainable development and safeguarding the global commons. This also appears to be a new notion, but in fact there is a United Nations Declaration on the Right to Development that seems already to cover this idea. In other words, the ideas, the values, the ethics are not anything that I would disagree with, but the report neglects existing accomplishments within the UN system.

It also suggests that these principles be embodied in a more binding international document, a global Charter of Civil Society. As a human rights specialist and a human rights activist, I find that quite frightening. I think there would be a danger in attempting to reformulate human rights in a new charter. I would certainly welcome an effort to make binding rules that enhance the capacity of civil society to express itself, but I would not support a reformulation of rights and responsibilities, especially along the lines listed in the report. I don't mean this observation to be a fundamental criticism at all. It is meant as constructive and friendly criticism.

Let me move now from the "what" of the report to the "how," which, for international relations specialists, is very exciting because of the nature of the reforms proposed as means of revitalizing the General Assembly, the Security Council, and the Economic and Social Council. Those of us in the human rights field have every reason to welcome giving a new mandate to the Trusteeship system and institutionalizing civil society. Since my time is almost up, I will only say more about the institutionalization of civil society. The report proposes to have non-governmental organizations, redefined as Civil Society, accredited directly to the General Assembly, and establish a Forum that would meet before each session of the General Assembly where a broad array of three hundred to 600 Civil Society organizations could meet and discuss the issues coming up before the General Assembly. More dramatically, it proposes to grant Civil Society access to the Security Council and the Secretary-General through the right of petition to a Council for Petitions.

These are very exciting ways for Civil Society to have a more genuine participatory role in the United Nations. The only observation I would make at this stage is that I had the rather uncomfortable privilege of representing an NGO during the recent efforts of the Economic and Social Council to reform relations between non-governmental organizations and the United Nations. The Economic and Social Council created an open-ended working group. We have seen innumerable cases in the history of the United Nations where a mandate is given to a body and then not much is accomplished. It's easy to paper over a contentious subject with sterile debate and declare a success. Most international conferences are of this type. The working group I recently attended though was an unmitigated failure due to its incapacity to implement the very clear mandate to reformulate the rules governing consultative status.

The reason that I mention this is that it is a sign of a political climate that is hostile towards what we assumed — two or three years ago — would be an upsurge of awareness of civil society and its participatory role in the United Nations. At a time when these very valuable proposals are going forward by the Commission, we must confront the fact that a modest reform of the existing rules governing relations between non-governmental organizations of the United Nations system failed even to generate a text that could go before the Economic and Social Council at its current session.

Saying this is not a sign of pessimism, but an effort on my part to urge all of you in this room to gird yourselves for a tougher political struggle if you want these valuable proposals to make any headway in increasing the participation of civil society in the United Nations system.

Response Panel #1

NANCY B. ROOF

• • •

Nancy B. Roof, a transpersonal psychologist, is the UN representative for the Center for Psychology and Social Change, an affiliate of Harvard Medical School. Since 1993, she has been the director of the Balkans Trauma Project, in which capacity she designed and implemented bicultural training programs on healing the traumatic effects of war. She is author of The Impact of War on Humanitarian Service Providers, *which is being distributed and utilized in war-torn regions around the world. She was co-chair of the Values Caucus at the United Nations, 1994-95, and is the Director of the Global Values Project at the Center for Psychology and Social Change.*

O ur *Global Neighborhood* needs wide distribution. Many people need to be part of the discussion on global governance. We were asked to give an overall impression of the report. It is very easy to feel positive about the very innovative ideas it contains. It is significant and relevant because it locates its ideas within the trends of the times and in a world characterized by rapid change. The quality of the people who participated in its preparation, and the process used to arrive at the final statement, give it even more importance. The number of actors brought in to help draw conclusions and make recommendations was inclusive. The report makes values

"We have a dark side as well as a light side, and I feel the report emphasizes the light side...I feel we have to build deterrence, restraints, and limitations upon the kinds of flagrant destructive actions that are going on in the world."

fundamental to all the recommendations, and it offers concrete plans of action. Most of all we feel refreshed by the spirit of innovation, truth, and integrity that permeates the report.

The breadth of the vision includes not only institutional changes, but also recognizes the needs of the people. It urges us to find some means of security for civilians, especially women and children. The report needs more elaboration of this increasingly urgent problem. Since the report was published, more civilians, women, and children are at risk. The most recent statistical indications is that nine civilians are killed for every one military person. Who will protect "We the People?"

The areas of deficiency, in addition to what I've just spoken about, are in not fully recognizing the need for deterrence and limits on the destructive tendencies of individuals and groups. We need to better understand human nature and our capacity for being either helpful or harmful in the world. We're on that razor's edge. We could go either way. In fact, our inner dialogue is often far more destructive than we reveal in the outer world. Human nature has a dark side as well as a light side. The report emphasizes the light side.

How do we deal with the dark side? At one point I felt that the only way to deal with it was by building the positive in the world. I have changed my mind about that. I now feel strongly that we must also learn to deter, restrain, and limit the flagrant, destructive actions that abound in the world. I think we do a very bad job of it, especially we who are on the idealistic side. We tend to be passive. We tend to enable, appease, understand, and remain neutral even in the face of blatant aggression. Positive ideals and values must be balanced with the ability to contain destruction. By better understanding our own dark side, we can better come to grips with the tendencies and actions that we need to restrain in the larger world.

I also want to make some remarks about mobilizing civil society. I've been with an involved NGO for seven years. Mobilizing civil society, although of great importance, is not a panacea for our global problems. Problems between NGO organizations are very similar to the problems between states. There is much division in the NGO and civil society communities. There's a tendency toward domination of the weak. There are tremendous turf battles. When I went to the former Yugoslavia to develop programs to heal war trauma, I felt that the best way to do it was to get representatives from all the humanitarian organizations together to share experiences and to be trainers of their own organizations. I discovered that this had never been done before. There was no conversation going on between the different humanitarian groups. There was nobody in command, there were overlapping tasks, and humanitarian organizations were just going their own way. This came as a startling surprise to me. NGOs must learn to relate better if we are to be effective partners with government. I think this might have to do with the way we structure grants, the way we give out money, the way we have to prove we've been efficient and effective, and various other things that are built into our system.

But that's not what I'm here to talk about today. I'm trying to get to the values part, but I also have a lot of ideas related to other areas. For NGOs to be effective, we need one body where pluralistic voices and special interests are represented and another that looks out for the whole of humanity. We need two bodies in order to adequately represent both the pluralistic nature of our society and the needs we have in common, the good of the whole.

Now, the values section: I had a lot of fun looking at the list the Commission came up with. I've looked at a lot of lists of values; I sort of fooled around with this one, added to it and tried a lot of things. Then I realized the value of this exercise was not in the listing of values as much as the fact that I was getting involved in the process. I found myself thinking deeply about values. The inquiry about values could be something that we might plan for many groups. My own Global Values Project will be working towards having forums, seminars, and workshops to offer people an opportunity to engage in the process, articulate the values they believe in, and act upon them.

We need a broadening of the inquiry about values. Our world is yearning for a time we can agree on shared values and practice them together. Are there intrinsic values that are good in their own right, values we don't have to justify? How do these differ from instrumental values that help us to reach a particular goal. By ethics we are talking about an area in between law and freedom where our inner conscience, our inner impulse comes forward to instruct us in what is right and wrong. We need to develop wise discrimination and these inner capacities. Values and ethics are involved when we ask questions about the fundamental area of choices, about what is meaningful, how we live our lives, and how we relate to one another.

Most people do believe in and profess certain basic values. It's when two important values clash that we run into problems. We then need to prioritize our values, a more difficult challenge. There are also gender differences in value choices that are not taken into account in the report. According to Carol Gilligan's research, women tend to put a higher value on love. And men put a higher value on principle. So when it comes to our behavior in the world, the criteria for our choice may be love or compassion, the greatest good for the greatest number, or our highest principle.

We must extend our inquiry into personal values to the morality of organizations and nations. It's not sufficient that we as individuals practice these values, they must be incorporated into the behavior of our institutions. We need to have a lot of discussion about how we can make that happen.

There is a major gap between our professed values and the values we live. How do we begin to close that gap? Two suggestions:

First, we need to move beyond our cultural conditioning through some form of meditation or spiritual practice, or education, to the point that we can transcend the behavioral habits that are now incorporated into our psyches. We need to change ourselves at a deep level because we are living in a world of materialistic values unbalanced by spiritual values.

Second, we need skills. We don't know how to get along with one another. To change this situation, we must undertake four important learning tasks. We need new ways of thinking — from dualistic (either/or) thinking to an inclusive, unitary mode of thought (both this and that). We need to think ecologically about whole systems and the interrelationship of parts. We need new understanding about the nature of change that synthesizes Eastern and Western views. We need flexible identity for changing circumstances. We need to understand layered loyalty between different levels in which we function — from family, to nation, to world, to cosmos.

While we're in the horizontal process of globalizing, we also need to deepen our roots and raise our vision. We cannot sustain a globalization process psychologically without also building security in terms of our roots and our ultimate place in the universe. We need skill building in human relationships, conflict resolution, listening, and nonviolent resistance. Already we are seeing the seeds of a new world in an emerging orientation to inclusive values. There is a new area of leadership called values-oriented leadership — an approach to leadership that stresses the fundamental importance of changing attitudes and values in the world today. Values-oriented education is being developed at Connecticut College by its innovative president, Claire Gaudiani.

The report ends with hope for the world through future generations. I think we are the future generation. It is happening now. New values, new skills, new ways of being are emerging even as the world seems to be most fragile and endangered. These value-oriented approaches are bringing clarity, inspiration, and hope amidst the complexity and confusion of our transitional times.

RESPONSE
By Mr. Ramphal

First of all, if the Commission, not just me and my co-chairman, but all the members of the Commission were here, they would tell you that we welcome constructive criticism. We do not pretend that this is the last word that will be spoken on global governance; it is the first word. Because it is the first word, we have offered some things which are new. Of course, saying they are new doesn't mean they haven't been said before, but we say them in ways that bring new nuances to the notions of rights and responsibilities. That is particularly true of the issue of responsibilities. Yes, if you go back to the Universal Declaration and through the Covenants, you can find references to responsibilities, but how deep is the commitment in human rights, law, and practice to responsibilities? Does not the question of responsibility lie in part at the root of the quasi-dichotomy that exists between sociopolitical rights and economic, social, and cultural rights? When speaking of human rights, how many people really understand economic, social, and cultural rights? How much of this lies at the divide — on human rights issues — that exists between the developing world and the rest? Between the Christian and Muslim worlds? How many understand that there has to be a balancing of interests for the sake of people and our global society?

To us, the fact that the notion of responsibility is built into what we've called the Charter of Civil Society is not without significance. We had no desire to undo all the tremendous achievements flowing from the Universal Declaration and all the efforts that people like Stephen Marks have undertaken. But as we move into a new era, a new attempt to formulate these values in ways that will build on and advance those others is appropriate. We're not at odds. In fact, my overall impression of their criticism was, "Well, if this is all, we're not going to have many arguments."

A People's Response to Our Global Neighborhood

In response to Nancy Roof, I simply want to say that you started with an indication that you really wish to see the report get out. Well, by the end of the year, it will have been translated into Danish, Spanish, Japanese, Chinese, Urdu, Arabic, and German. And there are many other translations in the pipeline. We would hope that by this time next year it will have been published in something like twenty languages. These translations were not, I must say, sponsored by the Commission, they were all self-generated. So there is a belief out there that there are things in the report that ought to reach the people. And there is no more significant way of doing this than publishing it in their language. Stephen Marks said he was troubled that it might be too difficult to understand in English. I must tell you that the word reaching the Commission is primarily in the form of a thank you for publishing a report that people can understand. So there are some who are getting the message.

I want to say something on civil society. Stephen Marks has rightly raised a question about the power of skepticism. If his effort with ECOSOC crashed, how are we going to manage to create a Forum of Civil Society? How are we going to get the Right of Petition? Well, I think that earlier effort crashed partly because what we're saying is wrong with the UN system is wrong with ECOSOC. He wasn't dealing with governments; he was dealing with ambassadors. We tend to believe they're one and the same thing. They're not. You're dealing with a class there, not with global society.

We presented the Forum of Civil Society as a recommendation which civil society should get governments to accept. Civil society came to us through several organizations and asked, "Are you sure we've got to get governments to agree to it?" And we said, "No, you don't have to get governments to agree. Do it!" And they're doing it to the point where a group of international NGOs has come together and decided, "We're going to have a Forum of Civil Society." They've gone to the United Nations system and said, "We want a trusteeship, we want space in the building." And the UN has said, "Well, we've got the Trusteeship Council which is vacant because it has reached its goal." The Global Governance Commission suggested that, psychologically, this thing ought to take place in the Plenary Hall in the General Assembly in August.

That's what we want, and that's what they're discussing now. So there is going to be a Forum of Civil Society. It may have to evolve and work itself out, but it's going to happen. Before the commemorative session (in which I do not have abundant faith, since it will be a session of governments bound to the status quo, very good at lighting up the candles, blowing them out, and putting them away), Civil Society will have met. And I suspect that the most important thing in the context of the celebrations is going to be that meeting of Civil Society — people startling leaders by saying to them, "There has to be fundamental change." So the situation is more positive even than you think. It can happen, and you can do it.

OPEN DISCUSSION

· · ·

Unidentified: I want to take up the question of the collective oppression in Nigeria and the many examples given by Helen Caldicott and Nancy Roof. We've got to deter, stop these things. There must be a forum where these topics can be brought up in a routine way. That would be terrific. I want to point to the fact that there is a forum coming up in the UN to which NGOs are invited. It's this September, around the 20th, for three days. It's the conference of the Department of Public Information and the NGOs. I think everybody, every organization that can possibly sign up should. You don't have to be accredited to the UN. You simply address your request to the Department of Public Information, UN. Get there, try to organize in a successful way, the way that people like Helen Caldicott, Shridath Ramphal, Nancy Roof, Dr. Marks, came to speak about.

Unidentified: We have heard some wonderful talks, but everything that has been said can be summed up by a poem that was written on the Fourth of July. You see, poems explain these complicated ideas quite simply. This poem is called "Inner Light." "Light outside overcomes fear of darkness. Light within removes defenses among rich and poor, white and black, man and woman, to understand that truth as different colors merge to make white light." Different people make up the human race. Is it the light within? Is it love? All is greater than the sum of its parts. Differences sublimate into cooperation. Brainstorming is subordinated through the spirit of "live and let live." That is what we are talking about. It is not possible to create a civil society until our differences become a bouquet of flowers and our brainstorming is subordinated to the spirit of "live and let live."

Vadim Perfiliev: I'm from the United Nations. I have a very short piece of information for Shridath Ramphal. Just after his comments this morning concerning Nigeria, the special representative of the Secretary-General, the Assistant Secretary-General for Public Affairs, left for Nigeria to address the issue.

Lawrence Campbell: One of the thoughts that came to me as I listened today is the concept of revisionist history and the part it has to play in the dynamic of people being pitted against one another — the part it might play in undoing some of the destructive behavior we see within nations and between nation-state and nation-state. Does anyone have some thoughts as to what part the UN can play in this? I ask because even here, in New York where I'm an educator, we're embroiled in a battle related to multiculturalism and how it affects the thinking, self-esteem, growth patterns, psychological development, and feelings of our young people. But I'm also thinking about how it affects the whole global perspective when you talk about global neighborhoods.

What might the UN be able to do to enter into that kind of dialogue or that kind of workshop? I think we can have such a distinguished group of people involved as we have here today. They say water runs down hill, and I think it still does. Maybe if we open such a dialogue, some kind of consensus of opinion will emerge. Because I think if we were to poll each other about our ideas on what history really is and what it really has to say, each of us is really completely different, but I think that somehow we can help work together on that. I'm wondering if maybe at some point you might be able to respond to that.

Caroline Sandhill: As I understand global governance, it's really about expanding access to the UN by non-governmental organizations, academic institutions, etc. My concerns are as follows. As we expand access, will those who gain access come mainly from the developed world? In Third World countries, isn't there a lack of nongovernmental organizations? So, as we expand access, will that replicate the situation in the UN, pitting North and South, but within the civil society?

Richard Jordan: I'm from Global Education Associates. One brief comment for Professor Marks, and two brief examples of holistic action that has been taken already. You may want to check for those normative developments in the work of Fatma Ksentini, who was the special rapporteur for human rights and the environment. Her report was completed last year for the Subcommission on Human Rights, and it deals with state constitutions that already have elements of environmental protection in relation to human rights. Now, the two examples from areas outside those NGOs usually work in. One stems from my work at the World Conference on Tourism in Lanzarota, the Canary Islands, where NGOs are incorporating conventions from Rio within tourist projects. The second relates to the International Olympic Committee. The Olympic Committee has put the environment in their constitution as a third pillar: sports, culture, and environment. I think we need to look for ways in which to involve youth in education through sports and other activities that they are particularly interested in.

John Washburn: United Nations, retired. The discussion has left me in some doubt as to how we should regard the role and position of governments in the nation-state as we undertake the tasks laid out today. We've had a number of very hostile references to governments and to the nation-state. On the other hand, however, Shridath Ramphal and the Commission report itself make it absolutely clear that the central role of the nation-states and governments is not going to disappear. These two themes leave me in some doubt as to whether we expect the growth of international society to deliver the changes that we want in national governments and their behavior, or whether we still retain responsibility as citizens — domestically — to bring pressures to bear on our governments through our domestic political processes to support those same objectives.

Unidentified: I'm from Teachers College. I want to underscore some of Nancy's remarks and raise some questions about the possibilities for action following the report and the possibilities for the continuation of this kind of inquiry. It seems to me that much of what has been said by way of criticism indicates that the report needs to be expanded — the inquiry needs to go further. One of the areas for such inquiry is what Nancy began by acknowledging — the need to look at the darker side within ourselves and the system. What the report didn't examine, and what we haven't yet addressed, is the way the darker side is rewarded by the system. I think that is nowhere more evident than in the fundamental inequities that exist between males and females in virtually all societies.

That inequity is maintained largely through the exclusive, "legitimate" control of force by one side of that division. I think that this control of force is a major issue that has to be addressed. What is legitimate force? By whom and how can it be controlled? And then Nancy, if we need, and I believe we do need, to move from this very question to the process of deterrence, then we also have to put much more emphasis on two things — on reconciliation as an integral, organic part of the conflict process, and on all the strategies that come from nonviolence. I think there has been insufficient attention paid to what we know about disputes — conflicts need not be destructive or lethal.

S'Alomi Richards: I'm going to speak as a mother of four children. I feel that we really have to have the courage in these kinds of settings to talk more about what immediate action we're going to take in our own families. Everywhere we look we can see that the strongest passions, both positive and negative, emerge in the family. Who's going to raise the world leaders but parents? I feel that the greatest contribution I can make as a human being is in trying to instill in my children a regard for other human beings. As we all go home — probably to segregated neighborhoods and to our segregated social events; as we go to our chosen, homogeneous environments, to people just like ourselves — we could begin by taking the immediate action of giving an example to our children of what it means to truly respect other people and truly begin an inner reformation. I believe that's how we will really bring change to the United Nations — not by just talking about it within the context of states and NGOs and other types of organizations, but in those most basic units, our own families and communities.

RESPONSES

. . .

To Open Discussion

Roof: I want to say a few words in response to the question about access. Many of you probably know that the technology that is bringing us an interdependent world is only available to ten percent of the world. The other ninety percent does not have access to the technology of what we call an interdependent world. This serious gap in access to information is a problem we have to address because it's going to create enormous increases in destructiveness. The question may have dealt with access to power, but access to information is a very, very important problem.

Marks: I'd like to free associate a little bit with some of the questions that were raised, starting with Mr. Ramphal's very valid points. I accept what he had to say. I'd like to clarify a point about the comprehensibility of the text, though. It is a very well and clearly written text. My observation really had to do with the level of education in this country, with a failing in the United States. I believe that many of the people who should be aware of these values and this vision of the world are incapable of reading the report, not because it is not well written, but because this society has failed to provide a level of education and a level of understanding that would make it meaningful. It is our responsibility towards our children to raise this level, but it is also our political responsibility to overcome generations of a failure to recognize the fundamental tasks of our society in education.

An observation was made regarding the need for appropriate redress for massive violations of the human rights, particularly of minorities, but also of groups and organizations. Since our subject is this report, I won't give a general statement about it, but another constructive criticism I have relates to the proposal in the report that allows the voice of the victims to reach the political decision-making bodies of the General Assembly through the Council for Petitions. The report also makes passing reference to the existence of the Commission on Human Rights and the fact that the High Commissioner might be able to reinforce the Commission on Human Rights, which I personally doubt. It nevertheless goes on to say that what we need is civil society's access to the Secretary-General and the Security Council.

I also think the report fails to develop the types of redress that are needed in the United Nations in the human rights field itself. It doesn't talk as other reform proposals do about the creation of a court on human rights and other mechanisms, or reinforcing the growing mechanisms of human rights. I know that Mr. Ramphal and most of the members of the Commission are well aware of these mechanisms and procedures. They need to be reinforced and the other proposals will, hopefully, make that possible.

Let me move quickly to a couple of the other observations that were made. I want to respond to the question that Richard Jordan of Global Education posed. Yes, human rights and the environment are in constitutions several decades old. I don't know how much could be done through this Commission in response to that. I think John Washburn made some very pertinent observations as to the importance of the role of citizens groups within their own society, their use of the political processes. You should not just act globally. You have to act locally, within your own society, to be meaningful. That's really the essence of what civil society means: functioning at the local level first.

Ramphal: First of all, to the gentleman who was uncertain about creating new mechanisms for the redress of wrongs, and who seemed to place importance on preserving the capacity to get these wrongs addressed by going to the state: we're not suggesting anything by way of substitution for what exists. But I'm really a little surprised that there is anyone who feels sanguine about the value or the effectiveness of the right to go to the state. In most of these cases we're talking about wrongs inflicted by states. Going to see them has never been a very effective way of redressing these wrongs. That is why we think the right of petition is very important. And it comes back to a point that Stephen Marks made just now. Yes, we want to give civil society access to the political process. That doesn't mean that the judicial process mustn't be developed. It doesn't mean that at all. There is another dimension in which the rule of law must operate. That's why we support the International Criminal Court, that's why we are for the Commission on Human Rights. I share some of your skepticism about how that is developing, but as long as international action is driven by the Security Council, we must have access to the agenda of the Council. Without that political access — well, we have in the Caribbean an expression to describe futility. We talk about spinning a top in mud. It goes nowhere.

I welcome the presence of the representative of the Secretary-General in Lagos. This is a very good development. I hope it's not too late. More of that is necessary. I hope it's seen, I hope it's known that the UN Secretary-General's representative is in Nigeria. The poem, sir, causes me a little trouble. "Live and let live" is not enough. Coexistence is not enough. Tolerance is not enough. Mutual respect, yes. We're beginning to get to it. Acceptance of interdependence, of linkages, of oneness, of an identity that is larger than our separate identities. That's why I talked about our country, the planet. Not that we were going to give up our countries, but we also have another country.

Revisionist history. Well, I'm not sure what is revisionist history. History ought to be the recording of truth. History has not been a record of the truth. I became the Foreign Minister of Guyana almost by accident. They didn't have anybody else. But what happened on our independence? Because we were a British colony on the tip of South America looking out to the Caribbean, looking to Britain and Europe, we didn't look over our shoulder toward Latin America. We studied French as a second language after English. In Barbados, they actually studied Greek. None of us learned Spanish. One of the first things I had to do as Foreign Minister of Guyana was visit our neighbors. We had a big border conflict with Venezuela. And what did I find in Venezuela? I found a whole different set of idioms and attitudes and assumptions.

One such difference was brought home to me very directly. What we had read was history written by the British, including the history of Sir Walter Raleigh and his great exploits. In the Parliament chamber of the colonial legislature was a great portrait of Sir Walter Raleigh. When I went to Venezuela, I found Venezuelan history — which I think was really rather nearer the mark — branded Raleigh one of the classic pirates of the colonial period. Both views take the name history but, of course, history very differently written. So we've got to be careful when we talk about revisionist history. We do want a revision of history that brings it nearer to the truth. And I don't think we're at odds on that. I think you are for that. Will it make for greater divisions? I don't think so. There's nothing worse than slavery, but the truthful recording of slavery is not going to make us the worse for it, it's going to make us the better, because it's going to put each of us in the situation where we can judge that past as the past and bury it.

Access. I understand what you're saying. Is this access for civil society mainly access for Western NGOs? No. One of the very interesting realities, and some of you must be aware of this because you are living with it, is the growth of non-governmental organizations in the developing world. Very, very substantial, though too much of it is funded still from the United States. I've told them, take the money and do your thing. But they are very substantial and playing a very important role at the local level in Africa, in Latin America, and now recently in Asia. A lot of the environmental movements, a lot of the women's movements are in the developing world. So I expect international civil society to provide access for voices from the developing world, and I think you'll see them coming forward.

To respond to the question that our retired UN colleague asked about governments and the state system: of course they're not disappearing. The world will continue to be primarily a state system. And governments aren't about to disappear either. But the emergence of civil society and finding space for civil society internationally does not mean — here I fully agree with what Stephen Marks said just now — that any of this is a substitute for local action, particularly for local action by civil society. What has to happen internationally, as more and more of the framework for the functioning of the state is influenced by what happens globally, is that you have to replicate at the global level a good many of the things that you're doing at the local level. So there's not a conflict at all.

Continuing the inquiry into the dark side of society and the things the report hasn't gone into in great depth: I hope we will come to talk this afternoon not just about denuclearization, but about the really dark side — militarization, the military culture. It's not just a question of the use of force against women by men, it's violence by people against people, and it's the violence implicit in a military culture in which economies are based on the production of weapons of mass destruction to be used on other people in other parts of the world. That's the dark side. All this talk of security and the Security Council, and the right of intervention on humanitarian grounds...Who is supplying the arms in Bosnia? We're talking about nice intervention from the air so that those who drop the bombs don't get hurt. Your nine-to-one ratio will be fulfilled in Bosnia. Who are the bombs falling on? Smart targets? People. That's what we've got to deal with.

When the United Nations was formed, the concept Roosevelt had in mind, along with national disarmament, was that the United Nations would be created as an organization with the capacity for the enforcement of peace. We were to gradually move toward a world in which the major military force was the collective force, not the national force. That was the vision. Of course, within two years the Cold War destroyed all that, and we've never come back to it — and probably never will. But what we have to do is to build up that collective side.

Finally, to the mother of four children: of course, you make a massive contribution that way. But that's not the only contribution you can make. You must do another thing as well. Because of time. We need those children to have the assurance that they can grow up to the age when they can exercise influence in their own right, without that future being stolen in the meanwhile. Time is very short. You heard this morning. That was not just a scare story. We are destroying the future. So by all means, yes, you're making a big, big contribution — go on making it. But we must, all of us, also strive to make sure that the rising water doesn't drown us in the short time that we have. We've got to do something quickly about it.

Response Panel #2
DR. GURURAJ MUTALIK

• • •

Gururaj (Raj) Mutalik is IPPNW's Director of Program Policy and the coordinator of their global program for Abolition 2000. Prior to joining IPPNW, Dr. Mutalik worked in India as Professor and Chairman of the Department of Medicine at the University of Pune in Maharashtra State, and worked for twenty years for the World Health Organization where he was most recently the Director of the WHO office attached to the United Nations.

M y first reaction to speaking now was that it's a little late for a physician. The physician should go first, not the last, but I have no mixed feelings there. In terms of the dialogue — the diagnostics and treatment — that has been carried out under the leadership of the co-chairman and speaker, it has been a model of diagnostic work. We are truly inspired. In fact, I told my colleagues the Global Commission's report is a very good book, one that should be in every American library. And by the same token, the members of the Commission should be awarded degrees in medicine.

I say this because one of the great teachers in medicine, Sir Bradford Hill, used to teach that the practice of medicine involved asking three simple questions and finding some accurate answers.

"If the people of the world... decide that enough is enough and the nuclear era shall end, and we shall bequeath a nuclear-free world to our children and grandchildren, it can be done."

225

First, what is wrong? — Diagnosis. Second, what is going to happen? — Prognosis. And, what can be done about it? — Treatment. The Commission has asked these very questions and given us a framework to which we all can relate our own activities. I think it's also the social responsibility of every scientist to ask why it happened, and can anything be done to prevent it. The roots of that, too, are in the Commission's report. My organization, IPPNW, came into being at the height of the Cold War when two of our founders, a Russian physician and a US physician, decided they could relate to each other across the political divide and took a leap of faith to found a movement. We broke some new ground in public awareness in establishing this international civil society, and soon we grew to be 200,000 physicians in eighty-four countries. Within five years we were further encouraged by the award of the Nobel Peace Prize.

How does the Commission's report relate to our work? Or rather, how does our work relate to the larger framework that the Commission's report has provided? I would say without hesitation that it is a remarkably creative framework although we, too, have some nuances of difference, especially when the Commission talks about the importance of the Nuclear Non-proliferation Treaty. As the Commission has highly emphasized, this is not a blueprint, but a basic framework for further thought and development. And I believe the most important part of the work is not what are suggested as prescriptions about global governance, but indicators for structural changes concerning the globalization of development — about getting involved in the globalization process, changing our thinking, developing some of the things that we want on an individual level. These are extremely important to us.

From the point of view of my organization, this is the kind of report needed by every single individual, every single NGO, in order to be more effective and to relate locally, regionally and globally. Non-governmental organizations can light a candle and brighten the surrounding area. They can be exceedingly important in relating the needs of the people and blazing new trails for development. But the problem with non-governmental organizations has been that we have not learned the art of going beyond coexistence, of relating to each other for concerted action. We have not learned real teamwork or joint initiative. That is the challenge of the next century, a century in which we can only change the world by working together.

Now the other thing that comes to my mind is that back in 1978, when we were taking part in an important conference in the medical context — the conference on primary health care and new principles of the health care in the world — there was a lot of argument about whether we should use the expression "community participation," or "community involvement." There's a lot of argument on the nuances of these words. Someone told me an enlightened story. He said a pig and a hen were walking together. They came across a sign board, "Bacon and Eggs Sold Here," on a cafe. The hen turned to the pig and said, "Look, my friend, we are jointly participating in this enterprise." And the pig said, "No, my dear friend, I am involved, you are participating." So mere participation is not enough, you must involve yourself and give a part of yourself. In terms of the globalization envisioned in the framework of the Commission's report, we all need to be truly invloved in order to produce a change.

I am going to spend the rest of my time presenting some transparencies that show how we are translating or actually implementing some of the valid principles in this report in the context of our own work. First and foremost, I think the Commission has given us a philosophical or intellectual underpinning for globalization, in all its facets.

This is a paradigm of a pyramid. It's not a coincidence that the Commission addressed the question of globalization — global values, global security, global development, and global governance. These represent the *four walls* of a pyramid. We are working on one of them — namely, global security. We truly believe that it's not just a question of nuclear weapons, it's the whole culture of violence. And that culture of violence is rooted at all levels. As this diagram shows, violence and insecurity exist within nations as well as between nations. Ever since World War II, over 150 wars or armed conflicts have taken place and some 123 million people have died as a result. And all these wars have been based on insecurity and intolerance. All conflicts that have not been resolved nonviolently perpetuate this vicious cycle. And only nations working together on the basis of equity, justice, and empowerment of the people can promote common security and ensure world peace. This, we believe, is the essential challenge for the global governance for the twenty-first century.

As depicted in the pyramid, one can say that nuclear weapons represent the very apex of the pyramidal facet of insecurity. Then come conventional arms conflicts, regional wars, civil wars, low-level conflicts, ethnic strife, and societal violence. If you look at this in geopolitical terms, the nuclear-related insecurities are largely produced by the nuclear states, and it is no coincidence that they also, in one way or another, are the countries that supply seventy percent of the world's arms. They also dominate the rest of the world through their economics and political clout.

This next slide indicates that there is also an ever-widening divide between industrialized rich countries and the poorer developing countries. The Commission cited some reports showing that the world's poorer people have become poorer while the richer people have become richer. This is another aspect of the challenge that we have to face in this century. Mr. Ramphal used a very graphic term. He talked about a top spinning in the mud. We have a similar paradigm. Through this pyramid we want to suggest that the world is upside down, and not just spinning in the mud, it's spinning in anti-clockwise manner because it sets the clock back.

These are the issues which need to be addressed: national security versus global common security, the widening gap between haves and have nots, the deteriorating environment and quality of life — population growth, increasing poverty, growing violence, the persistence of hegemonies in the world that pit those who have the power, those who have the means, those who have the technology against those few countries who hold the vast majority of the persons living in this world.

We think that this present pre-millennium period is the right time to address this global disorder. By focusing on nuclear weapons we think we can initiate a process of change. In this pre-millennium period a window of opportunity has opened. You need one good victory to reverse this whole process, and the nuclear issue is pivotal in this regard — that's our thesis. The United Nations Development Program and other bilateral and multilateral development programs are trying to redress poverty in the South and to ensure development, but even today Africa loses out to the North by a reverse flow of resources from the African continent to the rest of the world. Our thesis is wherever we turn there are major hurdles to cross. But one decisive victory could make a difference. We think the nuclear issue could lead to such a victory. Forty-six thousand nuclear weapons that exist today have no reason to exist. There are no enemies left after the end of the Cold War, so why are they there? If the people of the world decide that enough is enough and that the nuclear era should end, we shall bequeath a nuclear-free world to our children and grandchildren. And that victory will provide just the strength to redress the entire issue of global security, global development, global governance.

We think that the time is right for abolition of nuclear weapons because there is increasing public demand, as many, many polls show. You might have heard of General Horner. He was one of the senior most commanders in charge of protecting the United States and Canada from a nuclear attack. He said, "I want to get rid of them all...they have no military value." He said that the United States should take high moral ground. General Pasteur, another US senior military commander, also said that all our security objectives can be met with conventional weapons and as such we don't need nuclear weapons.

We also think that an economic factor has come into play. Recent studies show that the United States alone has spent 4.3 trillion dollars, the equivalent of a national debt, on nuclear weapons. What would that money mean in terms of the vaccination of children, what would it mean in terms of schools, what it would mean in terms of education and poverty? I'm not just singling out the United States. It is true for Russia, Great Britain, France, and for China as well. Millions still need all kinds of basic needs satisfied.

Finally, Victor Hugo said that there is one thing more powerful than all the armies in the world — that is an idea whose time has come. We believe that abolition of nuclear weapons is such an idea. Its achievement will truly pave the way for a better global neighborhood.

Response Panel #2

VIRGINIA STRAUS

• • •

Virginia Straus is Executive Director of the Boston Research Center for the 21st Century. As a public policy specialist, she formerly directed and helped found Pioneer Institute, a state and local policy institute. Ms. Straus served as an urban policy aide in the Carter White House and as a financial policy analyst at the US Treasury Department.

I t's not all that easy to understand what civil society is. What does it feel like to live in one? Even after reading *Our Global Neighborhood* a couple of times, I still wasn't sure, so I found a book called *The Idea of Civil Society* by Adam Seligman, and breathed a huge sigh of relief. Seligman's basic thesis is that the term "civil society" implies a harmony of individual and social good, a balancing of private interest and public responsibility. He concludes that the problem of creating civil society, a term invoked increasingly by contemporary thinkers, revolves around how to constitute real trust in society, in human relationships, and in institutions.

Seligman says this is particularly difficult in America because although the country was founded on principles of equality and justice,

"The Commission has done NGOs a great service by presenting a vision of hope for a more humane world based on the empowerment of the people's voice. In response, let's find that voice and create something whole from all the fragments that are now the NGO community."

231

"...we still feel lack of solidarity, mutuality, and trust in our hospitals, schools, and places of employment. The public space of our citizenship still seems to be characterized by abstract legal formulae and not by moral affections."

This absence of a shared public space in America — and its excessive devotion to private space — is not new. Toqueville recognized it as a danger to life in America more than 150 years ago. He remarked that:

> *The first thing that strikes the observation is an innumerable multitude of men all equal and alike, incessantly endeavoring to procure the petty and paltry pleasures with which they glut their lives. Each of them, living apart, is as a stranger to the fate of the rest, his children and private friends constitute to him the whole of mankind; as for the rest of his fellow-citizens, he is close to them, but he sees them not; he touches them, but he feels them not; he exists but in himself and for himself alone; and if his kindred still remain to him, he may be said at any rate to have lost his country.*

This, almost by itself, explained my difficulty. No wonder it's hard for me to understand what civil society means. I'm an American!

I do feel, though, a need for and a connection to civil society in my spiritual life. Through my spiritual practice, I am able to look within and bring up a universal self that feels palpably connected at the deepest level with all living beings. I've also felt an incredible solidarity and atmosphere of caring at religious and cultural meetings sponsored by the Buddhist organization I belong to — most especially, on the global scale when members get together from the hundred or so countries in which we practice. On the other hand, the first time I ever experienced anything close to these deeply peaceful and socially unifying feelings in a secular context was when I attended the NGO forum at the Social Development Summit in Copenhagen last March, which was infused with a special kind of connectedness and shared compassion. This was my first experience of a global civil society in the sense invoked by the Commission on Global Governance.

I direct a research center that was established in 1993 to sponsor peace-oriented dialogues. As our mission statement says, the Center "aims to combat the powerful disintegrating forces of mistrust among people and pessimism about the future by fostering reverence for life." Its founder is Daisaku Ikeda, the president of a lay Buddhist organization called Soka Gakkai International (the US branch of which is the primary sponsor of today's gathering). At the founding of the Center, Mr. Ikeda said that, "Through the workings of genuine dialogue, opposing perspectives are transformed from that which divides and sunders people into that which forges deeper union between them."

I thought we were doing a fine job at carrying out this high-minded mission until I got a phone call from an elderly gentleman who comes to our conferences, and who seems to enjoy them. He said, "I've figured something out! You're not really holding dialogues. You're holding discussions."

"What's the difference?" I asked.

"Well, I've been reading David Bohm, the physicist, and he says the word discussion comes from the same root as the word percussion and this happens when you just knock ideas together and nobody changes their view. Dialogue, Bohm says, has to do with trust. To have true dialogue, people have to trust each other enough to reveal the deeply held beliefs that lie behind their surface opinions. Then, they can question each other's assumptions and begin to establish a context for shared thinking and action."

That sounds good in theory, but I had to ask exactly how you make that happen. I hoped for a simple answer. "Very difficult, very difficult," said my friendly critic. "We'd have to have a long talk about this." I put off this possible meeting of the minds and went on with the business of the Center, but as I prepared this presentation, and began thinking more deeply about trust and how trust relates to dialogue, my friend and his distinction between dialogue and discussion kept popping up. I don't have time to learn a whole new technology, I said to myself. But trying to ignore this caveat was impossible; if someone tells you, "Don't think about a pink elephant," that's all you can think about.

What he said didn't seem to square with my own observation of our dialogues — or whatever they were — because I've seen dozens of people leave the Center inspired and engaged after our sessions. Perhaps, I thought, both discussion and dialogue were taking place at the same time. My friend may remember the collisions, but I remember the trust — and the nurturing of group spirit. So, maybe we're halfway there. Haunted, nevertheless, by the pink elephant, I finally broke down and read some David Bohm in Peter Senge's popular book, *The Fifth Discipline*. Bohm's theory is that wholeness is what is real in the world. Fragmentation results from man's dealings with this whole. Analytical thinking, especially in the West, teaches us to divide the world in order to create meaning for ourselves. Eventually we become hypnotized by the distinctions we've made and forget that we're the ones that created them in the first place. This way we lose touch with the wholeness of things. True dialogue, in which we inquire into the roots of our thought, into the assumptions and the distinctions we've forgotten, creates a condition of learning together where we can actually experience *shared thinking*.

Bohm contrasts this dialogic method of inquiry with an advocacy approach, which is much more common. In advocacy, you push your own point of view. But being willing to fully reveal and then suspend your point of view is the first step toward inquiry. This step toward dialogue among people allows the wholeness of things to re-emerge. "Inquire," he points out, means to "look within." In a genuine dialogue, everyone gets to look within and share what's there.

This, I realized, is what I find so appealing about the Commission's report. They state their values, their deeply held beliefs, at the beginning of the book and hold them up for everyone to see, and then they create a broad vision of global governance based on these values. They invite us to share the values and the vision. They also issue a call to action — especially to the NGOs of the world — to bring this vision about.

Nonetheless, they don't underestimate the profound transformation in global consciousness that will be necessary. They say, "People have to see with new eyes and understand with new minds before they can truly turn to new ways of living." In other words, in America for example, we won't be able anymore to be the person that Toqueville observed: "he is close to them [his fellow citizens], but he sees them not; he touches them, but he feels them not..."

Suppose representatives of the five countries with monopoly power in the UN were asked to respond in kind to the Commission's view. What would their implicit assumptions be? I suspect one of their core beliefs, if stated honestly, would have to be "Might makes right."

How then, realistically speaking, can we so boldly hope to overturn by the year 2000, as the Commission proposes, such a firmly embedded authoritarian structure in the UN? I would say Gandhi knew how; it has first to do with having the courage to trust ourselves. In the book *All Men Are Brothers,* he said: "You have to stand against the whole world although you may have to stand alone. You have to stare the world in the face although the world may look at you with bloodshot eyes. Do not fear. Trust that little thing that resides in your heart..."

Once we have the courage to trust ourselves, then we need to engage in true dialogue among NGOs, the core of the civil society, so that each of us can move beyond our narrow focus and mission and find common ground by being open to learning and respecting each other's deeply held beliefs.

United together, NGOs will have the power to challenge the authority structure that now resists change. I think the most important recommendations in the Commission's report have to do with civil society. And there's nothing except lack of solidarity among NGOs preventing the fruition of such ideas as a Forum of Civil Society Organizations, a Council for Petitions, and a World Conference on Global Governance.

The Commission has done NGOs a great service by presenting a vision of hope for a more humane world based on the empowerment of the people's voice. In response, let's find that voice and create something whole from all the fragments that are now the NGO community. Today's conference is a step in that direction.

RESPONSE
By Mr. Ramphal

What a marvelous way to bring this talk — not discussion or dialogue — to an end. I want to say something about the Nuclear Non-proliferation Treaty (NPT), about the military country, about denuclearization, and about its bearing on global governance. One of the rather more controversial recommendations in the Commission's report was that we were for an indefinite extension of the NPT. We were a very varied Commission. We had people on it from countries that were very deeply opposed to the notion of an indefinite extension of the NPT. We had members who couldn't quite square the circle about the concept of non-proliferation while senior members of the international community retained nuclear weapons. We had all those inevitable conflicts, and yet as a commission we came to the conclusion that, in the context of the dangers posed by nuclear weapons, we had to take the step towards non-proliferation that is implicit in the indefinite extension.

However, we set conditions on that recommendation in two very important respects. We did so by calling for a commitment by all countries — in the context of the extension — to the abolition of nuclear weapons. Not necessarily tomorrow or overnight, but a commitment to abolition in a time-bound framework of ten to fifteen years. This means that you would not be asking people to make the commitment not to develop nuclear weapons without yourselves making the commitment to get rid of yours — and in a time frame we thought was feasible. The physicians have said by the year 2000. Fine.

The second condition for agreement on the indefinite extension of the NPT was agreement on the covenants of the Test Ban Treaty — the agreement that the testing of nuclear weapons would end — and that the latter agreement would come within the context of agreement on the indefinite extension of the NPT. We believed that was a reasonable package, one that would fulfill both principle and practicality. What happened? There was no commitment to the total abolition of nuclear weapons. There was a kind of vague expression that this was the direction in which we ought to go. And there was an agreement to agree on a Comprehensive Test Ban Treaty.

In 1996 we will agree on a Comprehensive Test Ban Treaty. But those who had nuclear weapons did not make the commitment together in terms of ten or fifteen years, or at all, and they did not agree to end nuclear testing. No agreement on the indefinite extension after arm twisting, baseball bats, the lot — the most intensive pressure on countries. What action did China take the next day? And the enormously more wrongful action by France in testing in the Pacific?

The countries that had their arms twisted to agree to the indefinite extension of the NPT feel that they were duped. They no longer feel morally bound. And can you blame them? The Security Council has five permanent members; all five are nuclear powers. When two of them — within weeks of that agreement — announce a program of nuclear testing, and when France (one of those five and, unlike China, right up front in the nuclear race) announces a program of testing in somebody else's backyard, with total insensitivity to the people of the South Pacific, no wonder the New Zealanders and the Australians are outraged as are all the scattered islands of the South Pacific. Since this was done with a kind of machismo and commitment to the security of France and the sovereignty of France, what kind of global governance can be expected?

This is why I say these events have larger ramifications than the mere outrage over nuclear testing and fallout. It calls into question the legitimacy of the entire Security Council process when you take account of the fact that those five nuclear states, as we just heard, are also centers of military culture, militarization. Those five who are entrusted under the Charter as the guardians of international peace and security are responsible for eighty-five percent of the arms transfers in the world. What kind of Security Council process can you have under those conditions?

I've already talked about demilitarization. We can get nowhere until we talk about efforts to *prevent* conflicts — efforts by the United Nations, efforts by the Secretary-General, pleas by the Security Council. But while all that is going on, those who are running the world's economy are producing weapons on a massive scale and then selling them to impoverished countries. What, I ask you, is the difference between poor countries sending drugs to rich countries, to the markets of rich countries, and rich countries sending arms that kill people to the countries of the developing world? What is the moral difference between the two? Yet we find it so easy to accept a sense of outrage with regard to drug transfers — and I share that outrage — but somehow it's all right to produce arms and to sell them.

Have any of you seen the effect of land mines? They cost a dollar apiece and they fit in the palm of your hands. In Angola, Mozambique, Cambodia, your lasting image of a visit to these societies is how many amputees there are. And that is to say nothing of the weapons of mass destruction, the automatic weapons, or the missiles that are being supplied everywhere. Nigeria today is facing deep political crisis. What is most of the money of Nigeria being spent on right at this moment? Arms. Who's supplying it? The Western economies. This raises the question of personal trust, because you will hear that the economies in Britain, in France, in the United States depend on arms production and arms sales. Jobs are involved, the welfare and prosperity of their society is involved. Do you want to pay that price for prosperity?

The world's governments must be made by their respective peoples to accept the end of the military culture. Otherwise, nothing we do will be of any use.

OPEN DISCUSSION

• • •

Melinda Kay: Mr. Ramphal, your remarks remind me so much of things that I've read by Daisaku Ikeda, I was wondering if you've read any of his books or have any contact with his writing and his thought?

Ramphal: No.

Dr. Harry Lerner: I represent Medical Action for Global Security, which is a UK version of the International Physicians for the Prevention of Nuclear War, and a communication coordination committee for the UN — one of those NGOs. Let me first begin by saying how thrilled I am to be here and to see again some of the friends who worked with us in CAMDUN — the Campaign for a More Democratic United Nations. I refer to the leaders and members of the Soka Gakkai. I also appreciate the contributions by the leadership of the Commission on Global Governance with whom we have been in contact for several years. We're very gratified with the contents of the Commission report, and also by the fact that the Commission participated with us in the previous CAMDUN event, and will, we hope, in the next one. This is in the nature of an invitation to a sequel to today's meeting which will be held October 6, 7, 8, and 9 at and near the United Nations. It will largely address the people's voice on various problems and reflects a partnership between the NGO community, united peoples, and the United Nations organization.

One particular point I'd like to make is that we of CAMDUN — which was formed in 1982, originally as an international network for a UN Second Assembly — have advanced a number of recommendations relating to grassroots participation of peoples' organizations. There are solutions that do not require amending the Charter and that reflect an opportunity for us to unite locally as well as globally to achieve the objectives which were so well advanced by the Commission on Global Governance and by the leadership of this meeting.

Phyllis Morrow: I have a research company in Manhattan. I'm struck by the enormity of today, and I'm very appreciative of the opportunity to be here and hear these comments, particularly those of Dr. Roof and your own, Shridath Ramphal. I want to add a comment about the resource of culture. We've talked about many of the other resources that we're concerned about. As a way to leapfrog the labyrinth of governmental constraints, we must never overlook the way in which culture moves people's hearts, and how it can get the people of the world to know more about the United Nations and about being world citizens. I think about great artists like Danny Kaye and his humor, and Jim Henson — what he did with Sesame Street being translated into so many languages. This is a great opportunity for us to think about a way to really resonate and move people's hearts in the process of this whole UN thing. If the United States is going to cut back on its commitment, we, as universal citizens, can certainly find ways to empower this message through cultural activities.

Suresh Bhamre: I'm with the Commission of Human Rights in Suffolk County, Long Island. Questions relating to human rights are a call of the really civilized society, and, as you see, we do not live in one. The crimes that are committed against the people and, in my native county, especially people who are lower class, are really often crimes committed by the upper classes. You may have seen a recent movie, *Bandit Queen*, about a woman who was born into the lower class and how she had been tortured and raped by many, many people in high class society. She revolted against it, and, therefore, they called her a bandit. If you see the movie, you will probably cry. We see what kind of a society we are living in, even here. Minorities have been tortured and beaten to death. If a minority person buys a house in a white community, it can be burned down. That is why I believe that the Commission, in trying to establish a stronger civil society, is taking the right direction. I applaud their efforts.

Emma Broisman: It's indeed been a pleasure to be here at this meeting and I'm very grateful. I'm a representative to the International Council of Women which has NGO observer status at the UN, and I belong to many NGO committees. I want to make two observations. First, while I agree with most of the conclusions of the Commission on Global Governance, I do not like the term Economic Security Council. I think it is too confusing, given the current existence of the Security Council. As it is now, many people do not even know what the Economic and Social Council is, so it seems to me it will be very hard to understand what the Economic Security Council is. I do feel that the Economic and Social Council needs to be restructured and strengthened, but the question of social issues needs to be taken into account much more than in your report. Unless we come to grips with the social conditions in the world today, we're not going to have any global governance, and we're not going to have sustainable development.

Secondly, as far as civil society is concerned, I've also been attending all the meetings relating to the open-ended working group on NGOs at the UN. It's been very confrontational and difficult. Part of the reason is that the relationships of the new NGOs coming into the UN is not clearly understood. We do not know whether they're advocating programs or policy, or whether they're just after their own personal benefits, advocating programs not related to the overall programs the UN is concerned with. I think the whole question of consultative status process has to be looked at much more closely before any decisions can be taken.

Robert Kauffman: Virginia, thank you very much for your comments on dialogue. This is one of the first times at a meeting such as this that I've heard dialogue described in what I would consider the more mature meaning of the term. I would point out, having had some experience with it, that it requires three things that are fairly difficult for me and for many other people to muster. It requires courage, a lot of courage, to sit down and really open your heart and talk without knowing where the conversation is going to go. It also requires time, often a lot of time. And perhaps more than anything else it requires that I give up any certainty that I know what the answer is. Because for me the root meaning of dialogue implies that the spirit of something speaks through the two or three of you, or however many are there. This is incredibly important. It may actually lead to solving some of the problems you're speaking about. If NGOs, for instance, could dialogue among themselves and begin to understand where they're coming from and then reach for solutions that derive from both or all positions, perhaps something relevant would happen.

RESPONSES

• • •

Mutalik: Virginia, you suggested that advocacy means you're trying to sell something, some of your own idea. I think that within the limits of the dialogue we should ourselves be willing to be vulnerable, to let our opinion be changed. And that brings up the earlier questions of whether there is something called evil or whether there's something called wrong. Can you have a dialogue with a confirmed murderer in which you are willing to be vulnerable enough that he can convince you what he did was right? Or does it have to be a value-based dialogue? In other words, we know nuclear weapons have no place on the earth. But to the extent that assumptions are to be questioned, we are willing to open ourselves and hear them and not be merely confrontational, nor moralizing, because confrontation may really derive from self-righteousness. Then it doesn't change anything. So I think that there are real conflictual aspects to dialogue. Maybe we should have a dialogue?

Straus: I agree with Raj. I feel that this morning my understanding was deepened a lot by what Mr. Ramphal said. I realized that he and the other Commission members are extremely vulnerable to people's suffering. And I was struck when he just now said that we must speak out against the militarism in those countries where the government is importing arms and those that are exporting arms. We have to feel people's suffering enough to overcome our own egos, to stand up and go beyond our private concerns to be a voice that confronts these activities. This is going on because of our own apathy.

As Raj was saying, I think there are answers I haven't yet thought of, and I don't know how I'm going to be able to act on what I've heard today, but I invite everybody to look within and think about what you can say and do to express your outrage about what's going on. We can't hold back anymore just to be polite. As Helen was saying this morning, we need leaders everywhere; we can't want to be popular. We have to be willing to make enemies, even very powerful enemies — and what could be more powerful than the governmental structures that are now oppressing people everywhere?

I don't want to blame it all on government because I believe that, as the Commission has stated, government reflects the will of the people. If the will of the people that isn't strong enough, we need to be able to share with each other and open up and create some solidarity. I really hope that we can remember everyone's suffering around the world and find a way to take action ourselves.

Hauber: I hesitate to call on him again, because we have asked Mr. Ramphal to speak so often, and he just finished speaking so powerfully. But I think in the interest of all, we would like to pull this conference together and ask you to please do that for us.

CLOSING REMARKS

• • •

By Shridath Ramphal

Thank you very much, but, you know, I do believe we can pull it together. I think we've had the beginning of a dialogue, just the beginning. We can differ on tactics and strategies and emphasis and priorities — many NGOs have, by definition, a narrow focus on certain issues. There's nothing wrong with that. But the collectivity has to be infused with wider concerns. I hope that one of the things that all of us will leave here with is the awareness that, whatever our particular preoccupation or concern, we really have to act together in responding to the challenges that all of us are facing beyond our particular missions.

I'd like to make a particular plea to the universities. This occasion has been made possible in a university context, thanks to the Boston Research Center and Columbia. I think for too long academics have just been academics. We need the intellectual strength of academia in the struggle for human survival. Academics cannot sit back and do their thing secure in the knowledge that other people are going to create national and global societies. That may have been acceptable in earlier times, but we're not in those times. None of us. And we desperately need that intellectual influence.

I had the opportunity two weeks ago in Spoleto, outside of Rome, to deliver the Aurelio Peccei Memorial Lecture. Peccei was the founder of The Club of Rome, and The Club of Rome was the first to give voice to limits on growth. They produced a controversial document, but they sounded the alarm long ago. And the Italians, in contrast with our image of Italy today as very confused and politically corrupt, fielded a group of academics of tremendous intellectual strength who bore down on issues of global governance. It was one of the highest levels of academic discussion I have heard on these issues. We need that all around the world. What has happened today is also a very important

247

demonstration of the way in which academic involvement can contribute to this discussion, this debate. I both applaud what has been done, and I ask you to do much, much more of it.

Finally, I ask you to believe that you do matter. I am utterly convinced that you matter more than anyone else. Human survival is too important to be left to governments. Left to governments, we may all go down the drain. And I say that as someone who has spent most of his life with and in governments. I am of that public sector, and by the same token, I know it. I know that what is going to happen in October in New York at the General Assembly when 150 heads of government come and each speak for five minutes will not have the slightest impact on human survival. But what might happen on that day — the 24th of October — might come a little closer to dialogue because of you. So in whatever you or your NGO is doing, whatever your activity, please know and convey to your colleagues the awareness that you matter, that your concerns are important, and that your accomplishments are vital to the totality of our success. Altogether they will make it possible for you to look your children in the eye come 1999. Thank you.

AFTERWORD

. . .

The Commission on Global Governance has woven a remarkable tapestry of ideas together in its report, ideas that can light our way out of the darkness of this century of war by illuminating the worldwide need to find better ways of managing our global affairs. The goals it has envisaged are formidable, but they are worth considering as we grope toward a saner tomorrow.

As the report acknowledges, the collective power of people to shape the future is greater now than ever before. And it is painfully clear that "mobilizing that power to make life in the twenty-first century more democratic, more secure, and more sustainable is the foremost challenge of our generation."

Cynics will say that the goals are too utopian, too far removed from the divisiveness, neo-isolationism, xenophobia and suspicion that are so much part of the current reality of our post-Cold War world. But as Goethe said, each step along the way must be a goal in itself and have its own value.

By showing us the way and urging us to join with them in taking more small steps, the Commission and this *People's Response to Our Global Neighborhood* inspire hope — the kind of hope the president of the Czech Republic, Václav Havel, spoke of in *Disturbing the Peace* when he said, "[Hope] is an orientation of the heart; it transcends the world that is immediately experienced, and is anchored somewhere beyond its horizons." He also said, "Hope in this deep and powerful sense is not the same as joy that things are going well, or willingness to invest in enterprises that are obviously headed for early success, but, rather, an ability to work for something because it is good, not just because it stands a chance to succeed. The more unpropitious the situation in which we demonstrate hope, the deeper that hope is."

With a new century only five years away, our collective efforts to continue and expand this public conversation among our friends and neighbors and colleagues can contribute in untold ways to the realization of the dream we hold so close to our hearts — peace and security for all the world.

Columbia University, site of the July 22nd conference.

The July 22nd event in the Kellogg Center at Columbia.

Jonathan Wilson

Participants from the general public directed questions to the panelists.

Jonathan Wilson

A sharing of perspectives.

252

Sir Shridath Ramphal (right), Co-Chairman of the Commission on Global Governance, exchanges viewpoints with young scholars (July 22nd).

Informal receptions provided an opportunity for further dialogue.

APPENDIX

• • •

SUMMARY AND ANALYSIS
OF *PEOPLE'S RESPONSE*
QUESTIONNAIRES

• • •

Introduction

The report of The Commission on Global Governance explores the idea of developing a global ethic that responds to the needs of civil society and non-governmental organizations (NGOs) alike. Participants in the dialogue necessary to formulate this ethic would, therefore, have to come from all walks of life: school teachers, students and parents, postal workers, grocery clerks, small business men and women, and all the other ordinary people whose lives —beyond governments and institutions — tend to be most deeply and traumatically affected by conflicts between and within nations.

Seizing the initiative in an effort to actualize the Commission's vision, the Boston Research Center for the 21st Century hosted a series of conferences and discussions during the Spring and Summer of 1995 to allow members of civil society to engage in a public conversation with members of the Commission, and to respond to, question, and to criticize *Our Global Neighborhood*. Speakers, panelists, and guests from our local neighborhood were invited to participate. They included celebrated academicians, representatives of the media and interested citizens.

The first of the day-long conferences took place at the Boston Research Center on May 13th, the second at Columbia University on July 22nd. An evening discussion was held at the Center on May 25th, co-sponsored by the United Nations Association of Greater Boston, and a luncheon seminar designed to hear women's perspectives on the report was held on July 10th. Some four hundred people attended these events and at the conclusion of each event, in order to make sure every voice had the opportunity to be heard, a questionnaire was sent to each participant asking them to respond to five questions.

Sixty-seven questionnaires were returned. What follows is a summary of the responses to each of the questions and a brief analysis. We point out the areas in which the participants found common ground, the suggestions they made, and instances in which the participants strongly disagreed with the Commission's vision and with each other.

The Questionnaire and the People's Response

QUESTION 1. *Have you encountered, at this conference, ideas for reforms in global governance in general, or for UN reform in particular, with which you strongly agree? If so, please give an example or two.*

In its report, the Commission makes a distinction between world government or world federalism and global governance. It makes it clear that global governance is not global government, and goes on to say, "no misunderstanding should arise from the similarity of the terms. We are not proposing movement toward global government, for were we to travel in that direction we could find ourselves in an even less democratic world than we have — one more accommodating to power, more hospitable to hegemonic ambition, and more reinforcing of the roles of states and governments rather than the rights of people." Although many of the participants in the conferences had not read the Commission's report, answers to the first question indicate that through their participation in the conferences, they clearly understood the distinction the Commission was trying to make as well as its purpose. Nearly fifty percent of the respondents to the questionnaire agreed that there is a need to strengthen or otherwise reform certain components of global governance such as civil society and also a need to identify shared values and engage in dialogue.

> *Jacques Baudot, United Nations Secretariat: Of first importance is the idea that there is no feasibility of a global governance within an ethical vacuum. Second is the observation that there is no good governance without good government. Third is the idea that "forgiveness" is a useful concept in international relations — North-South in particular.*

Abdul Hye Mondal, Research Fellow: I strongly agree with most of the ideas for reforms in global governance, especially on the emergence of international civil society and creation of shared values.

Karen Drozdale: The voice of the people must not just be heard but must be listened to!

Gregory B. Julian, Ph.D.: Empowering civil society to advance the ideas of citizen diplomacy is essential for a global political consciousness.

Takao Kato, Associate Professor of Economics: I strongly agree with the necessity to recognize a growing global interdependence and thus the increasing need for cooperation. I also strongly echo the call for recognizing core values that all humanity can uphold such as respect for life, liberty, justice, and equity, mutual respect, caring, and integrity. Moreover, I am in strong agreement with the need to balance the rights of states with the rights of people, and the interest of the nations with the interests of the global neighborhood. Finally, I was very pleased with the general tone of the conference: critical yet optimistic.

Fifty percent of the respondents found ideas related to United Nations reform discussed in the conference with which they strongly agreed. Nearly a third of those interested in UN reform ideas endorsed greater NGO involvement in the world body. Many respondents also connected an expanded role for NGOs with the idea proffered by the Commission regarding a Right of Petition "for promoting the security of people." The Commission calls for the formation of a Council of Petitions—a high-level panel of five to seven persons, independent of governments, to entertain petitions and forward recommendations to the Secretary-General, the Security Council, or the General Assembly.

Sara Sue Koritz, Board of Directors of Community Church of Boston: The coupling of Rights and Responsibilities; the stress on Right of Petition which enables ordinary citizens or groups to make their needs known and to seek help; institutions must be built on the needs of the people — not imposed on them by outside powers.

> **James W. Moore, Attorney-at-Law:** *I agree with the proposal regarding Right of Petition for promoting the security of people and with the formation of a Council of Petitions. These are interesting proposals and deserve more attention.*

Another area where many respondents agreed with the Commission was in its suggestion to create an Economic Security Council as can be seen in the following responses gleaned from the questionnaires.

> **James W. Moore:** *Yes, I agree with the concept of an Economic Security Council and the recommendations regarding the management of economic interdependence. This is a good start, but it appears to me that more specific proposals will be required and that proposals regarding representation and voting will have to realistically reflect the interest involved.*

> **David Walter, consultant:** *The UN has to recognize the conflict of interest of the Security Council's structure and welcome the suggestions of the creation of an Economic Security Council and Right of Petition.*

QUESTION 2. *What about ideas with which you strongly disagree?*

There were 50 responses to this question, and here numerous differences of opinion were evident. For example, disagreement about the Economic Security Council emerged in ten percent of the responses.

> **Emma R. Broisman:** *I do not like the term Economic Security Council — too easy to confuse with the Security Council and does not take into account the importance of social issues, which, in my mind, are presently even more important than economic issues. They are interrelated but the underlying problems arising from social conditions and finding solutions are fundamental to the solving of world problems in the context of global governance and sustainable development.*

Other dissenting respondents connected the idea of an Economic Security Council more directly with the proposed elimination of the Economic and Social Council

> **Louise M. Des Marais, author/editor:** *I find the emphasis seemed to be more on economics than on humanitarian objectives. Therefore I found the idea of eliminating ECOSOC not good. There is a suggestion to set up an 'Economic Security Council,' but what happens to the social problems?*

> **Betty Reardon, professor:** *The abolition of ECOSOC; restructuring and reform, yes, but specialized agencies should be strengthened and unleashed from states' restraints.*

And while one respondent had trouble with the notion of civil society, a number of those responding to the questionnaire encountered nothing that they strongly disagreed with during the conferences.

QUESTION 3. Do you think the US should support efforts to strengthen the UN? If so, how?

Everyone who responded to the questionnaire agreed that the US should support efforts to strengthen the UN. There was also a great deal of congruence as to how that support should manifest itself. More than fifty percent of the respondents, for example, agreed that the most important action that can be taken is to provide financial support to the UN. There were also some creative ideas about what to do beyond financial support.

> **Abdul Hye Mondal, Research Fellow from Bangladesh Institute of Development Studies:** *Yes, the US can and should take the initiative to organize, manage, and monitor global governance within a new UN system as suggested by the report and provide greater financial support to conduct research on the creation of human values and the welfare of humankind.*

Maria Guajardo, Executive Director of a non-profit organization: *Most definitely, by supporting the discourse of a global neighborhood, by financing at a higher level the work of the UN, and by formulating a process for the direct participation of global citizens.*

Joseph Baratta, historian: *Yes. We should lead in establishing more equitable institutions, like an Economic Security Council and a Council on Petitions, as we did in establishing the universal organization itself in 1945.*

A little over one third of the respondents, while endorsing financial support for the UN, also expressed awareness of US's indebtedness to the world organization.

Albert Ornstein: *Pay up what it owes and promptly - end sales of weapons, cut the Pentagon budget and apply it to human needs at home and abroad and set an example for good faith and courage at all times!*

Michael Simpson, Fellow Harvard University, Captain US Navy: *Yes, we should first pay overdue assessments. Then we should make an effort to put the UN on a solid financial basis through reform of the budget process. Further reform will then be possible, but very little can be done to strengthen the UN if resources continue to be grossly inadequate.*

Beyond financial assistance approximately ten percent of the respondents identified education as a way to strengthen the UN.

Alison Cucchiara, secretary: *It's the only World Forum we have. Let's strengthen it, not divorce ourselves from it. Continue education about the UN; its activities must be accessible to the common people and highly visible. More forums to express the voice and will of the people.*

Courtenaye Lawrence, teacher: *1) Development of educational materials to be used on the elementary, secondary, and university levels. 2) Establishment of a "youth" UN with participants from all*

*over the world encouraging them to hold dialogues on the issues that
they will face as adults.*

QUESTION 4. *If you had been a member of the Commission that
prepared the report,* Our Global Neighborhood, *what other recommendations or observations would you have made?*

Twenty percent of the respondents did not answer this question,
either because they had no suggestions or because they had not yet
read the Commission report. Of those who did respond, each had an
insightful suggestion. No patterns emerged except in one case where
nearly ten percent of the respondents would like to have seen a discussion of culture and the arts in the report.

> **Louise Roche, artist-designer, peace activist:** *I would have
> included reference to culture and the arts. Through the arts of each
> nation we learn about the people and their societies, ancient and
> modern.*

> **Melinda Kay, educator:** *I would have included the arts and
> culture as a topic, and perhaps, education.*

Other observations ranged the gamut from the suggestion to create a social council and a UN Army to the inclusion of an analysis of
global resource ownership and management. The following comments
are representative.

> **J. Peter Kulka, retired physician:** *Neither the generally admirable
> report of the Commission on Global Governance nor the thoughtful
> presentations of the panelists have directly addressed underlying psy-
> chodynamic aspects. Fragmented as such understanding may still be,
> it is basic to wise leadership and to affecting change in our way of
> thinking, which is needed for the realistic achievement of global
> neighborliness. Accordingly, an educational program (responsive to
> change) should be launched by the UN or an appropriate NGO. A
> first step would be the recruitment of an advisory council to design a
> largely experimental, self-generating learning system which would*

mesh with existing educational institutions. Particular emphasis would be given to the practice of dialogue.

Robert Kaufman, designer/builder, writer: *I would have pursued an investigation into 'non-social' indicators inhibiting social development. Greed would be one; corruption, antisocial behavior would be others.*

Abdul Hye Mondal, Research Fellow: *Apart from an ideological and humanitarian foundation of human values, innovative and creative premises for human values need to be developed that could be instrumental in neutralizing the impact of evil forces that are the outgrowth of distorted human values.*

QUESTION 5. *What would you be willing to do to further the kinds of reforms in global governance, or in the UN, that you would like to see? (Examples: telling friends and neighbors about Our Global Neighborhood; bringing up these ideas in conversation with others; initiating a discussion meeting at your civic, religious or other association; speaking at gatherings; writing articles, writing to representatives; teaching a course.)*

Out of 55 responses to this question, a majority of the answers fell in the category of writing, speaking and education. A little over thirty percent of the respondents to this questionnaire said they will write. An equal number said they will find opportunities to speak as is indicated in the following samples of their comments.

Gail Jacobson, mediator and host of a public affairs cable show: *Writing letters, articles — all of the above. Have people on my cable show who could talk about their work with global governance issues.*

H. Jones: *I have been spurred to write to my representative and senators about the non-proliferation treaty and the need for a comprehensive test ban treaty, etc.*

Twenty-five percent of the respondents combined the idea of writing with that of education and dialogue.

> ***Robert Kaufman, designer/builder, writer:*** *I am currently involved in speaking locally about the UN in general, and the report in particular. I am also writing articles which are beginning to gain an audience. This is one way to do it. What's probably most effective for me, is to bring up the subject with everyone I meet in face-to-face dialogue. I know I've reached someone.*

In addition to the twenty-five percent mentioned above, another fifteen percent combined education with writing and speaking.

> ***Gail Thomas, professor of sociology:*** *Writing letters and including issues more extensively in my teaching materials; support Boston Research Center and other NGOs that are moving towards greater humanism and equality and the public good.*

> ***Nancy Wrenn, environmental planner:*** *Act on my own principles of furthering inclusive dialogue within a global perspective. I recommend that this report be a required course for young adults — the future world citizens.*

Final Segment of the Questionnaire

Finally we asked each respondent to share any other suggestions or comments that he or she thought might be relevant to the concept of global governance. Those who replied to this segment of the questionnaire, with a handful of exceptions, said they would need more time to think about the question before responding. The others said they would respond in writing. One of those was Scott C. Mohr, from Boston University's Department of Chemistry, who submitted a paper that we decided to include in full. His presentation is indicative of the feelings expressed by those who did respond to the questionnaire. It also exemplifies the spirit of *A People's Response to Our Global Neighborhood* as well as the spirit of the Commission's report as articulated by Virginia Straus, the Executive Director of the Boston Research

Center for the 21st Century. At one of the four events she said, "First of all, the report gets the source and direction of social change right. It says, in many different ways, that peace in the world begins in the hearts and minds of people: change in people's consciousness and values are really what transforms institutions." Whether we agree or disagree with Mr. Mohr's thoughts is not the point. That he, like the more than 400 people who attended the conference series, accepted the Commission's challenge to lend his voice to bring about change is.

A United Nations of the People, by the People, and for the People

by Scott C. Mohr

In his discussion of *Our Global Neighborhood*, Barber Conable stressed the indispensability of the UN in the world today. Despite all its weaknesses and shortcomings it is 'the only game in town.' He and others, however, echoed the theme from the Commission on Global Governance that reform of the UN is urgently needed and requires major political effort, particularly in the United States. The focus of my comments is that such a political effort cannot take place until the movement for UN reform becomes a genuinely popular movement. Only when ordinary people feel that they have a direct stake in and influence on the United Nations will there be sufficient political will to enact the reforms which will bring about global governance. At the present time very few people — including the highly-educated, progressively-minded minority in America that works for social and political change — feel any strong, direct connection to the UN. And sadly, maybe even tragically, the vast majority of Americans seem to think of the UN as at best irrelevant, and in many cases as downright inimical to their interests. Jesse Helms' chairmanship of the Senate Foreign Relations Committee is profoundly symbolic of this political reality.

Why do we face such a sad state of affairs? After all, the United States was established by rational idealists who saw themselves creating a noble experiment in self-government to serve as a model for the whole world — and it was preserved in the face of its deep-rooted inner contradiction of slavery by a president who believed it to be 'the last, best hope of earth.' Surely the noble aspirations of the American past cannot all have vanished! In my opinion, the current swing of the political pendulum towards isolationism and ostrich politics where world problems and the UN are concerned, stems from a combination of ignorance, disappointment, fear…and reluctance to confront complex issues.

Most Americans know little of the activities of the UN and related international organizations; in the era of sound-bite politics and ratings-conscious TV news, the UN only comes to the fore in the context of violent crises, and then attention soon wanders elsewhere. The typical US citizen would be hard-pressed to name three successful UN projects and probably couldn't describe a single way in which the existence of the UN benefits his or her life directly.

Moreover, there is little doubt that the high expectations for the UN which greeted its founding 50 years ago have been followed by great disappointment and disillusionment, not only in the United States, but in the whole world. Hobbled by the Security Council veto and dominated by Cold-War politics for the first 45 years of its existence, the UN has a reputation as a debating society, not a potent force in world affairs. Its role in peacemaking and other international endeavors has been perceived as more of a hope than a reality. Part of that perception can be attributed to ignorance of its actual accomplishments, but in all honesty that is the lesser part.

Xenophobia — fear of the foreign — manifests itself to varying degrees in all nations in all epochs. It may seem ironically out of place in a nation like the United States, whose people represent an amalgam of virtually all other nationalities, but perhaps in our eagerness to define ourselves as Americans we all the more readily fall prey to xenophobic tendencies. Thus we automatically view with suspicion any proposal to cede control of our affairs (worse still, of our money!) to others. It's important to remember that for more than four decades the biggest bogeyman in American politics was the international communist conspiracy. Evidently for many Americans the UN represents foreign powers whose motives are suspect — despite the fact that the United States exerted the dominant influence over the UN at the time of its creation (in San Francisco, an American city) and continues to control many aspects of its operations (permanently headquartered in New York…another American city.)

Related to the aspect of fear of the foreign is reluctance to confront complex issues. Americans by and large are remarkably ignorant of the histories, languages and peoples of other nations and seem unconcerned by this fact. We tend towards the same type of smugness which long characterized China: confident of its own superiority, the 'Middle Kingdom' felt no need to learn about the rest of the world, and expected proper obeisance from foreign representatives. Rather than struggle with the ever-changing kaleidoscopic complexity of the international scene, Americans tend to indulge in a form of denial which replaces the details and particulars of the real world with simplistic stereotypes. The UN with its 184 member states (many of which most Americans would be hard-pressed to situate on the right continent, let alone in an exact geographic location) inherently contradicts a simple-minded world view. To some people this undoubtedly makes it a subject they would rather not have to think about, an unwelcome intrusion upon their otherwise comfortable world view.

How can inroads be made on these powerful negative attitudes which impede any attempt to rally support for a reformed UN from the broad mass of the American people? Unless this question can be answered and the answer(s) acted upon, the effort to reform and strengthen the UN will be futile. (I address myself strictly to the situation in the United States since that is my country, and also because, realistically, if UN revitalization cannot arouse popular support in the US it will certainly fail. That's not to say, of course, that support need not be sought elsewhere or that such support would count for naught. Indeed, many of the considerations which apply to the political situation here in the United States will probably apply elsewhere as well.) It's fair to say, I think, that reform of the United Nations has to begin with reform of the attitudes of average Americans; they must be persuaded to adopt Mr. Conable's point of view, and so thoroughly persuaded that they eventually believe that deep down this is what they have believed all along.

First of all, those of us who strongly believe in the cause of effective global governance must find ways to carry our message beyond the already-converted. This will require imagination and persistence. Above all it requires an awareness that "the broad mass of the American people" are harried, worried, and skeptical (even cynical) about the ability of institutions of all kinds to deliver on their promises. They will reject fancy language and abstract concepts, they will be impatient with bureaucratic details, and they will be on the lookout for genuine answers to palpable problems. (It is hardly coincidental that the phrase 'get real' has invaded the language just at the time that public alienation has reached an all-time high.) If we want to rally these constituents, we will need a down-to-earth approach, couched in simple language and using concrete illustrations. Best of all, we should tell stories, human stories which move the emotions and cut across barriers.

Of all the UN agencies and activities, UNICEF has come the closest to what I am trying to advocate. It has been widely accepted across the US, and with Halloween boxes and holiday greeting cards it can be said to have succeeded in becoming part of the popular culture. We should analyze the methods taken by UNICEF and try to expand them. Perhaps one way would be to move up the generational ladder a bit and promote more youth travel and exchange study, perhaps recruiting existing programs to move under a UN umbrella — in return for some type of assistance which would benefit the programs. Another would be to spread the UN logo (accompanied by some simple slogans), perhaps by encouragement of UN-sponsored postage stamps, travel brochures, calendars, etc.

This brings up an old idea, but one which might still be implemented successfully in the year 2000: devote one day per year to an international holiday/day of peace. In the original concept, "world day" would be the last day of the calendar year and not have a name as a day of the week. By dropping the number of normal days to 364 (exactly 52 weeks) the calendar would be fixed instead of variable (particular dates would always fall on the same day of the week.) That idea has not been accepted thus far, perhaps out of reluctance to change the system and perhaps out of a desire to maintain variety (and certainly out of a desire by calendar manufacturers to have a 100% annual replacement of their products). It could be suggested again, but if not popular enough, it need not prevent the adoption of a world holiday, perhaps called World Peace Day (Peace-on-Earth Day having too-obvious sectarian overtones). Such a day could be used for attention-getting UN-related activities, and as most holidays are welcome respites for ordinary folk, this one would doubtless win friends! [An obvious point here, of course, is that sharing a (political) holiday with everyone on the planet would build a sense of mutuality and solidarity — analogous to that felt by citizens everywhere on their country's national day].

Another way to encourage association of the UN with world solidarity — crass though it might seem — would be to have explicit involvement in international sports. Academics and would-be intellectuals (among whom I number myself) often ignore the power of sports to involve large masses of people - and bond them together. The Olympic Games are a towering example of this phenomenon with every indication being that they will grow in importance in the years ahead. Could a closer connection be — tactfully — forged between the International Olympic Committee and a revitalized UN? Perhaps this could arise from mutual benefit, with the UN providing assistance in the on-going process of operating the Olympics. And other international, sports-related activities might take place under (well-televised) UN auspices.

As a scientist, throughout my entire career I have been part of what I would like to think is the world's most open, egalitarian and successful international endeavor. From its beginnings 500 years ago, modern science has crossed all national, political, ethnic and religious boundaries and forged vital, trusted bonds between scientists everywhere. As with the sports world, the scientific community has in place many international connections and organizations. They could be more tightly and overtly affiliated with the UN to the benefit of both parties. Some specific ways to accomplish this might be publication under UN auspices of general journals, both technical and popular, which would emphasize outstanding scientific achievement and new discoveries pertinent to the solution of world problems. The UN logo would be on their covers. I think it's fair to say that the recognized world leaders in most scientific fields would be willing to lend their names and talents to this kind of project. It also should be possible to involve the UN in international scientific meetings and conferences — perhaps by such a mundane device as creating an Office of International Conferences whose staff would be able to provide cost-effective management superior to that now afforded by the scientific societies and universities which presently conduct such conferences.

Our Global Neighborhood addresses ways in which world economic affairs would benefit from more effective international organization and regulation. In addition to those 'hard' issues, it seems to me that there might be 'soft' aspects of international cooperation and community building which could go on through trade associations, professional societies, etc., analogous to what I have discussed above for science.

Above all, I want to stress the need for involvement of the UN in people's lives — as directly as possible, and in practical ways. There is, however, another aspect of human life which needs to be faced: the need for myths. I don't mean this term in the now-common, somewhat degenerate, pejorative sense, but rather in the classical sense of deep psychological truth. Every human being lives constantly in a reality informed by myth. We are acculturated to our communities' myths as children and they account for a large proportion of our political behavior. In America we have national myths about our history and government — and about our actors and musicians. Towering mythic figures ranging from George Washington and Martin Luther King to Elvis Presley and Marilyn Monroe give us concrete images to which we attach key ideas and beliefs. Any attempt to win the allegiance of the multitudes to a better form of world governance must include myth-making (in the positive sense) if it is to succeed. There are certainly heroes of the movement for world peace and human solidarity. Their stories must be told and retold until they are as familiar to young and old as Washington's cherry tree, Lincoln's honesty, and Jacqueline Kennedy's courage. They should be sung about, acted out, painted, and celebrated in poetry. I know this suggestion isn't high-brow, but neither are the masses of people whose loyalty and support are essential to any UN reform.

Analysis and Summary

An overall summary of the responses to the questionnaire indicates that, with these conferences, a significant and valuable step has been taken. Four hundred people came together and participated in a public conversation, the result of which allowed them to connect a number of concepts that will get us to our destination of a saner future. They saw the need for greater involvement of youth and women in the process of strengthening the UN; and the need for a global dialogue and discourse to promote the concept of global neighborhood.

Appendix

The responses of those who answered the questionnaire indicate that there is also congruence in terms of their support of the idea of global governance and reform to strengthen the UN. Most refer to the importance of some kind of Universal Declaration of Rights and governance based upon values, ethical considerations and responsibility to humankind. Most also believe that the US should offer increased support to the UN and support for the idea of global governance. Finally, most respondents said that they would like to be active in helping to bring global governance into being.

As would be expected, there were some differences, both concerning what the role of the UN should be in this post-Cold War era and how to achieve reform. Some, for example, stress economic changes, youth education and greater involvement of women. Others stressed rights, petitioning and legal solutions. Some believe that war should no longer be an option in settling national differences; while others stress the practicality of a military arm to the UN.

The ideas for reform that have been articulated by the Commission give us an opportunity to forge a better framework for the future. Lack of political will may well obstruct and delay their implemetation, but nothing can obstruct the growing chorus of the voices demanding a saner future.

A CALL TO ACTION:
SUMMARY OF
OUR GLOBAL NEIGHBORHOOD

• • •

The Report of
The Commission on Global Governance

A CALL TO ACTION

• • •

Extracts From Co-Chairman's Foreword

The Charter of the United Nations was written while the world was still engulfed in war. Face to face with untold sorrow, world leaders were determined never to let it happen again. Affirming their faith in the dignity and worth of the human person, they set their minds on the advancement of all peoples. Their vision produced the world's most important political document.

Half a century has passed since the Charter was signed in San Francisco. There has been no world war in that time, but humanity has seen much violence, suffering and injustice. There remain dangers that could threaten human civilization and, indeed, the future of humankind.

But our dominant feeling is of hope. We believe the most notable feature of the past fifty years has been the emancipation and empowerment of people. People today have more power to shape their future than ever before; and that could make all the difference.

At the same time, nation-states find themselves less able to deal with the array of issues — some old, some new — that face them. States and their people, wishing to control their destinies, find they can do so only by working together with others. They must secure their future through commitment to common responsibility and shared effort.

The need to work together also guided the visionary men and women who drew up the Charter of the United Nations. What is new today is that the interdependence of nations is wider and deeper. What is also new is the role of people and the shift of focus from states to people. An aspect of this change is the growth of international civil society.

These changes call for reforms in the modes of international

Reprinted with permission of the Commission on Global Governance.

cooperation — the institutions and processes of global governance.

The international system that the UN Charter put in place needs to be renewed. The flaws and inadequacies of existing institutions have to be overcome. There is a need to weave a tighter fabric of international norms, expanding the rule of law worldwide and enabling citizens to exert their democratic influence on global processes.

We also believe the world's arrangements for the conduct of its affairs must be underpinned by certain common values. Ultimately, no organization will work and no law will be upheld unless they rest on a foundation made strong by shared values. These values must be informed by a sense of common responsibility for both present and future generations.

The members of the Commission, all serving in their personal capacities, come from many backgrounds and orientations. Yet, over the last two years together we have been united by one desire: to develop a common vision of the way forward for the world in making the transition from the Cold War and in managing humanity's journey into the twenty-first century. We believe this report offers such a vision.

Each member of the Commission would have chosen different words, if he or she were writing this report alone. Everyone might not have fully embraced each and every proposal; but we all agreed on the overall substance and direction of the report. The strongest message we can convey is that humanity can agree on a better way to manage its affairs and give hope to present and future generations.

The development of global governance is part of the evolution of human efforts to organize life on the planet, and that process will always be going on. Our work is no more than a transit stop on that journey. We do not presume to offer a blueprint for all time. But we are convinced that it is time for the world to move on from the designs evolved over the centuries and given new form in the establishment of the United Nations nearly fifty years ago. We are in a time that demands freshness and innovation in global governance.

Global governance is not global government. No misunderstanding should arise from the similarity of the terms. We are not proposing movement towards world government, for were we to travel in that direction we might find ourselves in an even less democratic world than we have — one more accommodating to power, more hospitable to hegemonic ambition, and more reinforcing of the roles of states and governments rather than the rights of people.

This is not to say that the goal should be a world without systems or rules. Far from it. A chaotic world would pose equal or even greater dangers. The challenge is to strike the balance in such a way that the management of global affairs is responsive to the interests of all people in a sustainable future, that it is guided by basic human values, and that it makes global organization conform to the reality of global diversity.

Many pressures bear on political leaders, as they seek both to be effective and to retain support at the national level. Notwithstanding the drawbacks of nationalism, however, the history of even this century encourages us to believe that from the very best of national leaders can come the very best of internationalism. Today, a sense of internationalism has become a necessary ingredient of sound national policies. No nation can make progress heedless of insecurity and deprivation elsewhere. We have to share a global neighbourhood and strengthen it, so that it may offer the promise of a good life to all our neighbours.

Important choices must be made now, because we are at the threshold of a new era. That newness is self-evident; people everywhere know it, as do governments, though not all admit to it. We can, for example, go forward to a new era of security that responds to law and collective will and common responsibility by placing the security of people and of the planet at the centre. Or we can go backwards to the spirit and methods of what one of our members described as the 'sheriff's posse' — dressed up to masquerade as global action.

There should be no question of which way we go. But the right way requires the assertion of the values of internationalism, the primacy of the rule of law worldwide, and institutional reforms that secure and sustain them. This report offers some suggestions for such responses.

Removed from the sway of empires and a world of victors and vanquished, released from the constraints of the Cold War that so cramped the potential of an evolving global system throughout the post-war era, seized of the risk of unsustainable human impacts on nature, mindful of the global implications of human deprivation — the world has no real option but to rise to the challenge of change, in an enlightened and constructive fashion. We call on our global neighbours, in all their diversity, to act together to ensure this — and to act now.

Ingvar Carlsson	**Shridath Ramphal**
Stockholm	London
November 1994	

Summary of Proposals

In setting out the major proposals made by the Commission, we wish to emphasize that all the proposals form a coherent body — not inseparable, but mutually reinforcing. We encourage their consideration as such.

Governance, Change, and Values

Global governance, once viewed primarily as concerned with inter-governmental relationships, now involves not only governments and intergovernmental institutions but also non-governmental organiza-tions (NGOs), citizens' movements, transnational corporations, acade-mia, and the mass media. The emergence of a global civil society, with many movements reinforcing a sense of human solidarity, reflects a large increase in the capacity and will of people to take control of their own lives.

States remain primary actors but have to work with others. The United Nations must play a vital role, but it cannot do all the work. Global governance does not imply world government or world feder-alism. Effective global governance calls for a new vision, challenging people as well as governments to realize that there is no alternative to working together to create the kind of world they want for themselves and their children. It requires a strong commitment to democracy grounded in civil society.

The changes of the last half-century have brought the global neighbourhood nearer to reality — a world in which citizens are increasingly dependent on one another and need to co-operate. Matters calling for global neighbourhood action keep multiplying. What happens far away matters much more now.

We believe that a global civic ethic to guide action within the global neighbourhood and leadership infused with that ethic are vital to the quality of global governance. We call for a common commitment to core values that all humanity could uphold: respect for life, liberty, justice and equity, mutual respect, caring, and integrity. We further believe humanity as a whole will be best served by recognition of a set of common rights and responsibilities.

It should encompass the right of all people to:
- a secure life,
- equitable treatment,
- an opportunity to earn a fair living and provide for their own welfare,
- the definition and preservation of their differences through peaceful means,
- participation in governance at all levels,
- free and fair petition for redress of gross injustices,
- equal access to information, and
- equal access to the global commons.

At the same time, all people share a responsibility to:
- contribute to the common good,
- consider the impact of their actions on the security and welfare of others,
- promote equity, including gender equity,
- protect the interests of future generations by pursuing sustainable development and safeguarding the global commons,
- preserve humanity's cultural and intellectual heritage,
- be active participants in governance, and
- work to eliminate corruption.

Democracy provides the environment within which the fundamental rights of citizens are best safeguarded, and the most favourable foundation for peace and stability. The world needs, however, to ensure the rights of minorities, and to guard against the ascendance of the military, and of corruption. Democracy is more than just the right to vote in regular elections. And as within nations, so globally, the democratic principle must be respected.

Sovereignty has been the cornerstone of the interstate system. In an increasingly interdependent world, however, the notions of territoriality, independence, and non-intervention have lost some of their meaning. In certain areas, sovereignty must be exercised collectively, particularly in relation to the global commons. Moreover, the most serious threats to national sovereignty and territorial integrity now often have internal roots.

The principles of sovereignty and non-intervention must be adapted in ways that recognize the need to balance the rights of states with the rights of people, and the interests of nations with the interests of the global context of a global neighbourhood rather than a world of separate states.

Against the backdrop of an emerging global neighbourhood and the values that should guide its governance, we explored four specific areas: security, economic interdependence, the United Nations, and the rule of law. In each area we have sought to focus on governance aspects, but these are often inseparable from substantive issues.

Promoting Security

The concept of global security must be broadened from the traditional focus on the security of states to include the security of people and the security of the planet. The following six principles should be embedded in international agreements and used as norms for security policies in the new era:

- All people, no less than all states, have a right to a secure existence, and all states have an obligation to protect those rights.
- The primary goals of global security policy should be to prevent conflict and war, and maintain the integrity of the environment and life-support systems of the planet, by eliminating the economic, social, environmental, political, and military conditions that generate threats to the security of people and the planet, and by anticipating and managing crises before they escalate into armed conflicts.

- Military force is not a legitimate political instrument, except in self-defense or under UN auspices.
- The development of military capabilities beyond that required for national defense and support of UN action is a potential threat to the security of people.
- Weapons of mass destruction are not legitimate instruments of national defense.
- The production and trade in arms should be controlled by the international community.

Unprecedented increases in human activity and human numbers have reached the point where their impacts impinge on the basic conditions on which life depends. Action should be taken now to control these activities and keep population growth within acceptable limits so that planetary security is not endangered.

The principle of non-intervention in the domestic affairs of states should not be taken lightly. But it is necessary to assert as well the rights and interests of the international community in situations within individual states in which the security of people is extensively endangered. A global consensus exists today for a UN response on humanitarian grounds in such cases. We propose an amendment to the UN Charter to permit such intervention, but restricting it to cases that in the judgment of a reformed Security Council constitute a violation of the security of people so gross and extreme that it requires an international response on humanitarian grounds.

There should be a new 'Right of Petition' for non-state actors to bring situations massively endangering the security of people within states to the attention of the Security Council. The Charter amendment establishing the Right of Petition should also authorize the Security Council to call on parties to an intrastate dispute to settle it through the mechanisms listed in the Charter for the pacific settlement of disputes between states. The Council should be authorized to take enforcement action under Chapter VII if such efforts fail, but only if it determines that intervention is justified under the Charter amendment referred to in the previous paragraph on the grounds of a gross violation of the security of people. Even then, the use of force would be the last resort.

We suggest two measures to improve UN peacekeeping. First, the integrity of the UN command should be respected; for each operation a consultative committee should be set up including representatives of the countries contributing troops. Second, although the principle that countries with a special interest in relation to a conflict should not contribute troops should be upheld, the earlier view that the permanent members of the Security Council should not play an active part in peacekeeping should be discarded.

New possibilities arise for the involvement of regional organizations in conjunction with the UN in resolving conflicts. We support the Secretary-General's plea for making more active use of regional organizations under Chapter VIII of the Charter.

The UN needs to be able to deploy credible and effective peace enforcement units at an early stage in a crisis and at short notice. It is high time that a UN Volunteer Force was established. We envisage a force with a maximum of 10,000 personnel. It would not take the place of preventive action, of traditional peacekeeping forces, or of large-scale enforcement action under Chapter VII of the Charter. Rather, it would fill a gap by giving the Security Council the ability to back up preventive diplomacy with a measure of immediate and convincing deployment on the ground. Its very existence would be a deterrent; it would give support for negotiation and peaceful settlement of disputes.

The international community must provide increased funds for peacekeeping, using some of the resources released by reductions of defense expenditures. The cost of peacekeeping should be integrated into a single annual budget and financed by assessments on all UN member countries, and the peacekeeping reserve fund should be increased to facilitate rapid deployment.

The international community should reaffirm its commitment to progressively eliminate nuclear and other weapons of mass destruction from all nations, and should initiate a ten- to fifteen-year programme to achieve this goal.

Work towards nuclear disarmament should involve action on four fronts:
- the earliest possible ratification and implementation of existing agreements on nuclear and other weapons of mass destruction;
- the indefinite extension of the Non-proliferation Treaty;
- the conclusion of a treaty to end all nuclear testing; and

- the initiation of talks among all declared nuclear powers to establish a process to reduce and eventually eliminate all nuclear arsenals.

All nations should sign and ratify the conventions on chemical and biological weapons, enabling the world to enter the twenty-first century free of these weapons.

For the first time, the dominant military powers have both an interest in reducing worldwide military capabilities and the ability to do so. The international community should make a demilitarization of global politics an overriding priority.

Donor institutions and countries should evaluate a country's military spending when considering assistance to it. A Demilitarization Fund should be set up to help developing countries reduce their military commitments, and global military spending should be reduced to $500 billion by the end of the decade.

States should undertake immediate negotiation of a convention on the curtailment of the arms trade — including provision for a mandatory arms register and the prohibition of state financing or subsidy of arms exports.

Managing Economic Interdependence

Globalization is in danger of widening the gap between rich and poor. A sophisticated, increasingly affluent world currently coexists with a marginalized global underclass.

The pace of globalization of financial and other markets is outstripping the capacity of governments to provide the necessary framework of rules and cooperative arrangements. There are severe limits to national action to check such polarization within a globalized economy, yet the structures of global governance for pursuing international public policy objectives are underdeveloped.

The time is now ripe to build a global forum that can provide leadership in economic, social, and environmental fields. This should be more representative than the Group of Seven or the Bretton Woods institutions, and more effective than the present UN system. We propose the establishment of an Economic Security Council (ESC) that would meet at high political level. It would have deliberative functions only; its influence will derive from the relevance and quality of its work and the significance of its membership.

The ESC's tasks would be to:
- continuously assess the overall state of the world economy and the interaction between major policy areas;
- provide a long-term strategic policy framework in order to promote stable, balanced, and sustainable development; and
- secure consistency between the policy goals of the major international organizations, particularly the Bretton Woods bodies and the World Trade Organization (WTO).

The ESC should be established as a distinct body within the UN family, structured like the Security Council, though not with identical membership and independent of it.

With some 37,000 transnational corporations worldwide, foreign investment is growing faster than trade. The challenge is to provide a framework of rules and order for global competition to the widest sense. The WTO should adopt a strong set of competition rules and a Global Competition Office should be set up to oversee national enforcement efforts and resolve inconsistencies between them.

The decision-making structures of the Bretton Woods institutions must be made more reflective of economic reality; gross domestic product figures based on purchasing power parity should be used to establish national voting strength.

The role of the IMF should be enhanced by enabling it to:
- enlarge its capacity to provide balance-of-payments support through low-conditionality compensatory finance;
- have oversight of the international monetary system and a capacity to ensure that domestic economic policies in major countries are not mutually inconsistent or damaging to the rest of the international community;
- release a new issue of Special Drawing Rights; and
- improve its capacity to support nominal exchange rates in the interest of exchange rate stability.

For some countries, aid is likely to be for many years one of the main ways to escape from a low-income, low-savings, low-investment trap. There is no substitute for a politically realistic strategy to mobilize aid flows and to demonstrate value for money, including cofinancing between official aid donors, the private sector, and NGOs with a view to widening the support base.

A false sense of complacency has enveloped the developing-country debt problem. Radical debt reduction is needed for heavily indebted, low-income countries, involving at least implementation of full 'Trinidad' terms, including the matter of multilateral debt.

In response to environmental concerns, governments should make maximum use of market instruments, including environmental taxes and traded permits, and adopt the 'polluter pays principal' of charging. We support the European Union's carbon tax proposal as a first step towards a system that taxes resource use rather than employment and savings, and urge its wide adoption.

It is time for a consensus on global taxation for servicing the needs of the global neighbourhood. A start must be made in establishing schemes of global financing of global purposes, including charges on the use of global resources such as flight lanes, sea lanes, and ocean fishing areas and the collection of revenues agreed on globally and implemented by treaty. An international tax on foreign currency transactions should be explored as one option, as should the creation of an international corporate tax base among multinational companies.

Reforming the United Nations

We do not believe the UN should be dismantled to make way for a new architecture of global governance. Much of the necessary reform of the United Nations system can be effected without amending the Charter, provided governments are willing. But some Charter amendments are necessary for better global governance.

UN reform must reflect the realities of change, including the new capacity of civil society to contribute to global governance.

Reform of the Security Council is central to reforming the UN system. Permanent membership limited to five countries that derive their primacy from events fifty years ago is unacceptable; so is the veto. To add more permanent members and give them the veto would be regressive. We propose a process of reform in two stages.

First, a new class of five 'standing' members should be established to serve until the second stage of the reform process. We envisage two from industrial countries and one each from Africa, Asia, and Latin America. The number of non-permanent members should be raised from ten to thirteen, and the votes required for a decision of the Council from nine to fourteen. To facilitate the phasing out of the veto, the permanent members should enter into a concordat agreeing to forgo its use save in exceptional and overriding circumstances.

The second stage should be a full review of the membership of the Council, including these arrangements, around 2005, when the veto can be phased out, the position of the permanent members reviewed, and account taken of new circumstances — including the growing strength of regional bodies.

The Trusteeship Council should be given a new mandate over the global commons in the context of concern for the security of the planet.

The General Assembly should be revitalized as a universal forum. Regular theme sessions, effective exercise of budgetary authority, and the streamlining of its agenda and procedures should be part of the process of revitalization. We also propose an annual Forum of Civil Society consisting of representatives of organizations to be accredited to the General Assembly as 'Civil Society Organizations.' It should be convened in the General Assembly Hall sometime before the Annual Session of the Assembly. International civil society should itself be involved in determining its character and functions.

The Right of Petition proposed for promoting the security of people requires the formation of a Council of Petitions — a high-level panel of five to seven persons, independent of governments, to entertain petitions. Its recommendations will go as appropriate to the Secretary-General, the Security Council, or the General Assembly, and allow for action under the Charter.

In the light of experience, the proposed Economic Security Council, and our other recommendations, we propose that the UN Economic and Social Council (ECOSOC) should be wound up. The UN system must from time to time shut down institutions that can no longer be justified in objective terms. We believe this to be true also of the United Nations Conference on Trade and Development

(UNCTAD) and the United Nations Industrial Development Organization (UNIDO), and propose an in-depth review to this end. Our proposals on these UN bodies are part of the integrated set of proposals we make for improving global economic governance including, notably, the setting up of an Economic Security Council. Balanced governance arrangements will not result if policy leadership is preserved in the hands of a small directorate of countries, while such institutions as UNCTAD set up to correct imbalances are dismantled.

To help put women at the centre of global governance, a post of Senior Adviser on Women's Issues should be created in the Office of the UN Secretary-General, and similar positions established in the specialised agencies.

The UN must assist regionalism and gear itself for the time when regionalism is more ascendant worldwide. Regional bodies should be seen as an important part of a balanced system of global governance. However, the continuing utility of the UN Regional Economic Commissions now needs to be closely examined and their future determined in consultation with the respective regions.

The procedure for appointing the UN Secretary-General should be radically improved, and the term of office should be a single one of seven years. The procedure for selecting the heads of UN specialized agencies, funds, and programmes should also be improved.

Strengthening the Rule of Law Worldwide

The global neighbourhood of the future must be characterized by law and the reality that all, including the weakest, are equal under the law and none, including the strongest, is above it. Our recommendations are directed to strengthening international law and the International Court of Justice in particular.

All member-states of the UN that have not already done so should accept the compulsory jurisdiction of the Court. The Court's chamber procedure should be modified to enhance its appeal to states and to avoid damage to the Court's integrity.

Judges should be appointed for one ten-year term only, and a system introduced to screen potential members for jurisprudential skills and objectivity. The UN Secretary-General should have the right to refer legal aspects of international issues to the Court for advice, particularly in the early stages of disputes.

The Security Council should appoint a distinguished lawyer to provide advice at all relevant stages on the international legal aspects of issues before it. It should also make greater use of the World Court as a source of advisory opinions, to avoid being itself the judge of international law in particular cases.

We do not emphasize formal enforcement measures but, failing voluntary compliance, Security Council enforcement of World Court decisions and other international legal obligations should be pursued under Article 94 of the Charter.

An International Criminal Court should be quickly established with independent prosecutors of the highest calibre and experience.

The International Law Commission or other appropriate body should be authorized to explore how international law-making can be expedited.

The Next Steps

We have made many recommendations, some of them far-reaching. We would like to go one step further by suggesting a process for the consideration of these and similar recommendations.

During the time the Commission has been at work, we have witnessed the currencies of Europe held hostage by forces of speculation themselves out of control. Powerful economies confronted each other on the threshold of trade wars, while marginal ones collapsed. There was ethnic cleansing in the Balkans, a 'failed state' in Somalia, and genocide in Rwanda. Nuclear weapons lay unsecured in the former Soviet Union, and neofascism surfaced in the West.

The United Nations faces much greater demands. Its existence is a continuing reminder that all nations form part of one world, though evidence is not lacking of the world's many divisions. Today's interdependencies are compelling people to recognize the unity of the world. People are forced not just to be neighbours but to be good neighbours.

Our report is issued in the year the UN marks a jubilee. It is not tied to that one event or to the UN system alone. It speaks to a longer time and a larger stage, but the UN and its future are a central part of our concerns. It is important that the international community should use the UN's anniversary as an occasion for renewing commitment to the spirit of the Charter and the internationalism it embodied, and establish a process that can take the world to a higher stage of international cooperation. This process must be centred on the UN but not confined to it.

Ours are not the only recommendations that will be considered in the anniversary year. The variety of reports and studies presenting the case for change and proposing the form it should take reflects wide recognition that change is needed. That itself does not guarantee action to bring about change. The will to change does not exist everywhere. It would be easy for all the effort to promote reform to be stalled by a filibuster or simply by inertia. Or, paradoxically, it could be overwhelmed by the onset of the very dangers that some of the changes proposed are meant to guard against.

We are prompted to recall the vision that drove the process of founding the United Nations and the spirit of innovation that ushered in a new era of global governance. We need that spirit again today.

We fear that if reform is left to normal processes, only piecemeal and inadequate action will result. We look, therefore, to a more deliberate process. The Charter has been amended on four occasions. But revision of the Charter is the final stage in a process of reform and is not required for many of the changes we propose.

The ultimate process has to be intergovernmental and at a high level, giving political imprimatur to a new world order whose contours are shaped to the designs developed for the anniversary year.

For such a process to have the best prospect of securing agreement on a new system of global governance, there will need to be careful preparation. Civil society must be involved in the preparatory process, which should reach out to even wider sections of society than the processes leading up to recent world conferences. Many views must be examined, and many ideas allowed to contend.

Our recommendation is that the General Assembly should agree to hold a World Conference on Governance in 1998, with its decisions to be ratified and put into effect by 2000. That will allow more than two years for the preparatory process.

Action on all recommendations does not have to await the final conference. Many of the changes proposed do not need an amendment of the Charter. Some changes are already under way. We encourage action on reform at all levels — provided, of course, that ad hoc decisions do not become a substitute for systematic reform through a fully representative forum.

A special responsibility devolves on the non-governmental sector. If our recommendations and those from other sources are worthy of support, international civil society must prevail on governments to consider them seriously. By doing so they would ensure that 'WE THE PEOPLES' are the instruments of change to a far greater extent than fifty years ago. We call on international civil society, NGOs, the business sector, academia, the professions, and especially young people to join in a drive for change in the international system.

Governments can be made to initiate change if people demand it. That has been the story of major change in our time; the liberation of women and the environmental movement provide examples. If people are to live in a global neighbourhood and live by neighbourhood values, they have to prepare the ground. We believe that they are ready to do so.

The Need for Leadership

Whatever the dimensions of global governance, however renewed and enlarged its machinery, whatever values give it content, the quality of global governance depends ultimately on leadership. Throughout our work, we have been conscious of the degree to which the realization of our proposals depends on leadership of a high order at all levels.

As the world faces the need for enlightened responses to the challenges that arise on the eve of the new century, we are concerned at the lack of leadership over a wide spectrum of human affairs. At national, regional, and international levels, within communities and in international organizations, in governments and in non-governmental bodies, the world needs credible and sustained leadership.

It needs leadership that is proactive, not simply reactive, that is inspired, not simply functional, that looks to the longer term and future generations for whom the present is held in trust. It needs leaders made strong by vision, sustained by ethics, and revealed by political courage that looks beyond the next election.

This cannot be leadership confined within domestic walls. It must reach beyond country, race, religion, culture, language, lifestyle. It must embrace a wider human constituency, be infused with a sense of caring for others, a sense of responsibility to the global neighbourhood

To a very particular degree today, the need for leadership is widely felt, and the sense of being bereft of it is the cause of uncertainty and instability. It contributes to a sense of drift and powerlessness. It is at the heart of the tendency everywhere to turn inwards. That is why we have attached so much importance to values, to the substance of leadership, and the compulsions of an ethical basis for global governance. A neighbourhood without leadership is a neighbourhood endangered.

When we talk of the need for leadership, we do not mean only at the highest national and international levels. We mean enlightenment at every level — in local and national groups, in parliaments and in the professions, among scientists and writers, in small community groups and large national NGOs, in international bodies of every description, in religious communities, in political parties and citizens' movements, in the private sector and among transnational corporations, and particularly in the media.

A great challenge to leadership today is to harmonize domestic demands for national action and the compulsions of international cooperation. It is not a new challenge, but it has a new intensity as globalization diminishes the capacity to deliver at home and enlarges the need to combine efforts abroad. Enlightened leadership calls for a clear vision of solidarity in the true interest of national well-being — and for political courage in articulating the way the world has changed and why a new spirit of global neighbourhood must replace old notions of adversarial states in eternal confrontation.

The alternative is too frightening to contemplate. In a final struggle for primacy — in which each sees virtue in advancing its national self-interest, with states and peoples pitted against each other — there can be no winners. Everyone will lose; selfishness will make genius the instrument of human self-destruction. But the leadership to avert this is not sufficiently evident. The hope must be people — people demanding enlightenment of their leaders, refusing to accept the alternative of humanity at war with itself. And that hope is balanced by the promise of the leadership that future generations will bring.

In a real sense the global neighbourhood is the home of future generations; global governance is the prospect of making it better than it is today. But that hope would be a pious one were there not signs that future generations come to the task better equipped than their parents. They bring to the next century less of the baggage of old animosities and adversarial systems accumulated in the era of nation-states.

The new generation knows how close they stand to cataclysms unless they respect the limits of the natural order and care for the earth by sustaining its life-giving qualities. They have a deeper sense of solidarity as people of the planet than any generation before them. They are neighbours to a degree no other generation has been.

On That Rests Our Hope for Our Global Neighborhood.

The Commission on Global Governance

The Commission on Global Governance was established in 1992 in the belief that international developments had created favourable circumstances for strengthening global cooperation to create a more peaceful, just, and habitable world for all its people.

The first steps leading to its formation were taken by former West German Chancellor Willy Brandt, who a decade earlier had chaired the Independent Commission on International Development Issues. A meeting he convened in January 1990 asked Ingvar Carlsson (Prime Minister of Sweden), Shridath Ramphal (then Commonwealth Secretary-General), and Jan Pronk (Netherlands Minister for Development Cooperation) to prepare a report on the new prospects for world cooperation.

Some three dozen public figures who met in Stockholm in April 1991 to consider this report proposed, in their Stockholm Initiative on Global Security and Governance, that an international commission should recommend ways by which world security and governance could be improved, given the opportunities created by the end of the Cold War for enhanced cooperation.

Willy Brandt, after consulting Gro Harlem Brundtland and Julius Nyerere, who had headed two previous commissions, invited Ingvar

Carlsson and Shridath Ramphal to chair the new commission. The Commission, with twenty-eight members all serving in their personal capacity, started work in September 1992.

The Commission held eleven meetings, six in Geneva (where its secretariat was established) and the others in New York, Cuernavaca (Mexico), Tokyo, Brussels, and Visby (Sweden). It commissioned a number of papers; it had discussions with several of their authors, a number of persons from public life, and representatives of many civil society organisations. Discussions on key issues on the Commission's agenda were arranged by the Common Security Forum, the Norwegian Ministry for Foreign Affairs, and the Centre for the Study of Global Governance at the London School of Economics. The UN University co-hosted a public symposium with the Commission in Tokyo. Regional consultations with experts were arranged with the collaboration of local organisations in San José (Costa Rica), Cairo, and New Delhi.

Support for the Commission's work was provided by the governments of Canada, Denmark, India, Indonesia, Netherlands, Norway, Sweden, and Switzerland, two UN Trust Funds established by Japan, the Canton of Geneva, the government of Mexico City, the European Commission, the Arab Fund for Economic and Social Development (Kuwait), the MacArthur Foundation, the Carnegie Corporation, and the Ford Foundation (all of the United States), the World Humanity Action Trust (United Kingdom), and the Friedrich Ebert Stiftung (Germany).

The Commission decided at an early stage to remain active in efforts to disseminate its report and to promote its ideas and recommendations. These will be pursued through speaking engagements, seminars, and workshops; work with governments, international organizations, NGOs, the media; and the distribution of material.

The Commission's secretariat will continue to function in order to coordinate this work:

The Commission on Global Governance
Case Postale 184
CH-1211 GENEVA 28
Switzerland
Tel: +41 22 798 2713
Fax: +41 22 798 0147

Commission Members

Co-Chairmen

Ingvar Carlsson	Sweden
Shridath Ramphal	Guyana

Members

Ali Alatas	Indonesia
Abdlatif Al-Hamad	Kuwait
Oscar Arias	Costa Rica
Anna Balletbo	Spain
Kurt Biedenkopf	Germany
Allan Boesak	South Africa
Manuel Camacho Solis	Mexico
Bernard Chidzero	Zimbabwe
Barber Conable	United States
Jacques Delors	France
Jiri Dienstbier	Czech Republic
Enrique Iglesias	Uruguay
Frank Judd	United Kingdom
Hongkoo Lee	Kenya
Sadako Ogata	Japan
Olara A. Otunnu	Uganda
I.G. Patel	India
Celina do Amaral Peixoto	Brazil
Jan Pronk	The Netherlands
Qian Jiadong	China
Marie-Angélique Savané	Senegal
Adele Simmons	United States
Maurice Strong	Canada
Brian Urquhart	United Kingdom
Yuli Vorontsov	Russia

The full report of the Commission, entitled *Our Global Neighborhood*, is available in bookstores worldwide. Copies can be obtained through the publisher, Oxford University Press, tel: (919) 677-0977 (USA), +44 1536 454 534 (international).